ARISTOTLE'S NICOMACHEAN ETHICS:
Commentary and Analysis

Francis H. Eterovich

University Press of America™

PREFACE

This book is an outgrowth of my lectures to graduate students at DePaul University, Chicago, Illinois. Its purpose is not to produce yet another textual commentary on Aristotle's Nicomachean Ethics--for many such commentaries, and excellent ones, already exist. Rather, as a commentary-- neither too short nor too long--its contents are designed to cover an analysis of the most important passages, a summary of the less important, and an explanatory paraphrase of Aristotle's thought. This is a companion volume for the student and the general reader of the Nicomachean Ethics. By making this basic and possibly greatest work of moral philosophy accessible and understandable, it is hoped that a sharpened awareness of ethical or human values will assist the reader to think critically on the overwhelming ethical problems of today and thereby to regain, at least partially, the moral wisdom which is rare today.

We are pleased to acknowledge our debt to the many experts in the Aristotelian text and its meaning: to the British commentators A. Grant, J. Burnet, H. H. Joachim, W. D. Ross, H. Rachkam, and J. A. Stewart; to the French Aristotelian scholar A. J. Festugière and two authors of the excellent commentary of the Nicomachean Ethics, R. A. Gauthier and J. Y. Jolif. Also, we must not pass over the outstanding German commentators, who preceded the British and French, including Fr. Susemihl, O. Apelt, H. von Arnim, and Werner Jaeger. Among the medieval commentators, St. Thomas Aquinas was consulted very carefully.

A few words on the composition of this book seem appro- priate here. The Introduction begins with a biography of Aristotle. Then, there is discussion on the kind of scien- tific knowledge found in Aristotle's moral philosophy and on the method of inquiry in Aristotle's ethics, on the proper students of ethics, on the composition and plan of the Nicomachean Ethics. The content commentary of the ten books follows. We have provided titles of the books and chapters The glossary of Aristotelian key terms used in the Nico- machean Ethics follows the commentary. Finally, a selected bibliography closes the book.

The Greek text we have used is that of Bekker, repro- duced very closely by I. Bywater in his critical text and by H. Rachkam in his translation of the Nicomachean Ethics. Other translations consulted are those of William D. Ross and Martin Ostwald.

iii

It is our pleasant duty to acknowledge and to give thanks for the editorial and advisory help we have received from our two distinguished colleagues at DePaul University, Dr. Thomas N. Munson of the Department of Philosophy and Dr. Zahava K. McKeon of the Department of English. And our sincere thanks is extended to Ms. Cathy S. Hampton for her patience in both language editing and typing the manuscript. My students should not be omitted from the long list of those who have inspired me to write these pages: their pertinent questions have gladdened by meetings with them and forced me to study further and deeper into the Aristotelian meaning of the work he dedicated to his son Nicomachus.

F. H. E.

TABLE OF CONTENTS

x

INTRODUCTION

ARISTOTLE
384-322 B. C.

Life

Aristotle was born in 384 B. C. in Stagira (today, Stavrós) on the northeast coast of the peninsula of Chalcidice. His father Nicomachus was the physician of Amyntas II, king of Macedonia. Thus Aristotle was raised at Pella, the capital of Macedonia. His mother, Phaestis, hailed from Chalcis, a town on the island of Euboea.

In 367 B.C. Aristotle went to Athens and entered Plato's school, the Academy. He remained there twenty years until Plato's death. In Plato Aristotle found a man worthy of great admiration. All of Aristotle's works carry the imprint of Plato's powerful influence; however, a disagreement evolved on several important points. Aristotle eventually created a system almost antithetical to Plato's.

After Plato's death in 347 B.C., and Speusippus' succession as the Academy's head, Aristotle left Athens with Xenocrates, a fellow Academic. Accepting the invitation of Hermeias, a former fellow student in the Academy and ruler of two towns in Asia Minor, /in the province of Mysia/ Atarneus and Assos, Aristotle organized at Assos a small Academic circle, married Pythias, the niece of Hermeias, who bore him a daughter by the same name. His wife Pythias died later in Athens. Aristotle then took a woman from Stagira, Herpillis, who bore him a son Nicomachus, from whom the Nicomachean Ethics received its name. He never married Herpillis.

Aristotle spent three years in Assos, but when Hermeias was killed by Persians he moved to Mytilene, on the island of Lesbos, where ne studied marine biology. He made a lasting acquaintance/ while on Lesbos/ with the native scholar, Theophrastus, who later became Aristotle's most famous disciple.

In 343 B.C., Philip of Macedon, the son of Amyntas II, invited Aristotle to Pella as a tutor to his son Alexander, then thirteen years old. Aristotle accepted the invitation. However, little is known about his

tutoring of Alexander except that he had probably revised the text of The Iliad for his pupil and had
composed two political treatises, On Monarchy and On
Colonies. At this time, Aristotle's attention was
drawn to political subjects, to the constitutions and
laws of many Greek city-states. Nevertheless, it is
interesting that in spite of Aristotle's admiration
for the Macedonian monarchy, he lived and died faithful to the Greek political ideal of the city-state.
Kingdoms and empires were left to barbarians.

When Alexander became a regent for his father in
340 B.C., Aristotle left Pella and for some time
settled in his native Stagira. Although a deep friendship never developed between Aristotle and Alexander,
a mutual respect was established. Alexander was a man
of action; he appreciated learning only as a guide to
action. During his tutoring of Alexander at Pella,
Aristotle also became a friend of Antipater, a regent
appointed by Alexander during his absence in Asia.

The most fruitful period of Aristotle's life began
when he returned to Athens in 335 B.C. He founded his
own school--the Lyceum (Lykeion)--gathered chosen
disciples from the city of Athens and walked with them
daily through the covered walks of the gardens and
corridors of the building; hence, the name peripatetics
(peripatos means walk and corridor) for his disciples.
In the morning he presented systematic approaches to
philosophical disciplines--logic, physics and metaphysics; in the afternoons or evenings, he lectured a
larger audience from Athens on less difficult subjects--
ethics, politics and economics. The former or the
esoteric were for the inner circle of students--advanced
lectures; the latter or the exoteric for the outer
circle, large audiences -- popular lectures. Unfortunately, works based on exoteric lectures are no
longer extant.

In the Lyceum Aristotle collected hundreds of
manuscripts, maps, and a museum of natural history.
Alexander is claimed to have given him 800 talents to
form this collection and also to have sent him specimens
from his Asian campaigns. The constitutions of all
Greek city-states (158), the names of all winners in
Olympic games, and other important items were carefully
placed there by students cooperating in this scholarly
undertaking.

Alexander's death in 323 B.C. created anti-Mace-
donian feelings in Athens. Aristotle was known as
having connections with the Macedonians--Alexander,
Antipater,and Hermeias, for whom he wrote an epitaph.
As Socrates before him, Aristotle was accused of
impiety. He was reported saying that he did not want
Athenians to sin twice against philosophy; he then left
Athens and settled in his mother's town, Chalcis.
Aristotle died in 322 B.C. Among others bequests, Ari-
stotle's will (preserved for us through Diogenes
Laertius) freed several of his slaves.

Antiquity portrays Aristotle as quite polished; he
liked jewelry, particularly rings, spoke with a lisp,
enjoyed teasing people,and loved a life of pleasure.

Works

In Lives of Famous Philosophers, Book V, Diogenes
Laertius (starting with the life and works of Aristotle)
states that Aristotle wrote nearly 400 works. Scholars
today agree that Aristotle had probably written about
200 treatises--only forty-eight of them still extant.
These lectures are almost all esoteric, written in the
thirteen years (335-322) when Aristotle was the head of
the Lyceum. We will divide Aristotle's works according
to his own division of philosophical knowledge--
theoretical, practical,and productive. At the beginning, however, the logical treatises are listed, not as
part of his philosophy, but as the tool (organon) of
his philosophizing.

Logical Treatises:

Categories (In Latin: Categoriae; in Greek: Kategoriai.
One book.

On Interpretation (De Interpretatione; Peri hermeneias).
One book.

Prior Analytics (Analytica Priora; Analytika protera).
Books 1-2.

Posterior Analytics (Analytica posteriora; Analytika
hystera). 1-2.

Topics (Topica; Topika) 1-8

Sophistical Fallacies (De sophisticis elenchis; Peri
sophistikōn elenchōn). One book.

Treatises on Natural Philosophy:

Physics (Physica; Physikē akroasis), 1-8.

On Heavens (De caelo; Peri ouranou), 1-4.

On Generation and Corruption (De Generatione et corrup-
tione; Peri geneseōs kai phtoras), 1-2.

Meteorology (Meteorologica; Meteorologika), 1-4.

Biological Treatises:

History of Animals (Historia animalium; Peri ta zōa
historiai), 1-10.

On the Parts of Animals (De Partibus animalium; Peri
zōōn moriōn), 1-4.

On the Movement of Animals (De motu animalium; Peri
zōōn kineseōs). One book.

On the Walk of Animals (De incessu animalium; Peri zōōn
poreias). One book.

On the Generation of Animals (De generatione animalium;
Peri zōōn geneseōs). One book.

Psychological Treatises:

On the Soul (De anima; Peri psychēs), 1-3.

Smaller Natural Treatises is a group of small works
dealing with psychological matters as follows:

On Sense and Perception (De sensu et sensibilibus; Peri
aisthēseōs kai aisthētōn).

On Memory and Reminiscence (De memoria et reminiscentia;
Peri mnēmēs kai anamnēseōs).

On Dreams (De somniis; Peri enypniōn).

On Sleep and Waking (De insomniis; Peri hypnou kai enrēgorseōs).

On Prophesying by Dreams (De divinatione per somnum; Peri tēs kata hypnon mantikēs).

On Long Life and Short Life (De longitudine et brevitate vitae; Peri makrobiotētos kai brachybiotētos).

On Life and Death (De vita et morte; Peri zōēs kai thanatou).

On Breath (De respiratione; Peri anapnoēs).

Problems (Problemata; Problemata), 1-38 is a collection of various problems--mathematical, musical, optical, physiological, and medical--not all of them written by Aristotle.

Metaphysical Treatise:

Metaphysics (Metaphysica; Ta meta ta physika), 1-14 is a series of lectures, some inserted (2, 5, 11, 14), whose chronological order is hard to establish. The name metaphysics (which means: after Physics) comes from the position of these lectures in the Aristotelian corpus as it was put together by Andronicus.

Treatises on Ethics and Politics:

Great Morals (Magna Moralia; Ēthikā Megalā), 1-2.

Eudemian Ethics (Ethica Eudemia; Ēthikā eudemeiā), 1-8.

Nicomachean Ethics (Ethica ad Nicomachum; Ēthikā Niko-macheiā), 1-10.

On Virtues and Vices (De virtutibus et vitiis; Peri arētōn kai kakiōn). One book.

Politics (Politica; Politikā), 1-8.

Of the collection of 158 Greek city-state constitutions only that of Athens has been discovered in Egypt, on papyrus, in 1891 under the title:

The Constitution of Athens (De constitutione Athenarum; Athēnaiōn politeiā). One book.

Treatises on Rhetoric and Poetics:

The Rhetoric (Rhetorica; Technē rhētorikē), 1-3.

The Poetics (De arte poetica; Peri poiētikēs), only partially preserved.

WHAT KIND OF EPISTEME ARE ETHICS AND POLITICS

Epistēmē or scientific knowledge in the Aristotelian sense is a demonstrative knowledge showing the universal and necessary connection between substances (subjects) and their attributes (predicates). This is done through the finding of a reason or cause for such a connection. Expressed in a syllogism, this reason or cause is called the middle term. Its universal and necessary conclusion follows from universal and necessary premises.

Each epistēmē has three objects distinguishing it from all others: its proper subject matter; its unique aspect, angle,or approach to the subject matter; and its proper reasons or causes determining the inherence of the properties (attributes, predicates) in their subjects.

Aristotle divides epistēmē into three large categories:

1. Theoretical epistēmē aims at grasping (theoria), the truth of being for its own sake. Aristotle singles out three of the theoretical sciences.[1]

a. Metaphysics. It investigates reality as a whole; the subject is approached from the most universal aspect--being-qua-being, i.e., being qua unchangeable, eternal, separate from any matter. Metaphysics inquires into the primary causes (reasons, principles) of all reality and its essential attributes: matter and form, substance and accident, quality and quantity, potency and actuality, unity and plurality.

b. Mathematics. Its subject matter is numbers and points as exemplified by lines, surfaces, and tridimensional bodies. Numbers and points are studied under a specific aspect, namely, being qua quantitative, either qua discrete (numbers) or continuous (figures) quantity. The study comprises quantified being qua unchangeable and separable from matter; i.e., quantity qua abstracted from sense-perceptible objects, although it can only be and exist in the objects of sense-perception. Finally, mathematics studies the first principles of quantified being, for example, geometry, which studies axioms and their derivative theorems, postulates,and corollaries.

c. _Physics_. A perceptible, physical body as such and its various kinds are studied in the _Physics_. The subject is approached through a specific aspect, body _qua_ changeable, or reality in process and inseparable from matter. Physics investigates the causes or constitutive principles of bodies: _physis_ and _techne_, matter and form, potency and act, change and rest, space, time, continuous magnitude.

2. Practical _epistēmē_ aims at understanding the truth of life in order to guide human action (praxis). Its subject matter is that which is done--human affairs (prakta), and human action (praxis) insofar as it springs from intelligent deliberation and free choice. Since _praxis_ is immanent to the agent, it cannot be separated from the acting subject: it is directed to the well-being of a man acting. We may say, man acting _qua_ member of his _polis_ (city-state), because Aristotle, as well as Socrates and Plato before him, insisted that ethical behavior is not possible outside of the _polis_.

Practical _epistēmē_ approaches its subject by detecting what is noble and base, right and wrong, good and bad in _praxis_. Aristotle approached the morality of _praxis_ existentially; he was interested not in the abstract theory of a good moral life, but in the morally good life of a man _qua_ member of his _polis_.

Practical _epistēmē_, finally, seeks to discover reasons, causes, or moral principles in order to show the link between the attributes of goodness and badness and corresponding human acts. In his two works, the _Nicomachean Ethics_ and the _Politics_, Aristotle outlined with great care the principles of the good moral life. Here only mention is warranted of great moral principles such as teleology, eudaimonism, intellectualism, virtuous mean, choice and its preceding deliberation, moral character, and moral habit. Justice and friendship rule life in the _polis_ in their manifestations of citizenship, statesmanship, constitution, revolution, and education.

Aristotle did not separate his two practical sciences, ethics and politics. Ethics studies man's individual conduct, moral character (_ethos_), and happiness (_eudoimonia_). Politics studies the social, economic, and political conduct of a citizen. However, since both aim at the morally good life of man and citizen, both are very close to each other. Ethics is undoubtedly concerned with the good moral life of man, but today one would have difficulty saying the same

for the study of political life. In many places of both
the Nicomachean Ethics and the Politics Aristotle is
clear on this issue. "As then our present study, unlike
the other branches of philosophy, has a practical aim
(for we are not investigating the nature of virtue for
the sake of knowing what it is, but in order that we may
become good, without which result our investigation
would be of no use), we have consequently to carry our
inquiry into the region of conduct, and to ask how we
are to act rightly. . ."[2] In the Politics, "It is therefore evident that, while all partnerships aim at some
good, the partnership that is the most supreme of all
and includes all the others does so most of all, and aims
at the most supreme of all goods; and this is the partnership entitled the state, the political association."[3]
Furthermore, the aim of politics is the existential,
good moral character and happy life of citizens: ". . .
for we stated that the supreme good was the end of
political science, but the principal care of this science is to produce a certain character in the citizens,
namely to make them virtuous and capable of performing
noble actions."[4] In this text, politics stands for
ethics; thus, politics is an outgrowth of ethics. Man
is not an isolated being. He lives in society, in the
Greek polis, and in the barbarian ethnos (tribe, ethnic
group). Ethics aims, then, at politics; politics at
ethical life, and ultimately at a good quality of life
for its citizens. Immediately, politics create the
necessary framework of laws and institutions for the
civilized, moral, and happy human life: "The good life,
then, is the chief end of society, both collectively for
all its members and individually."[5]

    3. Productive episteme (arts, skills, applied
sciences) aims at understanding in order to guide the
production (poiesis) of both useful and beautiful products (ergon) according to a preconceived ideal and
planned course of production. Aristotle has elaborated
upon the rules of only one such productive science--
poetics. Even in poetics he is a master; writers, poets,
and literary critics cannot ignore his Poetics.

    Productive episteme does not study the medium
(i.e., the rock or wood) an artist or artisan uses to
make his product in order to know what they are, what is
the truth about them. Only those features of the rock
or wood necessary for the production of an artist's

work are studied. An artist is not a scientist in the sense that a mineralogist or biologist is; he is the maker of his product. His concerns are the production and the product that is its outcome. Although products are intended to satisfy human needs, the artist is incapable of prescribing the use of his product. That is the task of practical science.

Why, then, should Aristotle call the practical art of living and the productive art of knowing how to make things, epistēmē? Neither one is epistēmē in it full demonstrative sense. However, both of these arts exhibit it. Both embody human thought or ideality on the one hand in action, and on the other in production.

The processes of thinking, acting (or living a virtuous life), and making things succeed each other in an uninterrupted manner. In thinking the intellect illuminates the essences of things by asking for the what and why of things; in acting (living a virtuous life) the agent's intellect embodies the ideal of goodness in human action; and in making things the artist's intellect embodies in the matter at hand the ideal of beauty and usefulness as he understands it. In each case, in thinking, in acting, and in producing, the intellect is alive. By analogy, then, both the practical and productive activity of man are epistēmēs because both are permeated with thinking.

Neither the practical nor the productive epistēmē pursues scientific knowledge (epistēmē) for its own sake (as the theoretical epistēmē does), but rather for the sake of an end, purpose, or an ideal to be embodied in human conduct and in a human product. Man's purpose of thinking is to get the right idea or right reason for acting in a certain way and for making certain things: not understanding except as a means to action and production. ". . . the end of this science (practical epistēmē) is not knowledge but action."[6] Similarly, Aristotle at the end of the Nicomachean Ethics says:

> Perhaps, however, as we maintain, in the
> practical sciences the end is not to attain
> a theoretic knowledge of the various sub-
> jects, but rather to carry out our theories
> in action. If so, to know what virtue is
> is not enough; we must endeavor to possess
> and to practice it, or in some other manner
> actually ourselves to become good.[7]

Both the practical and productive sciences are concerned with process and change. In this case, a thinking
man is not interested in understanding the unchangeable
nature of things except insofar as knowledge of it may be
necessary to help him produce and control changes in the
variable field of human acts and products. He is intent
on guiding and improving action and production, evidently
areas in which things can be other than they are.

In both sciences, man is the source of the change or
process of human affairs and products. Man is not only
a spectator or observer watching processes taking place
with no desire for change as in theoretical sciences,
but he can also alter human acts and products according
to preconceived ideals.

The preconceived ideal in man's mind as well as the
preplanned course of action and production direct action
and production; both the intellect and the will join
forces in this planning. The will of the agent or its
deliberate decision or choice produces the action and
production, and the intellect plans, guides or directs
the course of action and production.

In practical knowledge, the purpose is to live and
act specifically according to an ideal. The object and
the agent, his state of mind, his will and activity are
inseparable. The activity is here immanent. It is
called action (praxis).

Still, the object or purpose of productive knowledge is to make things a certain way according to a
certain ideal. The object or product (ergon) is separated from the artist, the artistic product stands
totally on its own merit, independent of its artist.
An artist's will, motives, mode of operation, and actual
techniques are important only as influences on a product's character. In this case, the action is transient
or outside   the agent. It is called production
(poiesis).

ARISTOTLE'S METHOD OF INQUIRY

IN THE ETHICS AND THE POLITICS

Ethics deals with human affairs, actions, and emotions "which may be otherwise." This is the realm of often unpredictable individual, particular, concrete, personal decisions. Ethics lies in the realm of human contingency; necessity or necessary laws ruling human actions are not to be found. Since human actions are particular, ethics and politics do not provide the same necessary proof that one would expect from mathematics.

What kind of certainty can one expect in the practical sciences of ethics and politics? Aristotle raises the same question and answers as follows: "For it is the mark of an educated mind to expect that amount of exactness in each kind which the nature of the particular subject admits."[8] Metaphysical and mathematical matters require and offer greater degrees of certainty than moral matters, that is questions of right and wrong, noble and base in human actions and emotions. Here, all that is aimed at are general or universal rules of conduct. Ethical and political principles and conclusions are generalizations, sufficiently proven guides for living. Thus, in the study of ethics and politics, we reach moral certainty based upon generally accepted opinions of wise and good men from which moral principles are reached and conclusions drawn.

What is the method of ethical and political study? In spite of many instances in which dialectical method is used and other instances in which highly scientific method is exercised in Nichomachean Ethics the right answer seems to be that the ethical method is neither dialectical, based upon mere opinions of others, nor scientific, based upon the necessary and absolute premises. However, both methods contribute to the unique, original ethical and political method. Dialectical method serves ethician and politician as the good start. They study generally and universally accepted opinions of wise and good men in moral matters: those opinions stem from the common experience and common moral sense of the good people. Those opinions are the legitimate premises for ethician and politician. On the other hand, scientific method is necessary in ethics and politics in order to build

up the true practical epistēmē. Ethics cannot hope to
reach necessity and absoluteness of truth as theoretical as
philosophy does whose premises express necessary facts,
essential attributes, and absolute truths. But ethician
and politician must have generalizations and universaliza-
tions, that is, general or universal moral principles
and conclusions in order to construct their practical
epistēmē. Aristotle does not study competent moral
opinions of the wise men to exercise in dialectical
reasoning for its own sake, or to pass on to us a history
of morals, or to construct metaethical theory of morality.
His analysis and synthesis in ethical reasoning aim at
general and universal rules of human conduct.

One may say that Aristotle minimized the accuracy
and exactness of ethical reasoning by putting emphasis
on the subject-matter of ethics, i.e., particular and
personal human actions and emotions. However, Aristotle
has not indulged in casuistry--on the contrary, ethical
matters are studied from the viewpoint valid for all
men. Beneath individual actions, emotions, and decisions
lies human nature, human needs, and human fulfillment
that are common to all. Thus, Aristotle analyzes and
defines the nature of happiness (eudaimonia), virtue
(aretē), moral choice (proairesis), moral weakness
(akrasiā), and individual moral virtues such as temperance and justice with such accuracy and seriousness that
the results are not looked upon as particular to his time
but as valid and lasting. The great principles of teleology, intellectualism, eudaimonism are expertly woven
into his entire ethical study. Only a thinker with a
comprehensive view of moral reality could be so con-
sistent in building ethical principles on such strong
pillars.

THE PROPER STUDENTS OF ETHICS

Proper students of ethics need sufficient life
experience with which to control conduct because controlled conduct is the basis of ethics and ethical
action. Therefore, young men who have not had sufficient
life experience, as well as adults who never learn from
life experience, are unfit for the study of ethics.
Furthermore, students of ethics should not be guided by
their passions since their intellect and willpower,
obscured and weakened by strong emotions, cannot make
proper moral decisions. This refers not only to the
young men who are, as a rule, more emotional and
passionate, but also to immature adults who never
mastered their emotions. Since the rational element is
so emphasized in Aristotelian ethics, students of
ethics should look for a logical connection of actions
and principles that may serve as a guide. In other
words, reflective experience, control of emotions, and
rational guidance of action are necessary for the profitable study of ethics. "Moral science may be of
great value to those who guide their desires and actions
by principle [logos]."

In addition, students of ethics need a proper moral
upbringing at home. Every science proceeds from what is
known to what is yet unknown. Students of ethics must
accept on faith or authority and carry in their soul
fundamental principles and common moral conclusions.
This, however, is not enough, but it is the beginning.
We may start a study of ethics by referring to these
known basics, while a student morally confused, hardly
knowing right from wrong or having distorted moral
beliefs, is unfit for studying ethics.

Those disposed for following moral discourse,
having appropriated basic moral principles and conclusions at home and in society, will benefit doubly from
the study of ethics. First, they will begin to understand the reasons for commands and prohibitions, and
second, they will begin to adopt good conduct by
intelligent habituation, i.e., by the steady practice of
good deeds controlled by right reason resulting in
virtuous habit and action.[10]

ARISTOTLE'S NICOMACHEAN ETHICS: COMPOSITION

The Nicomachean Ethics is Aristotle's mature
ethical treatise. Nicomachus was Aristotle's son.
The treatise was composed in Athens at the Lyceum.
Another treatise, the Eudemian Ethics was written
earlier in Assos, Asia Minor. Eudemus was a disciple of Aristotle and edited his work after Aristotle's
death. Books V, VI, VII of the Nicomachean Ethics are
the same as Books IV, V and VI of the Eudemian Ethics
and originally belonged to the latter work. The first
study of the concept of pleasure found in the Nicomachean Ethics, VII, 12-15, originally belonged to the
Eudemian Ethics. Finally, the third ethical treatise in
the Aristotelian corpus is the Great Ethics (Latin:
Magna Moralia; Greek: Ta Megalā ethikā) whose content
is found in Aristotle's other ethical works and was
written, in all probability, by a first generation
peripatetic.

The Nicomachean Ethics is not a strictly unified
and finished work. Several parts (lectures) can be
discovered in it. However, its content can be logically
unified as is evident from the plan of the work shown on
page XXVII.

Aristotle says: "Human good (well-being or happiness) turns out to be an activity of soul in accordance
with virture (moral virtue); and if there are more than
one virtue, in accordance with the best and most complete /intellectual virtue of wisdom/."[11] Thus,
Aristotle will search for the activity or life consisting of man's ethical well-being. But before such
search can be started, one must inquire into the nature
of virtue because only a virtuous life is worth living
and conducive to human well-being. "Since happiness is
an activity of soul in accordance with perfect virtue,
we must consider the nature of virtue; for perhaps we
shall thus see better the nature of happiness."[12]

Aristotle intended to examine three human lives
/perhaps more than three/ in order to find the most
worthy. He will not exclude from human happiness the
life of pleasure, or virtue, or contemplation. "For the
most notable kinds of life are three: the life just
mentioned /that of pleasure/, the political life, and
the contemplative life."[13] But he will judge the worth
of each according to its contribution to human well-being.

To the three human lives one could also add the life of
friendship (Books VIII and IX) as a special type of
happy life, or even more,   lives such as those of
various moral heroes, the wise man (Book VI), the just
man (Book V), the courageous and the temperate man
(Book III). However, all of these types are one man
in the highest expression of ethical life, the contemplative, the thinker, the philosopher, the wise man of
Book X of the Nicomachean Ethics.

     Aristotle points to the basic division and plan of
the Nicomachean Ethics when he says: "Now that we have
spoken of the virtues, the forms of friendship, and the
varieties of pleasure, what remains to discuss in outline is the nature of happiness [contemplation]."[14]

     The life of pleasure for its own sake is childish
because pleasure detached from activity and its achievements is empty and unfulfilling. But pleasure in the
service of activity and human development is a legitimate and necessary ingredient of human happiness, especially when pleasure accompanies virtue and
contemplation.

     The life of virtue (moral virtue) is the life of
the happy, magnanimous, just, temperate, courageous,and
friendly man. Moral virtues are practiced in the framework of the participatory Athenian democracy, in
assembly, jury,or council.   However, political life
also involves outside disturbances in actions and
inside disturbances in passions so that peace of mind,
a necessity for true happiness, cannot be reached in
that life.

     The life of contemplation is the highest expression
of man's well-being. Freed from the cares of life and the
disturbances from outside and inside in the life of contemplation, the intellect--the highest human faculty--grasps
directly the highest eternal truths. However, man is
both mind and body.   As a result, contemplation
is a privilege of a few and only at rare moments.

ARISTOTLE'S NICOMACHEAN ETHICS: PLAN OF THE WORK

Introduction

Book I, 3. What kind of <u>episteme</u> is ethics? Who
are the Proper Students of Ethics?

The problem of human good and end

Bk. I, 1-2, 4-12. All human action aims at some good--
Ends and means--What is the good and
the highest good or well-being for
man?

I. THE LIFE OF VIRTUE

Theory of virtue

Bk. I, 13. Kinds of virtues and their psychological
foundations.

Bk. II, 1-9 Pleasure and pain are tests of virtues.
Definition of moral virtue. The mean of
moral virtue.

Conditions of moral responsibility for human conduct

Bk. III, 1-5 Types of human acts--Obstacles
to volunatary acts. Choice.

Individual moral virtues

Bk. III, 6-9.   Courage

Bk. III, 10-12   Temperance

Bk. IV, 1-2   Liberality and magnificence
     3-4   Magnanimity and ambition
     5   Gentleness
     6   Friendliness
     7   Truthfulness
     8   Wittiness
     9   Modesty

Book V.   Justice
     1-7   Its objective nature and divisions
     8-11   Its inner or subjective nature.

INTRODUCTION
Footnotes

[1]Metaphysics, Book VI (E), Ch. 1.

[2]N.E., Book II, ii, 1-1130b 25.

[3]Politics, Book I, i, 1-1251b, 5.

[4]N.E., Book I, ix, 8-1099b 30.

[5]Politics, Book III, iv. 3-1278b, 20.

[6]N.E., Book I, iii, 6-1095a 5.

[7]N.E., Book X, ix. 1-1179b 1.

[8]N.E., Book I, iii, 4-1094b 25.

[9]N.E., Book I, iii, 7-1095a 10.

[10]N.E., Book I, 7, 30-1098b 5.

[11]N.E., Book I, ch. 7-1098a 15.

[12]N.E., Book I, ch. 13-1102a 5.

[13]N.E., Book I, 5-1096a 3.

[14]N.E, Book X, ch. 6-1176a 30-34.

BOOK I

THE PROBLEM OF HUMAN GOOD AND END

Chapter 1

The General Meaning of the Good and End

The teleological tenor of Aristotle's ethical theory is set in the opening sentence of the Nicochean Ethics:

> Every art (techne) and every investigation (methodos), and likewise every practical pursuit (praxis) and undertaking (proairesis), seems to aim at some good: hence it has been well said, that the good is that at which all things aim.[1]

The textual terms, techne, methodos, praxis and proairesis are not used in a strictly Aristotelian sense (see the Glossary) but are more Platonic in meaning. In fact, the two doublets are easily united: techne means any art, and methodos is the knowledge that directs art making. First, we have the art of making and then applied science, the knowing how to produce things of art. The term techne means any productive art and skill. In a way the two terms are synonyms. Another doublet is praxis and proairesis, that is, exterior action and its interior motivation, intention and choice. The first doublet expresses the world of techniques, the second, the world of moral action.

Two other important ethical terms are found in the above opening text of the Nicomachean Ethics. They are the good (agathon) and the aim or end (telos). The two terms are similar: the good is the quality making everything attractive and desirable; the end is the completion or perfection of anything.

Aristotle offered both concepts of good and end in his Metaphysics. The good (agathon) is desirable not only because it pleases us, but also, and in the first place, because it has value of its own, because it is perfect. "Perfect" is not taken in an absolute sense, but in the sense relative to good things. Perfection means that things have all their parts; that things

1

and persons function well in their won particular
excellence, such as a physician or flute-player; that
things or persons arrive at the end of their development and so become fulfilled. For example, the perfection of man's life does not consist primarily in the
practice of virtues but in the possession of happiness
toward which the virtuous life strives.[2] The two first-
mentioned perfections, completeness of parts and excellence in functions, refer to the physical good. The
third one, when humans are concerned in reaching the end
of their lives, refers to the ethical or moral good. On-
tological goodness, we may add, consists in the actuality
of the existence and power of being.

Thus, the good as end, completion and perfection
is the Aristotelian conception of good. In Books II
and III we will see the morality of means, of human
actions and passions, but their morality will be judged
in the light of the ends of human action. Goals or ends
are the leading principles, rules and laws in moral affairs; as a result, these ends are freely and consciously
sought by humans.

Every man must know not only what is good for
human nature as such, but also what is morally good for
him. Here we enter into the objective and subjective
approaches to morality. Men disagree in their judgment
as to what is good for them individually. However, no
man voluntarily pursues what is evil for him. In other
words, men always pursue what at east <u>seems</u> to them
to be their good. This <u>apparent</u> good may be, in reality,
evil for those men. That which pleases our senses, ex-
cites our imagination, stirs up our feelings, and inclines
the reason to form a favorable judgment of it is oftentimes only an apparent good. If this, and only this,
were the approach to morality, every man would be the
sole judge of moral good and evil. We would have complete
relativism. There would be no way of knowing what men
should desire; we would know only what men do desire.
But the <u>real</u> good for man, corresponding to real human
needs and desires, is what ethics tries to ascertain as
objectively as possible.

Finally, there are degrees in the series of goods.
Some are <u>useful</u> for furthering ends, some are <u>pleasant</u>
feelings of satisfaction in the possession of a good
object (thing and person), and some are <u>noble</u>, honorable,
righteous goods enobling man as man, contributing to the
perfection of the whole human being. The useful and
pleasant are morally good but only insofar as the useful and

2

the pleasant lead to the noble good, the moral good.
The useful and pleasant, detached from their direction
to the noble good, are constant temptations to human
deviation from life goals. There is a need for
constant, willful and conscious striving towards the
noble ends of human life.

The end (telos) is "that for the sake of which a
thing is done."[3] Aristotle listed the end among his
four causes. For him all change is a process whereby
some given underlying substratum (matter) acquires a
new specification or perfection (form) through the
action of an agent (efficient cause) which is moved to
act by the attraction of some good (the end). Ultimately, the end attracts and leads an agent to fashion
a new perfection from an indeterminate matter. Thus
the end is the supreme cause of action, change and
growth. Such a view of the primacy of ends in the universe makes the world a place in which all things have
a purpose.

In Aristotelian terms one might say that everything
in the universe strives to actualize its potentialities
or capacities. Omnipresent in Aristotelian ethics is
the focus on development or growth, taken originally
from the biological sciences with which Aristotle
was well acquainted. Growth points to the maturity or
fullness of things. This completion of hidden potencies
is the good (agathon) at which everything aims, mineral,
plant or man. Teleology or purposiveness therefore rules
Aristotelian ethics, although as we shall see, deonto-
logical elements--those pointing to duties--are not
absent from it. But moral obligation is only the consequence of man's good or virtuous life.

This is the law of teleology or purposiveness.
Each being is so constructed in its nature (physis) that
it acts only according to a particular pattern and in
a certain direction. But this direction presupposes
a definite nature or essence from which a determinate
action starts. Moreover, there is no random action; on
the contrary, every action points to the end or target
towards which it aims. Therefore, determined nature produces determined action; this action in turn produces
or reaches a determined end. Thus nature, action and
end are correlative terms. Everything has its function
to fulfill, and this fulfillment of its function is its
proper end.

Men are not exempted from this universal striving

3

for self-fulfillment, possessing as they do potencies, needs and corresponding desires. The proper role of man's rational faculty (logos) and its appetite (orexis) is to conduct him from the imperfect state of potency in which he is born to his fullest possible actualization.

As applied to human beings, teleology may be summarized as follows: human action springs from human nature and human action in turn leads to an end. However man's striving for self-fulfillment is not merely an unconscious impulse. Rather , it is a conscious and free effort. Ethical goodness is rooted in the rational human nature and its permanent needs.

In order to avoid misunderstanding, it is necessary to point briefly to the four meanings of good-end in human life. One meaning is subjective, the other objective, and both may be either factual or normative, as follows:

a. Subjective-factual is what someone believes to be his good or his end and then tries to achieve it. This kind of good may be, in itself, real or apparent. One may strive for such good either consciously or unconsciously.

b. Subjective-normative is what one's conscience dictates to be his good or his end. This good may not necessarily be good, objectively speaking.

c. Objective-factual is what someone does achieve in fact. This achievement can be good or bad when examined in the light of objective ethical principles.

d. Objective-normative is what someone ought to achieve. This is the meaning of end-good-value in Aristotelian ethics and politics.

The ethical and political life states goals or purposes in view of objective-normative values to be achieved. This does not mean that Aristotle neglects the subjective side of morality. As we shall see in Books II and III, he is very careful in pointing to the role of one's personal moral character, habits, knowledge or ignorance of circumstances and consequences of moral acts, the choice, and the intention that the agent has in mind while acting morally. His ethics, however, finds morality principally in the nature of acts, the nature of humans, their goals, circumstances and consequences of their acts. The human mind dis-

4

covers the rightness and wrongness of human acts by
referring them to objective moral principles and rules.

Let us continue with the text of Chapter 1.

> (It is true that a certain variety is to
> be observed among the ends at which the
> arts and sciences aim: in some cases
> the activity (energeia) of practising the
> art is itself the end, whereas in others
> the end is some product (ergon) over and
> above the mere exercise of the art; and
> in the arts whose ends are certain
> things beside the practice of the arts
> themselves, these products are essen-
> tially superior in value to the activities.)[4]

One would expect Aristotle to pass over techniques
(art and applied science) and concentrate in the Ethics
on moral action (praxis and proairesis). However, he
continues proving that every activity is done for an
end precisely in the line of techniques. In fact, every
example in the first chapter is taken from the world of
techniques. Thus, moral action (praxis) is taken as
production (poiesis), activity (energeia) as immanent
activity, and epistēmē as nothing but methodos that is
productive knowledge. Certain arts such as flute
playing are ends in themselves, but the art of building
has the end product (ergon) outside itself in the house
that is built. In the last case, the products stand
out on their own merit even after the artist is gone or
dead; they outlive their maker's activity.

The above parenthesis has no particularly important bearing on the analysis of ends and means that
Aristotle intended to carry out in the following text.
Both action and production are evaluated in view of
the produced results.

Chapter 1 ends by pointing to the order among arts,
pursuits and applied sciences.

> But as there are numerous pursuits (praxis)
> and arts (technē) and sciences (epistēmē),
> it follows that their ends are corres-
> pondingly numerous: for instance, the end
> of the science of medicine is health, that
> of art of shipbuilding a vessel, that of
> strategy victory, that of domestic
> economy wealth. Now in cases where

several such pursuits are subordinate to
some single faculty (<u>dynamis</u>)--as bridle-
making and the other trades concerned
with horses' harness are subordinate
to horsemanship, and this and every
other military pursuit to the science of
strategy, and similarly other arts to
different arts again--in all these cases,
I say, the ends of the master arts are
things more to be desired than all those
of the arts subordinate to them; since
the latter ends are only pursued for the
sake of the former.[5]

Aristotle   uses examples from the world of
techniques (arts and applied sciences) to show the
subordination of one to another and of their ends to
each other. He uses the arts to illustrate moral
action and its means-ends subordination. In the first
place, all arts mentioned in Chapter 1 have ends beyond
their activity: medicine's end is health, shipbuilding,
a vessel, strategy, victory, and of domestic economy,
wealth. Furthermore, there is a hierarchical subordination among the arts and applied sciences: some are
higher, some lower, and the latter serve the higher.
Finally, each mentioned art has several auxiliary arts
subordinated to the master art. Strategy, for instance,
uses the skill of horsemen, archers, and sailors in
order to win the victory.

Chapter 2

Ends and Means

The world of techniques presented in Chapter 1 is
now being applied to before moral action; in both cases
there is a subordination of means-ends. Aristotle,
however, presses his analysis of means-end subordination
to the point where there must be some ultimate intrinsically desirable end of human life. If there is no
such end, our desire would go on ad infinitum, pursuing
an indefinitely receding object, so that "all desire
would be futile and vain."[6] Such aimless desire and
action is impossible since all desire and all action
must terminate in its object or in its end.

We have seen that all human endeavor aims at an
end, but in order to reach his end man must use means.
These means are only immediate and intermediate ends:
their real significance cannot be discovered except in
terms of the ends at which they aim. Thus, all
immediate and intermediate ends receive their meaning
from the supreme end of man's action and life, the end-
in-itself, which does not admit of further activity.

The whole meaning of end consists in the attractive good it offers to the agent. Both the immediate
and intermediate ends aim at further ends, which owe
their attraction to the one end that is the highest
goal of man's striving. Since all ends receive their
goodness, and consequently their attraction, from the
last one, there must be a last end--the supreme source
of goodness and its attraction--initiating every other
subordinate end in a series of meaningfully connected
ends or there would be no series at all. If there
were no last, there could also be no first. Since it
is impossible to string out to infinity a series of
ends and means, there must be a supreme end of human
conduct and life.

It is important for us to define the ultimate
goal of human life and to see which science or art
studies it. The answer to the former will be given
starting with Chapter 4 of Book I, whereas the answer to
the latter is given here. Politics is the most outstanding practical science of human conduct; it offers
humans conditions of self-sufficing life, civilized
existence and well-conducted lives in the frame-

work of the city-state (polis). All arts mentioned
above and many others, such as strategy, domestic economy and oratory, ultimately aim at the good human life
in the polis. Their master science is politics because
their ends are subordinated to its highest end, the
good of man.

In essence, the reasoning of Chapters 1 and 2
is Platonic. Not surprisingly, politics is made a
queen of practical and productive sciences. In fact,
from the following, one is tempted to think that ethics
is a subordinate species of politics and that the good of
the individual man or ethic's goal is subordinate or
even, perhaps, as some see the text, absorbed into the
state or into the public and political good of the
citizens.

The text reads as follows:

> Therefore, the good of man must be the end
> of the science of politics. For even
> though it be the case that the good is the
> same for the individual and for the state,
> nevertheless, the good of the state is man-
> ifestly a greater and more perfect good,
> both to attain and to preserve. To secure
> the good of one person only is better than
> nothing; but to secure the good of a nation
> (ethnos) or a state (polis) is a nobler
> and more divine achievement.[7]

Politics may be taken in two senses: either the
art of governing the polis, or, and this seems to be the
text's meaning, the practical science that sets laws,
norms and rules of human conduct. As such, moral
politics guides humans to happiness, to the good human
life and therefore it is political ethics. What ethics
does to the individual by pointing to his supreme goal
of life, politics does to all individuals, to the
society, to the polis. Such politics is political ethics.
Since politics gives the moral law support by making it
a law for all to follow, politics is the supreme practical science, an architectonic science to which all
others are subordinated in achieving the fullness of
human good in the polis.

Chapter 3

What Kind of Episteme are Ethics and Politics?
Aristotle's Method of Inquiry in the Ethics and the
   Politics
The Proper Students of Ethics

The subject matter of this chapter has been commented
   upon in the Introduction, pp. XVII - XXIV.

Chapter 4

What is the Good and the Highest Good for Man?

   The most universal answer to the question, "What
is the good and the highest good for man," is that all
men desire happiness; hence, happiness (eudaimonia) is
the supreme good for man. However, not all men agree
about the meaning or nature of happiness. Some men
equate happiness with pleasure, wealth, health and
honors. Before the meaning of happiness is examined,
Aristotle confronts various opinions on the subject
that his predecessors have formulated.

Chapter 5

Various Opinions on the Good

and the Highest Good for Man

Men lead basically one of three lives--pleasure,
moral virtue and contemplation. The latter will be
discussed in Book X. Let us examine various goods that
fit into the life-style of pleasure and moral virtue.

More about pleasure will be said in Book VII and X;
here only a few words will suffice. Pleasure stimu-
lates, accompanies and rewards activity and achievements.
Pleasures do have a legitimate place in human life but
tend to something else, to activity, and, therefore,
pleasures cannot be the highest good of man.

Honor is a recognition of virtue or excellence in
the honored. Virtue, then, is better than honor. Honor
cannot be the good,and less can it be the highest good
of man.

Virtue or excellence itself cannot be the highest
good of man. Its practice is not easy; suffering and
privation are involved. Virtue is really maturation
and preparation for a life of balanced personality,
peace of mind and the contemplative life which is the
highest happiness.

Wealth is a means to the acquisition of things that
might, we hope, make us happy. Money, in particular, is
a means of buying the means of sustenance of the body
and of the education of the soul.

Since all the above-mentioned goods, and the list
is by no means exhaustive, are means to further goals,
they cannot be the good of man and even less his highest
good.

Chapter 6

Plato's View of the Highest Good

To Plato, the many goods, including the good human
life, experienced in our lives are only participations,
images or reflections of the one and only supreme Form
of Good. The Form of Good is to the world of particular good as the Sun is to the universe: it is the source
of all good. Such was Plato's doctrine. Aristotle
says, ". . . and it has been held by some thinkers
/Plato and the Academy7 that besides the many good
things we have mentioned /pleasure, honor, virtue,
wealth7, there exists another good, that is good in itself, and stands to all those goods as the cause of
their being good."8

In the Ethics Aristotle looks for a specifically human
good, and therefore, the Platonic Form of Good which is
so universal that it is separate from any individual
good, is not and cannot be the basis of the ethical good
of man. Aristotle differs from Plato by putting forms
in individual things, whereas Plato sees them as self-
subsistent entities, separate from the individual
things of which they are perfect embodiments. Consequently, he disproves the Platonic doctrine of the Form
of Good as the highest good of man by means of the following reasons:

a. Plato's Form of Good is a substance. But good
    as we know it is rather a quality of substance,
    a   relation of one to another substance.
    Such is not Plato's Good; it is the Good in
    itself, by itself, of itself, and not the pro-
    perty of something else.

b. The Good applied to many goods in various
    categories--quality, quantity and relation--
    cannot mean one and the same thing in each one
    of these cases the unity of the Good cannot
    stand the real diversity of goods.

c. If there is one Form of the Good and all good
    things are included under it, there should be
    a single science dealing with all good things
    as Plato understood his dialectics to be. But
    that is not possible. There are several
    sciences dealing with various goods, such as

11

medicine with health, strategy with victory
and gymnastics with bodily exercise. In fact,
even within a single good such as health several sciences are found within what is known
generally under the title of medicine.

d. There is no self-subsistent entity whose being
    is goodness and nothing but goodness which is
    the cause of all goods in the universe. The
    Form or Ideal Good coincides in fact with the
    concept of good we have in our minds, but it is
    not an entity separate from its particular
    manifestations. There are ten categories of
    being, and not only one, substance. As far as
    substance is concerned, there are as many sub-
    stances as there are things in the world.
    Thus, there is no place for Platonic Forms; no
    place for the Platonic Form of Good either.

e. Even if there were the Form of Good it would be
    useless for practical purposes. The good of
    man should be practicable and attainable. The
    Form of Good is neither, it cannot be attained
    by man and it cannot be realized in human
    action.

Finally, Platonists might raise the following
objection: Platonic doctrine does not refer to every
kind of good; it refers to that kind of good pursued
and loved for its own sake as being intrinsically good.
It does not refer to the useful goods that are means to
the intrinsic goods.

Aristotle retorts: What sort of things are intrinsically good? According to Platonists, things are
intrinsically good by reference to the Form of Good.
Therefore, the definition should be the same for every
good that has a value of its own, such as health, wealth,
virtue and wisdom. But as it was said above, that
is not the case. If, on the other hand, intrinsically
good things are those that are pursued only for their
own sake, such can be, in a Platonic context, the Form
of good only.   But, as was said above, the Form of
Good does not exist separate from individual good things.

The solution is that there are many different good
things. What do they have in common? They all have a
certain affinity: they are good substance and/or good
properties. By analogy they are all called good.

Chapter 7

What is Happiness for Man?

Aristotle did not see happiness as a feeling, even
if the feeling was deep and permanent, purified of gross
bodily pleasures; nor did he see it simply as a disposition of temperament. To him happiness was an activity
through which a man develops his capacities by living
well, doing and faring well, and is thus on the way to
reaching his well-being in mind and body. And since,

> activities are of two kinds, some merely
> necessary means and desirable only for the
> sake of something else, others desirable
> in themselves, it is clear that happiness
> is to be classed among activities desirable
> in themselves. . .[9]

Happiness, the activity that is desirable in and for
itself, is characterized as follows:

First, it must be something final, that is, something "for the sake of which anything else is done."[10]
In the long run, man looks for the complete fulfillment
of all his desires; nothing less will satisfy him. But
complete fulfillment, if and when it is reached, leaves
man nothing more to strive for. Therefore, happiness
is man's chief end and the supreme good.

Furthermore, happiness must be self-sufficient.
Aristotle explains the meaning of self-sufficiency:
"We take a self-sufficient thing to mean a thing which
merely standing by itself alone renders life desirable
and lacking in nothing."[11]

Finally, happiness must be a lasting state and must
occupy a complete lifetime.[12]

But we must still discover what happiness really is.
First, Aristotle took up the question of man's function:
What kind of function is man designated by nature to
fulfill? He answered by inquiring what man alone
can do. Man shares nutrition and growth with both
plants and animals;he shares a sentient life with animals. "There remains therefore what may be called the
practical life of the rational part of man."[13] Man is
the animal with the rational principle, called logos,

which understands the end and directs man's acts to it.

Man's proper function thus consists in the exercise of an activity that is in conformity with man's rational part. Furthermore, it is not enough for man to live merely according to reason, but he must also aim at attainment of excellence. He has to strive and reach for maximum human development. Thus we now have the ground prepared for the definition of human happiness.

> The good of man is the active exercise of
> his soul's faculties in conformity with
> excellence or virtue, or if there be
> several human excellences or virtues,
> in conformity with the best and most
> perfect among them.[14]

The concept of virtue is being introduced in order to define human happiness. The reason for that introduction is simple. Virtue is closely connected with the concept of function first introduced as the key term in the definition of happiness. Virtue is nothing but an excellence at fulfilling any function. In the case of men, the practice of moral virtue fulfills man's capacities and makes him happy. However, the best and the most perfect virtue is the intellectual virtue of theoretical wisdom. Its exercise will make man the happiest, as Book X will show.

Chapter 8

The State of Happiness

After showing the essence of happiness, Aristotle then proceeds to analyze its ingredients. Popular thinking of his time defined happiness by identifying it with one good or another. According to the following conditions, Aristotle found a proper place for each good in his own concept of happiness.

a. Those goods must be real goods that satisfy natural human needs.

b. A hierarchy is found among the goods--some goods are higher, some lower, some are means and some are ends.

c. Man is not made happy only by simple possession of the goods that make him happy, but also and above all by the activity for and about them.

There are three broad categories of goods in which humans tend to place happiness:

a. External goods. Aristotle is realistic enough to see that a sufficient amount of external goods--lands, cattle, slaves, money and what it buys, food, shelter and clothing--is necessary for man to develop bodily and mentally. Moreover, good reputation, honor and good luck, enhance happiness. External goods, however, are means to happiness. In fact, it is not their possession as the activity about them, a working for a living, conducting one's own business, securing the material prosperity for oneself and one's family and the polis that makes man happy.

b. Bodily Goods. Health, beauty, vigor and agility and good old age are ingredients of human happiness.   Sick,   ugly, weak and clumsy   bodies cannot be called proper companions to happy living. Thus, biologically necessary activities to maintain health such as eating, drinking, bathing as well as rest and sleep used for the restoration of lost energies,

are parts of happiness. Moreover, play and
exercise enhance bodily fitness and contribute
to man's happiness.

    c. Goods of soul. Moral virtues such as temper-
        ance, courage, justice; and intellectual
        virtues such as skills and fine arts, practical
        wisdom /prudence/, understanding, theoretical
        wisdom, and conteplation--in the proper order,
        contribute to human happiness. In fact, the
        goods of soul do it in the highest degree.
        "...the good of the soul we commonly pronounce
        good in the fullest sense and the highest
        degree."[15]

All forms of activity conducive to pleasure, sensual,
intellectual and aesthetic, are ingredients of happiness.
Truly speaking, pleasure is a stimulus of, companion of,
and reward for, activity. Thus, good activity or virtuous activity is naturally pleasant. Joy found in the
virtuous life is, in fact, a sign that man is truly
virtuous.

The practice of moral and intellectual virtues is
the highest degree of human happiness. Possessing the
habit of virtue is not enough; virtue must be put into
practice. The temperate, the brave and the just man is
a happy man, especially if he is simultaneously the
skillful, the prudent, the understanding, the wise and
the contemplative man. Then, he is fully a happy man.

Aristotle could not omit in his historical and
sociological Greek context, happiness in social and
political life. The active cultivation of friendship
does enter into the cumulative state of happiness as
Books VIII and IX will amply prove. Next, marriage
and family life, i.e., a good wife, good mother, and
good children add very much to man's happiness; just
as a bad wife, bad mother, and bad children make man
unhappy.

The component parts of happiness, external goods
and internal goods both of body and soul, are listed by
Aristotle in his Rhetoric.

    If, then, such is the nature of happiness, its
    component parts must necessarily be noble birth,
    numerous friends, good friends, wealth, good
    children, numerous children, a good old age;
    further, bodily excellences, such as health,

> beauty, strength, stature, fitness for
> athletic contests, a good reputation,
> honour, good luck, virtue.[16]

Aristotle defined each of the component parts of happiness in the same place. Finally, an Athenian citizen experiences happiness in his active political, legal, administrative, and military endeavors by which he builds up the common well-being of the city-state /polis/. He participates actively in various forms of democratic political processes as an assemblyman, jury-man, councilman, and as soldier or sailor defending his country. Aristotle, as we have seen already, calls such activity "...nobler and more divine achievement."[17] He will show in Book X that political, forensic, and military life involve a participant in distractions so that contemplation is offered as the peak of human happiness. However, contemplation is properly divine happiness, and humans live lives of variety, change and struggle. It is human to find happiness in the middle of a struggle for individual and common well-being.

Chapter 9

How is Happiness Acquired?

Is happiness a gift from the gods? It is reasonable to suppose that it is since everything that men have--of which happiness is the best--is a gift from gods. Is it acquired by chance? Hardly so. The noblest thing in human life cannot be left to chance. Is it the result of learning? Not quite so. Happiness is not only knowledge but is also fulfillment of all human faculties, appetitive, as well as cognitive. Is it the result of a virtuous life? Definitely. Happiness is life in conformity with virtue both moral and intellectual. Effort and habituation is needed to make one virtuous and consequently happy. However, neither animals nor children can be called happy. They do not use intellect and free choice for acquiring and sharing happiness.

Chapter 10

Should Any One Be Called Happy While He Lives?

The question can be understood in two ways; first,
is a man actually happy when he is dead? Since Aristotle
defines happiness as a kind of activity, we cannot
accept the opinion that man is happy when he is dead.
It is true that in his work On the Soul, Book III, Aristotle presented an interesting theory of man's active
intellect surviving the death of its body; but a second
question was then raised: how can the active intellect,
without its passive counterpart, conceive ideas, make
judgments, think and contemplate alone? If, on the
other hand, the meaning is that no one can say that a
living man is happy before the course of his life is
terminated--because then, and only then, after death is
he beyond the reach of misfortune--even the latter
meaning is unacceptable. Aristotle insisted that although man undergoes changes of fortune in his life, we
need not wait for the end of his life to call him
happy. Virtue makes man happy, not fortunes. The virtuous man is not easily affected by the vicissitudes of
fortune.

> The happy man therefore will possess the
> element of stability in question and will remain
> happy all his life; since he will be always or
> at least most often employed in doing and con-
> templating the things that are in conformity
> with virtue.[18]

Surely, great successes in life will make life
more perfectly happy. On the other hand, frequent
great misfortunes may crush happiness. Still, the virtuous man bears the vicissitudes of fortune most nobly
and with great dignity and high-mindedness.

Chapter 11

Do the Fortunes of the Living Affect the Dead?

In the preceding chapter, Aristotle examined the question how much effect, if any, the lives of descendants have on the dead man. There he was skeptical that the dead are aware of the lives and fortunes of their descendants. He repeats the same opinion here regarding the lives and fortunes of the friends of the dead man. However, in both cases, he admits that such effects may be small and insignificant, making the unhappy descendants happy and depriving the happy departed of their bliss.

Chapter 12

Virtue is Praised, but Happiness is Prized

Praise of anything involves its quality and its standing relation to something else. For example, we praise a just man on the grounds of his actions and achievements and also on a comparison between his and other men's justice. Praise is proper to virtue because its excellence makes men capable of performing noble deeds.

Prize involves the honoring of something for its own sake. Such is our honoring of gods and god-like things. Human happiness is the most god-like thing and so it is prized above all other things. Happiness is the final good, the first principle and goal of life. We do everything else for its sake.

Chapter 13

The Psychological Grounds for the Division of Virtues

This subject introduces the reader to Book II of the Nichomachean Ethics. In fact, the definitive division of moral virtues will be given in Chapter 7 of Book II and of intellectual virtues in Book VI. In this place Aristotle describes the psychological background for the division of virtues. But even this psychology will be reformulated in On the Soul. An important insight, however, can be acquired from this chapter: the difference betwwen the rational and irrational part of man and its reflection on man's ethical life.

The virtue we study is human virtue. No animals or gods participate in this kind of excellence. Animals are incapable of it; gods do not need it.

Human virtue is not an excellence of the body, but one of the soul. Happiness, the result of the practice of moral and intellectual virtue, is the activity of the soul.

The soul consists of the irrational and the rational. The irrational element is subdivided into the vegetative, which is capable of nutrition, growth and reproduction and common to all living things, and the appetitive, which is the seat of appetites and desires. The former has no share in reason at all; in a morally strong man, the latter accepts the leadership of reason.

The rational element of the soul is also subdivided into two parts: "the one having rational principle /logos/ in the proper sense and in itself, the other obedient to it as a child to its father." [19] The logos is taken here not primarily in a logical sense of the reason comprehending, judging and concluding to theoretical truth but in a normative [practical] sense, as the reason that understands and formulates ethical principles and this guides the conduct of the good man. The other part of the soul's rational element is the appetitive part, first in the will, and second in the sense appetite.

Consequently, virtues are divided into the intellectual and the moral. Intellectual virtues belong to the rational part of man; the moral virtues dispose the irrational part of the soul to obey reason and so to form a good character.

The essence of Aristotelian ethics consists, then, in that reason (<u>logos</u>) understands and formulates moral principles and thus guides unreasons or appetite (<u>orexis</u>) to act well. Man, an animal possessing rational control of his conduct, is supposed to introduce measure, order and harmony into his complex being and into his social intercourse.

BOOK I

FOOTNOTES

1

  Nicomachean Ethics, Book I, i, 1-1094a 1-4. The
quotations from *Nicomachean Ethics* in this book are
taken from Aristotle: *The Nicomachean Ethics*, translated by H. Rackham (Cambridge: Harvard University
Press, 1926, 1934, 1962). Each quotation gives, besides
Rackham's divisions of the *Nicomachean Ethics*, the
standard reference numbers of the Berlin edition of
Aristotle's works.

2

  Metaphysics, Book VI, ch. 16, 1-1021B 10-30

3

  The Basic Works of Aristotle, ed. by Richard
McKeon (New York: Random House, 1941). *Physics*, II,
iii - 194b 3ss; *Metaphysics*, V, ii - 1013a 33.

4

  N.E., Book I, i, 2-1094a 5.

5

  N.E., Book I, i, 3-4-1094a 7-16.

6

  N.E., Book I, ii, 1-1-1994a 20.

7

  N.E., Book I, ii, 8-1094b 10.

8

  N.E., Book I, iv, 3-1095a 25.

9

  N.E., Book X, vi, 2-1176b 1-5.

10

  N.E., Book I, vii - 1097a 22.

11

  N.E., Book I, vii, 7-1097b 14.

12

  N.E., Book I, vii, 16-1098a 20.

13

  N.E., Book I, vii, 13-1098a 2.

14
   N.E., Book I, vii, 15-1098a 15.

15
   N.E., Book I, viii, 2-1098b 10.

16
   Rhetoric, Book I, v, 4-5 - 1360b, 19-26

17
   N.E., Book I, ii, 8-1094b 10.

18
   N.E., Book I, x, 11-1100b 15.

19
   N.E., Book I, XIII, 19-1103a 1.

BOOK II

THE THEORY OF VIRTUE

Aristotle studies in this book the nature and kinds of virtues. However, his primary concern is not to elaborate a theory of virtue for its own sake but to find out how to live a virtuous life. "We are not investigating the nature of virtue for the sake of knowing what it is, but in order that we may become good, without which result our investigation would be of no use."[1] In practical sciences--like ethics and politics--it is of the utmost importance that theory be carried out into action.

Furthermore, it must be noted here that virtuous and happy (fulfilled) lives are identified in Aristotelian philosophy. The virtuous man lives fully the functions of his nature, moral and intellectual.[2] Therefore, "The good of man is the active exercise of his soul's faculties in conformity with excellence or virtue..."[3]

Chapter 1

The Acquisition of Moral Virtue

How do we acquire virtue (arete)? There are three possible ways: by nature, by instruction and by habitual practice. "Now some thinkers hold that virtue is a gift of nature; others think we become good by habit, others that we can be taught to be good."[4] The problem of whether excellence or virtue is acquired by nature, by teaching or by habitual practice, has been raised by Plato at the opening of Meno. Plato looked at virtue as the knowledge of good, and hence something that it could be taught. Aristotle first studied this question in his Eudemian Ethics.[5] His definitive answer is to be found in the Nicomachean Ethics.[6] Moral virtues, Aristotle believed, are not the gift of nature, "for no natural property can be altered by habit," as are virtue and vice.[7] It must be said, however, that "nature gives us the capacity to receive them (virtues), and this capacity is brought to maturity by habit."[8] One does not become virtuous in his moral life by studying the theory of virtue, although a well-disposed listener might profit greatly from such a study.[9] Therefore, while not totally excluding natural inclination and instruction in moral virtues,

26

one must say that they are acquired by practicing good
deeds that create in the human mind an established
habit of doing well. Until developed into actual
moral excellence by the steady practice of good acts,
the virtuous habit remains latent. Purposefully repeated, these same acts will deepen the habit, form
the moral character, and lead to a fulfilled or happy
life.[10] Examples of practice creating moral virtues
are just, temperate and brave acts. "Similarly we
become just by doing just acts, temperate by doing temperate acts, brave by doing brave acts."[11]

It must be noted, however, that just as practice
builds up good habits, so the lack of practice and
vicious practice destroy good habits or virtue. "It
is by taking part in transactions with our fellow-men
that some of us become just and others unjust, by
acting in dangerous situations and forming a habit of
fear or of confidence we become courageous or
cowardly."[12]

Aristotle concludes this chapter by pointing out
the importance of habits inculcated in us from early
childhood. Since both children and adults should
continue cultivating a set of good habits by steady
practice, Aristotle studies here, and even more so
at the end of the N.E.[13], the importance of state
legislation. To him laws are guides of men's lives;
they inculcate good habits in citizens. They educate
citizens for good lives, both those citizens needing
only persuasion and those needing compulsion to choose
the good way of life.

Chapter 2

What Kind of Actions Lead on a Virtuous Life?

Not every action, but the right action in conformity with right reason is a virtuous action.[14] Virtues are destroyed both by deficiency and excess in actions and emotions and are preserved and increased by the mean or proper measure in action and feeling. Just as in the bodily world, "Strength is destroyed both by excessive and by deficient exercises, and similarly, health is destroyed both by too much and too little food and drink, while they are produced, increased and preserved by suitable quantities."[15] Similarly, in matters of virtues, courage, for example, is destroyed both by either too little or too much of it. In the former case we become cowards; in the latter, we become reckless. The right amount of readiness to withstand obstacles for the right reason makes us courageous. "And so with courage: we become brave by training ourselves to despise and endure terrors, and we shall be best able to endure terrors when we have become brave."[16]

It is the role of man's rational faculty (logos) to find the proper measure for actions and emotions, the mean between excess and deficiency both of which are vicious. Moral virtue lies midway between the two extremes. We shall later return to this important point in the study of virtue.[17]

Chapter 3

Pleasure and Pain: Tests of Virtue

The criteria for judging whether or not one is virtuous are supplied by tests of pleasure and pain. He who controls his propensity to pleasure and fear of pain is a virtuous man; he who habitually succumbs to the lure of pleasure and avoids pain at virtue's expenses, is a vicious man. Aristotle listed several reasons for his theory that pleasure and pain are tests of virtue and vice in men.   These reasons are here summarized.

1. Virtue is concerned with pleasure and pain, because pleasure makes us do what is base and pain prevents us from doing what is noble.

2. Virtues and vices have to do with actions and feelings, both of which are accompanied by pleasure or pain and both of which virtue must keep in check.

3. The excess of pleasure causing wicked conduct must be cured by pain, a medium of punishment.

4. The object determines the nature of habits and acts; the wrong or right pursuit or avoidance of pleasure and pain are decisive factors in the corruption or improvement of man.

The above reasons sufficiently prove Aristotle's point that pleasure and pain are tests of virtue. What follows further illustrates the same thesis.

5. There are three motives for choosing or avoiding actions according to three kinds of goods: the noble, the expedient (useful), and the pleasant. The last is the best test of the good and bad man, for pleasure tends to lead us on the wrong path in life.

6. Love of pleasure is ingrained in us from birth and is hard to eradicate when it turns to wrong objects.

7. Pain and pleasure are not only the sources of our feelings but also the standards by which we

regulate, to a greater or lesser degree, our actions. "On this account therefore pleasure and pain are necessarily our main concern, since to feel pleasure and pain rightly or wrongly has a great effect on conduct."[18]

8. Resisting the lure of pleasure is more difficult than checking the impulse to anger; but after all, the primary concern of virtue is located precisely in that which is difficult to achieve.

It would be wrong to infer that virtue is freedom from both pleasure and pain. The whole point is not to suppress our tendency to pleasure, but to moderate it according to rational rule.

Chapter 4

How is Virtue Formed by Acting Virtuously?

Aristotle has established in Chapter 1 that in order to acquire moral virtue one has to practice the acts of that virtue. "We become just by doing just acts, temperate by doing temperate acts, brave by doing brave acts."[19] Aristotle himself raised the question that this conclusion involves the following difficulty: if one cannot *become* virtuous unless he does the same acts as one who *is* already virtuous, is not this a vicious circle?

The difficulty is solved by distinguishing the objective acts that are or look temperate, just and brave from the subjective elements of a virtuous act. Intention, choice, and habitual disposition are the three subjective conditions for acts flowing from virtue. A good action must be done knowingly, deliberately and must spring from a permanent disposition of good moral character. In other words a man must know what he is doing and he must know that what he is doing is right; he must choose to do what he is doing; finally, his acts must flow from a habitually good disposition of moral character. Knowledge alone is not enough in a virtuous act. Two other conditions are here of utmost importance; they are choice and good character.

Therefore, virtuous acts externally practiced are not yet a guarantee that a man is virtuous. Virtuous acts are truly so by a deep connection with the human mind, its intellect and will. "Thus, although actions are entitled just and temperate when they are such acts as just and temperate men would do, the agent is just and temperate not when he does these acts merely, but when he does them in the way in which just and temperate men do them."[20]

31

Chapter 5

The Genus of Moral Virtue

Of all the nine accidents virtue fits best into
that of quality. But Aristotle lists four types of
qualities:[21] habit (hexis) and disposition (diathesis),
capacity and incapacity (dynamis, adynamiā), affective
quality and emotion (pathetikē poiotēs, pathos), and the
shape and form of things (schēma, morphē). Since shape
and form are qualities of bodies, they obviously have
nothing to do with virtue; therefore, only the first
three are mentioned here. Now, virtue cannot be either
an affective quality or an emotion. The former means
that we are affected by qualities of things such as
sweetness, coldness, and the like; the latter means that
we have emotions such as love, anger, fear. But we do
not call men good or bad for being affected by various
qualities of things either pleasantly or painfully, or
for having different emotions, for these are neither
good nor bad in themselves. Both of these are given to
us; they are not chosen; they do not express an attitude,
a motive, or knowledge. Virtue is neither capacity nor
incapacity; for we are not called good or bad, we are not
praised or blamed simply because we are capable of feeling or acting this or that way. We actually have to feel
and act to become good or bad. Therefore, having elimi-
nated other kinds of qualities, virtue must be either a
disposition or a habit. Aristotle concludes that, since
a disposition can be easily lost, virtue must be a good,
permanent disposition called habit (hexis), fixed by the
steady practice of good acts and disposing the mind to a good
action. Habit is then the general category (genus) of
virtue. It makes a virtuous man good and it makes him
perform his function well.[22]

Chapter 6

The Differentia of Moral Virtue

In general, moral virtue is a habit of mind. However, what is its specific, distinguishing characteristic? Or, what kind of habit is moral virtue? For Aristotle, moral virtue is a good habit of choosing the proper mean in actions and feelings. The following is his
explanation of the virtuous mean.

In every continuous quantity that is infinitely
divisible and found in things, as well as in human actions and emotions, there is a larger, smaller and equal
or middle (ison, meson) part. The larger and the
smaller parts in things are measured by the middle. Let
us present it graphically by the line:

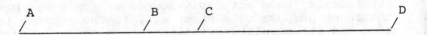

A-B is a smaller part, and B-D is the larger part, while
A-C and C-D are the equal part. The middle point C is
the measure for two other parts.

The middle or equal part in things means a part
equal to the left part, i.e., a half. Let us look at the
line again and bissect it at the point equally distant
from its two ends.

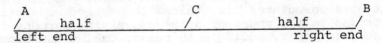

Now, the middle point in actions and feelings is
the middle point between too much and too little of them.

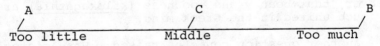

Since every individual human agent is different
from others in many ways, Aristotle introduces, besides
the objective mean in things, actions and emotions,
which is the same for all, the mean relative to us, i.e.,
to each individual. Thus, taking a middle part

33

of actions and emotions relative to the moral agent
means taking the proper amount for the recipient, lying
between two other amounts that happen to be one too much
and the other too little for him. For example, if ten
pounds of food per day is too much for adults and two
pounds of food too little, it does not follow that all
adults must eat six pounds of food per day. Six is an
objective or arithmetical middle point between two and
ten, because 6-2 = 10-6=4. On the contrary, the mean
between excess and deficiency in eating will be different for each individual.

```
A           D D  D    D D       D D            B
/      ---        1 2 /      3 4 5 ---        /
Too little                       Too much
```

Why does Aristotle introduce the concept of quantity to measure a quality or good habit which apparently
cannot be measured? The application of a quantitative
standard can hardly be applied to all elements entering
into morally good actions. How do we apply the mean to
the inner purpose of a human act, to the agent's intention and its moral circumstances, and to the character
of the person has the right intention and performs what
is right for the right reason?

The partial answer to Aristotle's quantitative
illustration of the virtuous mean comes from his Greek
background. Greeks used to see the quantity of proportion, harmony, measure, equality, or moderation in their
sculpture, painting, and architecture. The canon of
proportion of the human body was well known to the educated and sensed by simple men and women. Accordingly,
Aristotle formulated his ethical concept of moderation
according to the model of arts--expressing harmony in
measurable lines, adding nothing nor taking anything
away from the perfect work of art without destroying it.
Arts aim ultimately at the harmony of invisible beauty.
Thus, the virtuous mean for Aristotle was a qualitative
concept of reasonable conduct. We should not forget,
moreover, that beauty and goodness (kalokagathia) are
very much united in the Greek mind.

Another question could be raised: Has Aristotle
introduced moral relativism into ethics by accepting a
virtuous mean relative to each individual? To answer
this question one may say that Aristotle was deeply aware
that human actions are individual or particular and that
each individual grows morally in a manner proportionate
to his individual self. However, regardless

of character, temperament, bodily constitution and endowments, individuals have the same human nature, and thus
a   common human function to achieve. Aristotle rightly
blends both objective and subjective morality.

Moral virtue is concerned with the proper choice[23]
of the mean of actions and emotions in order to avoid
the vicious extremes of excess or deficiency. Who will
determine what is the proper mean relative to us? We
will first take our feelings, then our actions. We can
be frightened or bold, experience pleasure or pain,
either too much or too litle, in both cases wrongly.
But "to feel these feelings at the right time, on the
right occasion, towards the right people, for the right
purpose, and in the right manner, is to feel the best
amount of them, which is the mean amount--and the best
amount is of course the mark of virtue. And similarly
there can be an excess, deficiency, and due mean in
actions."[24]

Logos--the rational principle, rule or plan to
which excess, deficiency, and the mean must be referred
  in order to find out how wrong or how right our
feelings and actions are--is a practical (praktikos),
right (orthos) logos that is the norm of virtuous mean.
Thus, virtuous mean becomes a reasonable mean, a rational
determination of the right circumstances of morally good
or bad feelings or action.

But how do we apply moral, practical and right
norms to each particular emotion and action? We do so
by using practical wisdom or prudence[25]--the intellectual
virtue without which moral virtue is incomplete, as
will be seen later.[26] Here, at least a brief remark
may be in order. Prudence directs (counsels, judges,
commands) the use of the right principles in choosing
the right means for reaching the right goals of life.
Justice, temperance, and courage dispose the passions
as well as the intellectual appetite (the will) to
follow the directives of practical wisdom.[27] For example, to act bravely, a man must possess courage; but to
act courageously, a brave man must have prudence.

To be morally virtuous one must either have practical wisdom or follow the example or precept of someone prudent. We call such a person whose conduct is an
example to his community a wise or prudent man.

Taking into consideration all the elements explained, we may finally define the virtue. "Virtue then is

a settled disposition (hexis) of the mind determining
the choice (proairesis) of actions and emotions, consisting essentially in the observance of the mean
(mesotēs) relative to us, this being determined by
          principle (logos), that is, as the prudent man
(phronimos) would determine it."[28]

Several of Aristotle's remarks are welcome at
this point. First, becoming a virtuous man is hard
because one has to have the right mean in his actions
and emotions, no more, no less. Becoming a vicious man
is easy; vice is both excess and deficiency in many degrees on both sides of the mean. Moral success is possible in one way only, while moral failure is possible
in many ways.

Secondly, the mean of virtue is not to be confused
with mediocrity. The virtuous mean is not a safe way
between extremes; it is not simply a middle-of-the-road
position, nor the line of least resistance. The virtuous mean is the most reasonable course of action to
be taken in a given situation. Avoiding two extremes is
already the high point of virtuous life; but sustaining
the mean of virtue in all human conduct is an extremely
difficult task habitually requiring one's judgment and a
building up of the steady moral effort necessary to keep
the proper balance between the two extremes. With respect to excellence, then, moral virtue is a high and
the highest point between the two extremes. Graphically,
one may illustrate this as follows:

                      Virtuous Mean

          Deficiency   Excess

Thirdly, Aristotle warns us that murder, adultery,
theft and feelings such as malice, envy, delight at
another's misfortune, do not admit of a mean. They are bad
in themselves, not only because of their excess or deficiency, but because they are always wrong and never
right. For example, depending on the person, time and
manner, adultery cannot be judged as either right or
wrong;   merely committing such action at all is wrong.
The mean is opposed to excess and deficiency; therefore,
there is no mean of excess or deficiency, and there is
no excess or deficiency of the mean. "There is no such
thing as observing a mean in excess or deficiency, nor
as exceeding or falling short in the observance of the
mean."[29]

                           36

Chapter 7

Division of Moral Virtues

Virtues are divided into two main groups: intellectual and moral. Intellectual virtues (discussed in Book VI) belong to the rational part of man, while moral virtues dispose the irrational part of the soul to form a good character. In Book II of the Nicomachean Ethics, Aristotle outlined moral virtues according to the feelings to be controlled and actions to be done. Although Aristotle's list of feelings and virtues is far from exhaustive, it is important to know that for each virtue there are two corresponding vices, or vicious extremes.

1. Division of Moral Virtues According to Feeling (Pathos)

Feeling	Virtue	Deficiency	Excess
Confidence	Courage	Cowardice	Recklessness
Fear	Courage	Fearlessness	Cowardice
Pleasures of Touch	Temperance	Insensitiveness	Self-Indulgence
Anger	Gentleness	Spiritlessness	Irascibility
Shame	Modesty	Shamelessness	Bashfulness

Aristotle also listed the following:

Feeling: Pain and pleasure felt at others' good or bad fortune.

Virtue: Righteous joy at others' deserved good fortune; righteous indignation at others' undeserved good fortune.

Deficiency: Malice or rejoicing in another's misfortune.

Excess: Envy or deep sorrow in view of others' good fortune.

But according to Aristotle, the feelings of pain and pleasure at others' good or bad fortune are intermediate states, not pure feelings, and, in the strict sense, their corresponding virtues are not virtues.

2. Division of Moral Virtues According to Action (Praxis)

Action	Virtue	Deficiency	Excess
Pursuit of Money:			
a) Giving and getting money on a modest scale	Liberality	Stinginess	Prodigality
b) Giving money on a large scale	Magnificence	Niggardliness	Extravagance
Pursuit of Honors:			
a) On a modest scale	Dignity	Lack of ambition	Pride
b) On a large scale	Greatness of soul	Smallness of soul	Vanity
Social Intercourse:			
a) Conversation	Truthfulness (sincerity)	Self-deprecia-tion	Boastfulness
b) Pleasantness in social inter-course	Wittiness	Boorishness	Buffoon-ery
c) Pleasant com-panionship	Friendliness	Obsequious-ness and flattery[30]	Quarrel-someness
Exchange of Goods:	Justice	Injustice	Injustice

Courage, temperance, justice and friendship will be taken up later.[31]Detailed explanations of the remaining moral virtues will be given in Book IV of the Nico-machean Ethics.

Chapter 8

The Relation Between the Mean and Its Extremes

The extremes, excess and deficiency, and the mean of virtue are related as follows. Each virtue is opposed to two extremes; the extremes are opposed to each other and to the mean. The middle is opposed to both extremes; it exceeds deficiency, and it is deficient in relation to excess. Thus, the people who act and feel at the extremes push the mean to the other extreme. For example, a coward calls a brave man reckless; a reckless man calls a brave man a coward.

The extremes, opposite vices, are more opposed to each other than to the virtue in the middle. Aristotle's teaching could be opposed on the ground that vices are closer to each other than they are to virtue. Vice is multiform, and the transition from one to another, even to the opposite extreme, is easier than bridging their distance from the virtuous life. However, there is a certain similarity between virtue and excess, as in the case of courage and recklessness.

In some cases the deficiency or in others the excess is more opposed to the mean (virtue). For example, the deficiency, cowardice, is more opposed to courage than the excess, recklessness; in the case of temperance, the excess, self-indulgence, is more opposed than the deficiency, insensitivity. There are two reasons for this. In some cases this result arises from the very nature of the facts. In its nature, courage is more opposed to cowardice than to recklessness, whereas in other cases, the result arises from ourselves--those things seem to us more opposed to the mean to which we are ourselves more prone. Thus, we oppose temperance more to self-indulgence than to a disciplined life.

Chapter 9

Some Moral Advice on How to Become Virtuous

To keep the mean of virtue, person, act and circum-
stance must be kept in view; for instance, who, what,
to whom, on what occasion, in what manner, for what
reason. "Anybody can become angry--that is easy, and
so it is to give and spend money; but to be angry with
or to give money to the right person,   to the right
amount, at the right time, for the right purpose, and
in the right way--that is not within everybody's power
and is not easy; so that to do these things properly
is rare, praiseworthy, and noble." [32]

In this chapter Aristotle gives three practical
moral counsels for achieving the virtuous mean.

1. First avoid the extreme that is more opposed
    to the mean. For instance, while driving, if
    you must choose between hitting a pedestrian
    or a fence, choose the fence.

2. Keeping in mind your strengths and weaknesses
    consider your natural inclinations and act
    accordingly. For example, if you are very
    brave, take care not to behave recklessly; if
    you drink immoderately, avoid drinking alto-
    gether.

3. Beware of immoderate pleasures; they are the
    real test of the virtuous man. Taking an ex-
    ample from Roman history, one may say that
    Anthony's downfall stemmed from overindulgence
    in sexual pleasures.

In spite of all advice, one becomes a virtuous man
only when the act or feeling is set and measured in its
proper circumstances. In the first place, practice
makes man virtuous, and only secondarily counsels make
possible learning to act right or wrong when an occasion comes again.

BOOK II

FOOTNOTES

1

  Nicomachean Ethics, Book II, ii, 1-1103a 27.
  See also N.E., Book X, ix, 1-1179b,1.

2

  N.E., Book I, vii, 14-1098a 10 ff.

3

  N.E., Book I, vii, 15-1098a 15.

4

  N.E., Book X, ix, - 1179b, 20.

5

  Eudemian Ethics, Book I, 4 - 1214a, 14ff.

6

  N.E., Books II and X.

7

  N.E., Book II, i, 2-1103a 20.

8

  N.E., Book II, i, 3 - 1103a 25.

9

  N.E., Book X, 9, 6-7 - 1179b, 25.

10

  Aristotle indulges here at the beginning of
Book II in a philological study, based not on the identity of roots of words but on their similarity. He
tells us that the Greek word for habit or custom ĕthos
is probably kindred to the word ēthos which means moral
character. Now, since the word ēthikos moral and morality, derives from ēhos   then the three linquistic expressions, habit, character, and morality are all kindred words.

11

  N.E., Book II, i, 4 - 1103b 1.

12

  N.E., Book II, i, 7-1103b 15.

13

  N.E., Book X, ix - 1179b-118 1b.

14
   This dictum will be discussed at length in Book VI.

15
  N.E., Book II, ii, 6-1104a 15.

16
  N.E., Book II, ii, 9-1104b 1.

17
  N.E., Book II, chs. 6-9.

18
  N.E., Book II, iii, 9-1105a 5.

19
  N.E., Book II, i, 4-1103b 1.

20
  N.E., Book II, iv, 4-1105b 5.

21
  Categories, viii - 8b 25-10a 25.

22
  N.E., Book II, vi, 2-3 - 1106a 20.

23
   The choice will be studied in Book III ch. 2.

24
  N.E., Book II, vi, 11-1106b, 15-25

25
   Prudence, phronesis, will be discussed in Book VI,
ch. 5.

26
  N.E., Book VI, 13.

27
  N.E., Book Vi, xii, xiii - 1143b-1144a, b and
1145a; N.E., Book X, viii, 3-1178a 16-20.

28
  N.E., Book II, vi, 15-1107a 1-5.

29
  N.E., Book II, vi, 20-1107a 20-25.

30
The obsequious man has no personal stake in a
matter, the flatterer aims at his own interests.

31
Courage: Book III, vi-ix; Temperance: Book III,
x-xii; Justice: Book V; Friendship: Books VIII-IX.

32
<u>N.E.</u>, Book II, ix, 2-1109a 25.

BOOK III

CONDITIONS OF FREE CHOICE AND MORAL RESPONSIBILITY

We have seen in the preceding section that the
very essence of moral virtue consists in choosing the
right mean between excess and defect in feelings and
actions. The nature of such a choice and the moral responsibility for it are the next problems we must consider. Is a man equally responsible for all his actions
and passions concerning moral virtues? The human act is
performed out of deliberate decision with knowledge and
consent. But not all knowledge is equally clear; man does
not consent in all cases in the same degree, nor is he
always allowed to make his own choices. An intelligent,
voluntary, and freely chosen human act involves full
knowledge of the intellect and free choice. Whatever
destroys or lessens either of these two elements destroys or lessens the voluntary character of the action.

Chapter 1

Types of Human Action

Obstacles to Voluntary Action

Aristotle distinguished between types of human
action, for the purpose of showing when the moral agent
is fully involved or when the man is a true efficient
cause of his action. A voluntary*/or willed/act (hekousion, denotes a voluntary action, and the person who
consents to perform such action is called hekōn) proceeds from the agent's knowledge and agreement. "...a
voluntary act wouldseem to be an act of which the origin
lies in the agent, who knows the particular circumstances in which he is acting." [1] A voluntary act, then,
is one "when the origin of an action is in oneself; it is
in one's own power to do it or not."[2] Aristotle more
explicitly defines voluntary action later on: "By a
voluntary action, as has been said before, I mean any
action within the agent's own control which he performs
knowingly, that is, without being in ignorance of the

*The words 'voluntary' and 'involuntary' as well as 'non-
voluntary' used here as translations of Aristotle's
terms are not appropriate. They presuppose the whole
philosophy of the will that Aristotle did not have.
However, other words are hard to coin.

44

person affected, the instrument employed, and the result (for example he must know whom he strikes, and with what weapon, and the effect of the blow): and in each of these respects both accident [mistake, ignorance] and compulsion must be excluded." 3

Aristotle pointed out two elements in the nature of a voluntary act: it is produced from within man by his deliberate volition, and it is done by man's knowledge of what he is doing. This latter element of knowledge should be again subdivided: the moral agent knows, or should know, by deliberate reflection on his desired end and means suitable to that end, that such and such an action, as a rule, will lead him to his end. But he must also know the particular moral circumstances in which his action must be affected in order to lead to his end. In other words, the moral agent must understand both the universal moral knowledge of human goals and means and the particular situation in which his action is to be projected in order to lead to his end. Thus ignorance of the general moral principles does not excuse; on the contrary, only the ignorance of particular moral circumstances renders an action involuntary.4 For example, there is no excuse for not knowing that stealing another man's horse is forbidden; but it is excusable if the man takes a horse he thought was his own. The involuntary, or unwilled act (akousion) for such an act; akōn for the moral agent who commits the act) is done under the constraint of external factors contrary to man's rational part, against his inner self, and consequently "it causes the agent pain and regret."5 A nonvoluntary, or nonwilled act (ouch hekousion for such an act, and   ouch hekōn for the person who performs this act) is done in ignorance of its moral circumstances and consequences, and the agent does not regret it. Aristotle points out here that out of ignorance of the moral circumstances (especially of a person affected by the action and the result coming out of the action), two kinds of action follow: involuntary--when the agent feels regret and pain for having done such an action; non-voluntary-when the agent feels no regret for having done such an action. "Acts done through ignorance therefore fall into two classes: if the agent regrets the act, we think that he has acted involuntarily; if he does not regret it, to mark the distinction we may call him a 'non-voluntary' agent." 6

Mixed actions (miktai praxeis) are partly voluntary and partly involuntary (although, strictly speaking, more voluntary than involuntary). A man performs such an action with the clear understanding that it is a reasonable thing to do it here and now, but he does it reluctantly in order to avoid a greater evil; e.g., a man consenting to have his leg amputated in order to save his life. "Such acts therefore are voluntary, though perhaps involuntary apart from circumstances-- for no one would choose to do any such action in and for itself." [7] Deliberate (proaireton) action refers to the means within one's power for reaching the end or ends set in his mind after reflecting upon them. For example, a student decides to go to the college of his choice.

Obstacles to Voluntary Action

Compulsion (bia) is an action exacted of a man under constraint by an outside use of force. "An act is compulsory when its origin is from without, being of such a nature that the agent, who is really passive, contributes nothing to it: for example, when he is carried somewhere by the stress of weather, or by the people who have him in their power." [8]

When a man performs bad actions under a pressure of violence that no one could withstand, he is not guilty; his actions are involuntary. But Aristotle here was careful to add that some acts are so repulsive that their repulsion should be stronger than any physical or other force exerted upon man to commit them; hence, if he commits them, he must be held as responsible as the one who has chosen to do so. "Yet there seem to be some acts which a man cannot be compelled to do, and rather than do them he ought to submit to the most terrible death."[9] Such might be the case when a tyrant tries to compel a man to kill his mother. Furthermore, there are degrees of outside violence put on man. Accordingly, there are degrees of voluntariness and involuntariness involved in the actions of the compelled man. In fact, actions done under pressure, but in view of some benefits, are voluntary actions performed on the initiative of the agent in the given circumstances.[10] The objection is sometimes raised that pleasant and noble actions are done under constraint, because the pleasant and the noble are external and have a compelling power. Aristotle answered that in this view all actions would be done under constraint; we are motivated in every one of our acts by pleasant and noble goods. But if we act consciously and willingly, our motivation is not compulsion.

46

Fear (phobos) is not a simple emotion but a gen-
eralized anxiety caused by an imminent or future danger.
Its origin may be within the agent (sickness) or without (the threat of blackmailers). Its intensity may be
serious (fear of death, public disgrace, or financial
ruin) or slight, depending on the immanent danger. As
for its influence, man acts from fear when fear precedes the action. Man acts with fear when fear accompanies the action without causing it--for example, a
soldier endures battle despite his fear.

Fear may render an act involuntary if the intensity of the emotion blocks man's rational control. But
not every act done out of fear destroys voluntariness;
circumstances are the determining factors. "But there
is some doubt about actions done through fear of a worse
alternative, or for some noble object--as for instance
if a tyrant having a man's parents and children in his
power commands him to do something base, when if he
complies their lives will be spared but if he refuses
they will be put to death. It is open to question
whether such actions are voluntary or involuntary."[11]
Hence, acts done from fear are less voluntary, but they
remain voluntary, and are involuntary only due to the
circumstances, such as in the case of a man who gives
money to a robber in the fear of being killed.

Ignorance (agnoia) is not a simple absence of any
knowledge, but a lack of the necessary knowledge that a
person should have in order to act morally. Ignorance
is involuntary when it causes the agent pain and regret.
The agent acts without his consent and his better judgment. Thus, he feels pain and regret. On the contrary,
if the agent feels no regret for the bad act done, he
is either unaware of what he really has done--in that
case his action is non-voluntary--or he knows well the
nature of his action and does not regret it. He would
have gone ahead (for example, shooting an enemy) even
if he had known what he had not known (the 'deer' at
which he was aiming was in fact his enemy hiding in the
bush). He is committing a voluntary bad act and is
guilty. Another distinction is also very important.
One kind of ignorance precedes the act, which then is
done through, out of, or due to ignorance. In that case
the action of the moral agent is involuntary, and he is
not guilty. We presuppose that the man would not have
done what he had done if he had known what he was doing
(we may substitute in our previous example of a hunter
killing not his enemy but his friend because he thought
he was firing at a deer). Another type of ignorance is

the one accompanying the act, which is then done in ignorance. Such an act is voluntary, and the man is guilty. Why? Either because a person neglects to acquire the necessary knowledge and to dispel the ignorance, or because by deliberately choosing ignorance, he pleads ignorance as an excuse for his action, or because by putting himself in a drunken state, for example, he acts in ignorance. Thus, "when a man is drunk or in a rage, his actions are not thought to be done through ignorance but owing to one or another of the conditions mentioned, though he does act without knowing, and in ignorance." [12]

People often excuse wickedness because of the ignorance in which wicked men live most of the time. But that is a gross over-simplification. We should expect every normal, adult man and woman to know what he or she has to do (the object), his or her identity as moral subject (person acting), the persons affected by an action, the circumstances of an action (time, place, manner, the means used in committing an act, the intention or purpose), and the consequences that will or could follow from his or her act.

However, among the above elements of a moral act we may distinguish two kinds: general moral determinants such as the act done, and the person acting (including a person's character, awareness, free choice, intention, and life goal). As a rule, everyone knows his identity as a moral agent and his good or end. As a result, he knows what to do and what to avoid in order to reach such an end. An ignorance of ends is not excusable, and is the sort of ignorance constituting vice.

As to the particular determinants of morality of action--moral circumstances and consequences--the agent may not be guilty when he cannot see particular circumstances or foresee certain consequences of an action. In these cases, if a person deliberately neglects acquiring the knowledge that would dispel ignorance, his ignorance is voluntary, and he is responsible for his action. If, however, he acts out of ignorance that could not be avoided (such as a hunter killing his friend when he thought he was firing at a deer) his ignorance is involuntary and he is not guilty.

Passion (epithymiā), especially the strong ones such as anger, love, hate and despair, modifies the voluntariness of a human act. Strong passions can

48

cloud the clear understanding of the circumstances,
thereby producing non-voluntary action. When passion
is not strong, it may even increase voluntariness.
Ordinary desires and emotions increase the voluntary,
but they also decrease free choice. When passion has
been voluntarily aroused, the action flowing from it is
not only voluntary but even more voluntary than it
would had there been no deliberate stimulus.

Chapter 2

Choice

Choice (proairesis) is a voluntary act, but implies an agent's wider and deeper involvement. Aristotle, as we know, ascribed the voluntary act to children and animals but choice is a truly human act and of crucial importance in moral life. This is the closest Aristotle came to the problem later to be called "freedom of the will." This concept was not completely clear to him in a Greek setting where Nature (physis), Necessity (ananke), and Chance (tyche) seemed to leave little to human freedom.

The study of choice involves an analysis of the moments through which the fully deliberate human act must pass. In the genesis of the human act, these moments must not be considered separate or isolated; they are psychological elements of a single whole. The whole man acts and every human act is a unit.

Before we answer what is choice, let us see what the choice is not. Thus, choice cannot be identified with the following:

a. Appetite (orexis). Appetite is found in animals, but choice is not; the acts of morally weak people are accompanied by appetite, but not by choice; the acts of morally strong people are accompanied by choice but not by appetite. The appetite deals with what is pleasant and painful, while choice deals neither with the pleasant or painful, but with the good or bad.

b. Passion (pathos). An act done out of passion is certainly not based upon choice.

c. Wish (boulesis). Wish is about the end (for example, health), and choice about means (for example, food, rest); a wish may have an impossible goal (for example, that a mortal man live the life of immortal gods), but choice refers to means within our possibility.

d. Opinion (doxa). Opinions are characterized not by their moral goodness or badness, but by their truth or falsehood. We make a choice of

things we definitely know as good, and we form
opinions about the things we do not quite know;
the same people do not make the best choices
and hold the best opinions; rather some hold
good opinions, but because of moral depravity
do not make the right choice.

"Choice is a voluntary action, preceded by deliberation, since choice involves reasoning and some process
of thought."[13] Both volitive and cognitive elements,
desire and thought, enter into the fabric   of
choice. "Choice will be a deliberate desire of things
in our power; for we first deliberate, then select, and
finally fix our desire according to the result of our
deliberation."[14]

Thus, choice involves the following elements:

a. perception of an end; b. desire of an end;
c. deliberation about means; d. practical judgment about
the means I can choose here and now; e. actual choice
(selection) of the means; f. an act performed.

The following illustration will give us a clearer
understanding of the elements of choice. Let us divide
the elements of choice into two groups: those that must
be done in the mind during, say, the planning phase, and
those that are done in practice in what we might call
the performing phase. Both will be subdivided as to
ends and means.

PLANNING PHASE

Concerning the End

Perception of the good as end - I see health as my good.

Desire of an end - I desire my health.

Concerning the Means

Deliberation about the means - I need good food, exercise, rest and clean environs for my health.

Practical judgment about the means to choose - Exercise
is something I can do here and now.

Actual choice of the proposed mean - I choose to exercise daily for my health.

PERFORMING PHASE

Concerning the Means

I use my powers (faculties) to fulfill the choice - I exercise daily .

Perhaps we may add one more element.

Concerning the End

Joy in the end attained - I enjoy that my health has considerably improved due to daily exercise.

Aristotle explains the fine interplay of thought and desire, built in every choice, as follows: "Choice may be called either thought related to desire or desire related to thought; man, as an originator of action, is a union of desire and intellect."[15] Hence, choice may be called either thought brought by desire (orektikos noūs) or desire guided by thought (orexis dianoētikē). The root of choice is then to be found in intellect or thought, and in the deep desire of goods to be chosen. The latter elements of desire should be rooted in the moral character of man: "Choice necessarily involves both intellect or thought and a certain disposition of character."[16]

Chapter 3

Deliberation

Deliberation (<u>Bouleusis</u>) is not only an important and indispensable precedent of choice but also of the virtue of prudence or practical wisdom. "The prudent man in general will be the man who is good at deliberating in general."[17] More about the connection between prudence and deliberation will be seen in Book VI. One[18] can learn what deliberation is there from the same book. Aristotle tells us that deliberation is not scientific knowledge (<u>epistēmē</u>) because men do not deliberate upon things certain and known but upon the uncertain and unknown. Deliberation is not a form of opinion because matters of opinion have been already settled in the mind of the one who accepted them, but the process of deliberation has not reached the stage of affirmation. Finally, deliberation cannot be thought of as shrewd guessing; deliberating takes time whereas the latter is done quickly.

The discussion of the nature of deliberation falls into three sections:

1. The Object of Deliberation

The term 'object of deliberation' presumably must not include things which a fool or madman might deliberate about, but those about which a sensible person would deliberate. For example, nobody deliberates about:[19]

a. Things eternal, such as the order of the universe.

b. Things that change but follow a regular process, whether by necessity or by nature or through some other cause; such phenomena, for instance, as the solstices or the sunrise.

c. Irregular occurrences such as droughts or rains.

d. The result of chance, such as finding a hidden treasure.

We do not deliberate about these things because they
are not within our power. Man is the source of his actions, and the province of deliberation is that of discov-
ering actions within one's own power to perform. We
deliberate then about matters which, though subject to
rules generally holding good, are uncertain in their
results and yet can be calculated with probability.

2. The Process of Deliberation

We deliberate not about ends but about the means
for attaining those ends. Aristotle's examples are
quite clear: no physician deliberates whether he should
cure, no orator whether he should convince, no statesman whether he should establish law and order. We take
some ends for granted and then consider in what manner
and by what means they can be realized.

When the mind weighs reasons for or against each
means, we are deliberating. If in the course of deliberation it becomes clear that several means are available for attaining the end, we take the easiest and the
best. If the end can be achieved by only one means, the
process will be halted with its consideration, since it
would be, perforce, the only one available for attaining
the end. In that case, we consider in what manner the
end can be achieved by that means and how that means
itself can be secured.

We continue the process of deliberation until we
come to the first link in the chain of causes, the last
in the order of discovery. This is the analytical method
of solving a problem: we examine the components of
the whole and come down to its first elements. The
latter are the last in the order of analytical discovery
but the first in the order of causes.

If in the process of deliberation we encounter a
difficulty impossible to overcome (for example, we need
money and none can be procured), we abandon our deliberation; but if it becomes possible (within our power) to
find means, we begin to act.

3. Deliberation and Deliberate Choice

The object of choice is that means to our end which
has already been found to be the best by deliberation
and which is within our power to perform here and now.
We may compare the part played by deliberation and
desire in forming a deliberate decision to the role

played by the kings and the people in the Homeric constitutions. The kings deliberate, select the policy
and set it before the people and the people adopt it.
Aristotle concluded that choice could be defined as
"a deliberate desire of things in our power." [20]

Chapter 4

Wish

A wish (Boulēsis) refers to an end not to a
means. Some believe that its object is always good
(Aristotle probably means Socrates and Plato); others
think that its object is what seems to be good (probably Sophists). Neither position can be supported. The
object of a wish is not always good; otherwise we must
say, as Plato did, that a man who makes a wrong choice
does not really wish what he chooses. Furthermore, the
object of a wish cannot be only what seems good because
then nothing is by nature the object of a wish (naturally desirable) but every object of a wish is simply
subjective. Thus, as there are many individuals, there
are so many different objects of wish. In fact, what
is good for one is bad for another.

Ethics as objective and normative practical knowledge hinges on the solving of this crucial problem.
The object of wish should be good for everyone. This is
its objective and normative meaning. The object of a
wish is good for an individual or what seems to be good
to him. This is its factual and subjective meaning.

Who is able to judge what the truly good object
of our wishes (boulēton) is? Aristotle pointed to the
man of high moral standards, the example and the model to
whom we look for the objective truth of so many decep-
tive wishes. "Perhaps what chiefly distinguishes the
good man is that he sees the truth in each kind of moral
question, being himself as it were the standard and
measure of the noble and pleasant." [21]

Why do so many err when satisfying wishes? They
are misled by pleasure. The pleasurable good is chosen
because to them it is the good and pain is avoided in
the belief that it is evil.

Chapter 5

Man as Responsible Moral Agent

The end is the object of wish but the means to
the end are objects of deliberation and choice. The deliberate choice of means is done in man's mind; it springs
voluntarily from within man. Consequently, man is responsible for both his good and bad actions. Since
virtues and vices are about means, man is responsible
both for his virtuous and vicious actions. Aristotle
is thus using deliberation and choice as the personal
factors making man responsible for his actions. Those
arguing for the absence of responsibility because of an
alleged absence of choice are clearly wrong.

An example will illustrate this. Lawgivers punish
evildoers, but not those who were under constraint or
acted out of ignorance for which they are not responsible.
The same lawgivers honor those who act nobly. Their intention is to encourage the latter and to deter the former. Yet nobody encourages us to do what is not in our
power to do.

Humans make several attempts to escape moral responsibility. One attempt is the pretext that ignorance
is responsible for most of human evil deeds. Aristotle
repeats what he said before of ignorance; neither ignorance of fact, induced voluntarily, say by drunkenness,
nor ignorance of law, excuse an adult and mature moral
agent.

Carelessness is another excuse for irresponsible
behavior. Carelessness, some say, is a part of man's
character. We are, perhaps, constitutionally careless
beings. Aristotle answers this objection in a very
straight way: each is responsible for carelessness when
he lives a loose and mindless way of life. A given type
of activity produces a corresponding character. This is
true of one who performs repeatedly unjust, intemperate,
unfriendly actions; he voluntarily becomes unjust, intemperate, unfriendly. It is true that acquired and
fixed habits become second nature and man follows them
almost irresistibly. But he initially had the possibility of not becoming unjust, intemperate or unfriendly. Those traits were voluntarily acquired.

The most serious objection to moral responsibility

is raised: "All men seek what seems to them good, but they are not responsible for its seeming good; each man's conception of his end is determined by his character, whatever that may be". 22

Aristotle answers that the individual is responsible for his moral habits and is hence responsible for the sum-total of his moral habits, i.e., for his moral character. Furthermore, he is similarly responsible for what appears to be good. Otherwise, no one is responsible for his wrongdoing but everyone is ignorant of his end, and of what is good and evil in his actions. Now, the end of life and the goodness and badness of our actions are not determined by the choice of the individual himself but by the moral sense and vision of the right logos that man, good and bad, is endowed with by nature. True, bad men have a distorted vision of what is noble and what is base, but they are responsible for such an incorrect vision. Somewhere along the road, they have allowed their healthy moral vision of right and wrong human actions to become ill or distorted. It follows that both virtue and vice are voluntary.

Finally, one difference must be stated: our actions and habits are not voluntary in the same sense. Insofar as we know the particular circumstances surrounding them, we are in control of our actions from beginning to end. But only the beginnings of our habits are controlled. All subsequent steps in the development of habits are quite hard to perceive. This, however, does not absolve anyone from responsibility for his actions. We deserve merit for virtuous and demerit for vicious habits, since the power to behave or not to behave in a given way was ours when our habits began to form.

Aristotle definitely rejected the Socratic view that no man is willingly bad. He is an outspoken advocate of human responsibility. He will, however, admit later on[23] the debilitating influence of many factors upon man's exercise of his actions. But to absolve a bad man from any responsibility for his deeds on account of his bodily constitution, education, inheritance, or environment is far from Aristotle's teaching on moral responsibility.

Here the discussion on free choice and moral responsibility ends, and Aristotle begins studying individual
moral virtues already listed in Book II, Chapter 7.
Courage and temperance will be studied in Book III and
the rest in Book IV. While some of these virtues have
been esteemed and deemed necessary in Aristotle's time,
they are not highly valued in ours; others more nearly
suit us and all of them are instructive for measuring
the moral quality of life. We will follow, as usual,
the text of the Nicomachean Ethics closely and explain
it succinctly.

Chapter 6

Courage: Its Subject-Matter

Courage (andreiā) is a mean with respect to fear
and confidence. Men most fear disgrace, poverty, dis-
ease and lack of friends. However, none of these constitute the supreme test of courage. Since death is
what men fear most, it is the test most befitting the
strength of the courageous man. However, men die
naturally and violently every day and not all of them
are courageous people. Aristotle believed that death
in battle was a truly courageous death.

> What form of death then is a test of courage?
> Presumably that which is the noblest. Now
> the noblest form of death is death in battle,
> for it is encountered in the midst of the
> greatest and most noble of dangers.[24]

The perils of war more than any others expose
the courageous man to death. The man of courage faces
terrifying dangers because his right principle
(logos) dictates that he must and will endure perils
for the sake of what is noble (kalon).

Chapter 7

Courage: Its Nobility and the Vices Opposed to it

To arrive at a definition of courage, Aristotle
stressed both the virtuous mean of a courageous act and
the end of courage.   As with other moral virtues,
courage demands that the courageous man follow the right
mean _ moderation. His right rule (logos) directs him.
He will endure those perils that are endurable for human
beings, but not those that are above human nature, that
no man can endure. Nevertheless, if the circumstances
call for it, he will not refrain from the supreme sacrifice of his life. "The courageous man then is he that
endures or fears the right things and for the right purpose and in the right manner and at the right time, and
who shows confidence in a similar way."[25]

The end of courage is the nobility of the courageous
act. The courageous man endures the perils of death for
the sake of acting nobly. Courage is a noble virtue
because its end, giving life for one's own country, is
noble. Telos shows the very nature of virtuous habits
and their corresponding actions.

> And every activity aims at the end that corres-
> ponds to the disposition of which it is the
> manifestation. So it is therefore with the
> activity of the courageous man: his courage is
> noble; therefore its end is nobility, for a
> thing is defined by its end; therefore, the
> courageous man endures the terrors and dares
> the deeds that manifest courage, for the sake
> of that which is noble.[26]

Vices Opposed to Courage

When a man cannot control his fear in the face of
death for a noble cause he is said to be a coward. But
a man who blindly rushes into death goes beyond courage;
his attitude is irrational because it is excessive. He
is reckless. While an excess of fear results in cowardice, an excess of confidence results in recklessness. On the other hand, the lack of fear results in
fearlessness, whereas a lack of confidence will result
in cowardice. Aristotle believed that reckless men are
basically cowards wishing to feign courage. "Hence most
rash men really are cowards at heart, for they make a

bold show in situations that inspire confidence, but do not endure terrors."[27]

Suicide is Cowardly

Courage controls both the deficient fear and the excessive confidence in view of the noble deed, such as death in war for one's country. But this motivation is lacking in men who kill themselves. In spite of the contrary view that such action shows courage in the face of death, Aristotle believed that the real motivation for suicide was a desire to flee life's sorrows. Therefore, suicide is cowardly.

Chapter 8
Other Kinds of Courage

This same term "courage" is applied to five dispositions, all somewhat similar to the virtue of courage:

1. Citizen's Courage, motivated by honors and
   rewards, aims at doing well as a citizen of
   one's country, enduring the dangers facing
   every country, especially during war. Since
   this is often followed by publicly awarded
   honors, courage motivated by a noble cause is
   closest to real courage. If a citizen shows
   bravery only because he fears the punishment
   laws inflict on cowardly citizens, he is too
   far from real courage.

2. The Courage of Experience is, for instance,
   that of foreign mercenary troops fighting
   for pay. But these men may easily prove
   themselves cowards when they are under-
   equipped with weapons or outnumbered by enemies. They fear death more than disgrace.
   Brave citizens would not fly because they
   are enduring dangers for the sake of honor
   and their country's safety.

3. The Courage of Temper is a courage originating in anger and pain, and can be observed
   not only in men, but in wounded wild animals
   who attack. This is not a real courage, although it seems to be the most natural. When
   in pain men feel angry, and when angry look
   for revenge. If, however, this kind of courage is motivated by deliberate choice and
   noble purpose, it can become true courage.

4. The Courage of Optimists (euelpides=high spirited). Optimists are not truly courageous
   because they act solely on a confidence derived from many successful encounters which inspire them to boldness in danger. Only in
   this way do they resemble a truly courageous
   man. A courageous man will act courageously
   when things go wrong. He is also capable of
   staying calm against unforeseen danger. If
   a sudden alarm or incident occurs, the courageous man will stay and face it, whereas the
   optimist would probably run until he had time

to weigh the risks involved. The ability
to confront the unforeseen springs from the
natural disposition (habit and character)
of courage.

5. The Courage of Ignorance. Another variety of
   what appears to be courage is displayed by a
   person who will face a danger without realizing that it is a danger. The ignorant man's
   self-confidence will disappear the moment he
   suspects the situation is not really what
   it appears.

Chapter 9

Pain and Pleasure in Courage

Men have and are credited with courage when they
are able to bear pain patiently. Pain is the test and
the regular companion of courage. Courage can be thus
commended on the ground that it is harder to bear pain
than to abstain from pleasure.

Pleasure is not expected in most virtuous acts unless the agent attains his end. Thus, the brave man is
not deprived of pleasure altogether; his real pleasure comes with victory over an enemy; or if he succumbs,
in the conviction that he has done his best for his
country. In spite of that, the fact remains that courage means enduring pain and strain while danger
threatens. The courageous man does not seek pain; but
if it is there and it usually is, he willingly endures
it as the right and noble thing to do. Death no doubt
is a great loss to the courageous man because life has
the most to offer him, and he realizes the great
blessings he is about to lose. This, however, does not
make him a coward. The appreciation of life he sacrifices for his own country makes him more brave, for he
would rather be courageous and noble than continue on
with life's blessings. Aristotle ends this section by
remarking that the truly courageous man does not
necessarily make the best professional soldier. Soldiers who may be in a professional army could be less
courageous men; but besides their lives they have
little value to lose, hence, they are ready to risk life
for a small gain.

Chapter 10

Temperance: Its Subject-Matter

Temperance (<u>sophrosynē</u>) is the observance of
moderation in relation to pleasures and pains insofar
as we experience these when deprived of pleasure. The
subject-matter of temperance is bodily pleasure not of
the whole body (massages and warm baths are quite per-
missible and good) but of the special parts of the body
which are seats of the pleasures of eating, drinking,
and sexual intercourse. The only senses involved here
are those experiencing these pleasures: the senses of
touch and taste. Taste, however, serves touch. We
taste food and drink not only for the enjoyment of
their flavors but also in order to eat and drink, i.e.,
to get in touch with food and drink. The pleasures of
seeing a landscape, hearing music, smelling aromas, are
excluded. Furthermore, the higher pleasures of the
mind, love for learning   truth of the aesthetic pleasure derived from the beauty of natural forms and man-
made art products are also excluded. Although both the
spiritual and sensual joys that contribute to the pleasures of touch in eating, drinking and sex are to be
governed by temperance, refinements in these pleasures
fall outside the field of temperance. Briefly,
Aristotle has narrowed the subject matter of temperance
to those pleasures common to men and animals which are
satisfied in a similar fashion. But humans are not
animals and their pleasures are not identical to those
of animals. Furthermore, moderation is called for in
every kind of pleasure, in that of mind, as well as
of body.

Chapter 11

Temperance: Its Nature and Its Opposite Vices

Aristotle draws the distinction between the natural and acquired pleasures of touch in eating, drinking and sex. All men share in the former and each possesses the latter in different degrees and manners. Natural pleasures are common to all men; they serve to stimulate and to satisfy our natural needs. In this sense all men when hungry desire food and feel pleasure in eating. However, tastes in bodily pleasures differ markedly from one person to another. Tastes in food, drink and sexual preference vary with individual temperaments and personalities, education and character. The extreme of self-indulgence in natural pleasures will result in gluttony, drunkenness and lust. All of these go beyond the measure necessary for the natural satisfaction of human needs. Accordingly, the self-indulgent man goes wrong in three ways: he enjoys some things that he should not or enjoys them more than most people do, or he enjoys them in a wrong manner. 28

The self-indulgent man feels pain while desiring pleasures that he cannot attain at the time. The temperate man feels no pain when the pleasure is absent or when he is abstaining.

There is little danger of a defective extreme in temperance, except in the case of unreasonable dieting leading to malnutrition or of abstinence from drink leading to dehydration of the organism. A person is not guilty of a defective extreme if he is naturally inclined to be spare in eating and drinking or is organically impotent in sexual intercourse.

Chapter 12

Self-Indulgence: More Voluntary than Cowardice

Self-indulgence (<u>akolasiā</u>) is a voluntary action because we choose pleasure. It is more voluntary than cowardice springing from fear of pain because we avoid pain when and where we can. Consequently, self-indulgence is more wrong than cowardice.

Cowardice as habit is not painful and could even be desirable, but particular cases throw the coward into unseemly behavior of painful non-resistance and escape. On the contrary, self-indulgence is not desirable but particular pleasures are. Therefore, particular self-indulgent acts are more voluntary whereas particular cases of cowardice are less voluntary.

It is extremely important to train humans at an early age to enjoy fitting pleasures and dislike immoderate pleasures. Children and adults are not too different from one another with regard to self-indulgence with the exception of sex. However, children do not reason things through and need guidance and even physical punishment in order to desire the proper pleasures and enjoy them in the right way. Otherwise, we will have spoiled, unruly children whose desire for pleasures, if unchecked, will grow to monstrous proportions.

Just as a child has to obey and follow his tutor, so the sense appetite's desire for pleasures must be controlled by <u>logos</u>. Briefly, "the temperate man desires the right thing in the right way, at the right time, which is what principle [logos] ordains." [29]

BOOK III

1   Footnotes
Nicomachean Ethics, Book III, i, 20-1111a, 20.

2
N.E., Book III, 1, 6-1110a, 15.

3
N.E., Book V, viii, 3-1135a, 20-25.

4
N.E., Book III, i, 15-1110b, 15-1111a.

5
N.E., Book III, i, 13-1110b, 15.

6
N.E., Book III, i, 13-1110b, 20.

7
N.E., Book III, i, 6-1110a 15.

8
N.E., Book III, i, 3-1110a.

9
N.E., Book III, i, 8-1110a 25.

10
N.E., Book III, i, 10-1110b 5-10.

11
N.E., Book III, i, 4-1110a 5.

12
N.E., Book III, i, 14-1110b 25.

13
N.E., Book III, ii, 17-1112a 15.

14
N.E., Book III, iii, 19-1113a, 10.

15
N.E., Book VI, ii, 5-1139b, 5.

16
N.E., Book VI, ii, 4-1139a, 30.

17
    N.E., Book VI, v, 2-1140a 30.

18
    N.E., Book VI, ch. 9.

19
    N.E., Book III, iii, 3-7 - 1112a, 20-30.

20
    N.E., Book III, iii, 19-1113a 10.

21
    N.E., Book III, iv, 5-1113a 30.

22
    N.E., Book III, v, 17 - 1114a 30.

23
    N.E., Book VII.

24
    N.E., Book III, vi, 8-1115a 30.

25
    N.E., Book III, vii, 5-1115-b 15.

26
    N.E., Book III, vii, 6-1115b 20.

27
    N.E., Book III, vii, 9-1115b 30.

28
    N.E., Book III, xi, 4-1118b 25.

29
    N.E., Book III, xii, 9-1119b 15.

BOOK IV

SELECTED MORAL VIRTUES

Book IV continues the detailed characterization
of the moral virtues listed in Book II, 7. Two of the
eleven, courage and temperance, have been covered in
Book III, 6-12, while the remaining nine are studied
in Book IV.

Four of these moral virtues are concerned with
the main pursuits of man in society: the pursuit of
wealth and money (liberality and magnificence) and the
pursuit of honor (dignity and the greatness of soul).
Three virtues moderate human relations in action and
speech: friendliness, truthfulness and wittiness.
Finally, two virtues require the right attitude first
towards angry feelings, gentleness, and then towards
shame and modesty. The mean and extremes of each virtue are first examined; similarities and differences
between these moral virtues are also commented upon.

One cannot help noticing Book IV's inductive and
dialectical method. Aristotle minutely describes the
characteristics of each moral virtue as recognized and
practiced in his time; thus he refers to public opinion
and wise men's example. This method shows the truth
of his theory of the virtuous mean. However, it is
necessary to repeat that the virtue is not always the
mean between extremes in any quantitative sense, but
the virtuous mean consists always in the most reasonable course of action and the moderation of feelings.
Thus, the emphasis should go rather to right reason
directing the   mean than to any median position
between two extremes.

Through a running commentary we will show the
essential characteristics and opposite vices of each
moral virtue studied in this book.

Chapter 1

Liberality, Prodigality, Stinginess

Liberality (<u>eleutheriotēs</u>) is a mean in handling-
-giving and taking--material goods of monetary value.
Wealth is the realm of useful things and can be used
well or wrongly. Liberty requires that the liberal
man, the Athenian free man, be a gentleman, and consequently, that he is not slavishly attached to his property. Material goods allow him to help others. He
will give to the right people, the right amount, at the
right time and for the right purpose. He will not take
another's possessions, but will take from his own pos -
sessions in order to give. Giving rather than taking
is more noble and praiseworthy because giving of one's
own wealth is a sign of an excellent disposition of
mind and generosity towards one's fellow man. The liberal man takes care of his possessions, but only to be
able to give them, reasonably and generously to others.
He does not expect return for his giving. He leaves
only a modest amount of property for himself. He is
not concerned, in the first place, for his own enjoyment of his wealth.

The measure of liberality is not how much a liberal man gives but his disposition in giving or helping
others even from smaller resources. "It is therefore
possible that the smaller giver may be the more liberal,
if he gives from smaller means." 1 Aristotle remarks
rightly here that those who have seen wealth and money
already established in their homes through inheritance
or gifts give more easily because they did not produce
it. On the contrary, having worked hard for it and
looking at it as their own creation, those who first
accumulated their own property hardly depart from it.
Everyone is fond of his own creation, just as parents
are of their sons and daughters or artists of their
art works.

The liberal man does not get rich easily: he is
a giver in the first place and values wealth not for
its own sake but as a means for giving. In fact, as a
rule the best people are the least wealthy. They do
not spend their time accumulating wealth and money.
They pursue higher goals. The liberal man is an easy person to deal with in money matters. He can be cheated
because he does not value money for its own sake. In
fact, "he is more distressed if he has paid less than
he ought than he is annoyed if he has paid more..."2

The prodigal (prodigality, asotia) man handles wealth wrongly. He squanders his money irrationally. He wastes his property and heads for self-destruction. True, the prodigal is prone more to giving than to taking but he gives wrongly. In fact, his resources eventually come to an end, and he may be tempted to take from others. He may develop into the self-indulging individual. Moreover, he may give excessively but wrongly to his flatterers and to those providing for his pleasures.

Stinginess (aneleutheria) applies to the people who are more prone to taking than to giving. Here deficiency is found in giving and excess in taking. The former is more prevalent among stingy people. In fact, most of them are satisfied to keep what they have and spend as little as possible even for their own needs.

There is, however, a type of a miser who takes excessively from others, for instance, usurers who lend small sums for high interest. Their motivation is profit, but profit from the wrong source (mostly poor people).

A tyrant who sacks cities, dispossesses the wealthy, and plunders temples is a different case. He is not stingy; rather, he is unjust and impious.

Chapter 2

Magnificence, Niggardliness, Extravagance

Magnificence (megaloprepeiā) is concerned, like generosity, with the handling of wealth. However, though a magnificent man is generous, a generous man is not necessarily magnificent. The difference between the two virtues is that magnificence gives money on a grand scale. Aristotle had in mind public services (leitourgiai), when the wealthy Athenians would volunteer to equip a warship, to finance a dramatic chorus in the theater, to buy votive offerings and sacrifices to gods, to build temples and stadia, and to defray the expenses of the delegation representing the state at one of the great Hellenic festivals.

The scale of expense is relative to the person giving, to the occasion, and to the amount of money given. A person is called magnificent (megaloprepēs) if he spends according to his ability and according to the occasion, some requiring truly great amounts of money, and others smaller but still substantial amounts of money. It all depends on the understanding and taste of the magnificent man how much, on what occasion, and for whom he is going to spend his money. "The magnificent man is an artist in expenditure: he can discern what is suitable, and spend great sums with good taste."[3] Suitable expenses fit his ability to spend, the occasion to spend, and the result or object that his magnificence produces. A result or object must be worthy of expense, and expense must be worthy or even exceed the result produced. As to the motive, the magnificent man gives large sums of money because it is noble to do so. He will spend gladly and freely without a strict calculation of costs. He is concerned with splendid achievements rather than with cost. Those achievements make him admirable in the eyes of others and in his own judgment. His great achievements are due to his great mind and heart.

By the very nature of magnificence it is very unlikely that a poor man will develop this virtue. He has no means to give on a large scale. On the other hand, the man who has inherited or acquired large sums of money has the facility to become magnificent.

The opposite of a magnificent man, on the side of
excess, is an extravagant (extravagance, banausia) man.
He spends more money than he should. He spends to show
off his wealth. The occasion on which he spends may be
banal or unworthy, such as lavishly equipping the comic
chorus in the theater. He spends little where much is
needed; he spends too much when less is needed. He
shows a lack of good taste in his spending endeavor.

A niggardly man (niggardliness, mikroprepeia) is
by deficiency opposite to the magnificent man. In
order to economize, he calculates too much while giving
large sums of money. He spoils the beauty of achievement for a small sum that he thinks he should save.
Most of the time, a niggardly man believes that he
spends more than he should.

Chapter 3

Greatness of Soul, Pettiness, Vanity

Greatness of soul (megalopsychia) is the lofty
pride and self-esteem of one who thinks he deserves
great recognition. Because he has done great things,
he actually deserves and claims great recognition. The
great-souled man is concerned with honor, but he is
looking at honor with moderation, and in spite of his
great deserts, he does not care too much when he is
deprived of it.

A truly great-souled man is an extreme; but since
his claim is right (he claims what he deserves), he
stands in the mean between extremes. The mean position
of the great-souled man is his virtuous height. The
truly great-souled man, inasmuch as he deserves the
greatest honor, that is,(the recognition of his
virtue) must be the best.   In fact, the greatness of
every virtue is the result of the great soul of the
virtuous man. "Greatness of soul seems therefore to be
as it were a crowning ornament of the virtues: it en-
hances their greatness, and it cannot exist without
them."[4] The great-souled man strives for excellence and
greatness in everything he does. It is, then, to be
expected that a truly great-souled man is good in every
aspect. Not surprisingly, Aristotle concludes this
section by stating that it is hard to be a truly great-
souled man.

Several things contribute to the greatness of the
soul. If he is good, a gentleman of noble birth, power
and wealth may develop greatness of soul more easily
than a man deprived of these qualifications. Of course,
many possess the goods of fortune without possessing
virtue. However, they cannot be called great-souled because great-souledness is a virtue acquired by noble
efforts. In fact, such people become easily arrogant
and vain because wealth and power corrupt when those who
possess them are deprived of virtue. Considering themselves superior, they look down upon others. They imitate the great-souled man in their external behavior
but only apparently so. Aristotle would allow that truly
great-souled men are right when looking down on unworthy
human beings, but fake imitators have no such right.
"For the great-souled man is justified in despising
other people--his estimates are correct; but most proud
men have no ground for their pride."[5]

Before concluding this section Aristotle delights in describing the great souled man's lofty mind. He will not run into danger for insignificant reasons, but will face great dangers for a great cause, even when doing so may cost him his life. He is fond of giving and ashamed of receiving benefits. He remembers the great things he has done, but not those he has received, the reason being that it is more excellent to give than to receive. Thus, he does not ask for favors but offers them readily. He is haughty with men of position and fortune, but simple and courteous towards those of moderate means. Why? There is nothing ignoble in asserting one's dignity among the great but to do so among the lower classes is as crude as to put forth one's strength against the weak.

The great-souled man is not pursuing the goals valued by the common people. He is slow in acting except when pursuing some great honor or achievement. His actions are few but they are great and distinguished. He is open in love and open in hate not of men but of their deeds and motives. He speaks and acts openly; he is frank; he is concerned with truth and not with what others say. He is incapable of living at the will of another unless he is a friend, for to do so is slavish. He does not admire people, for he lives in greatness; greatness is normal to him. He does not bear a grudge, for recalling things against people when they have tried to hurt him is not a sign of a great soul. Rather he overlooks such attacks. He does not gossip or say evil about others. He has only scorn for his enemies. He is not a complainer. He prefers beautiful and useless possessions to profitable and practical possessions because the former make him self-sufficient and the latter would make him dependent. His step is slow; his voice deep; his speech moderate and to the point.

The petty or small-souled (pettiness, mikropsychia) man underestimates himself and claims less than he deserves. He deprives himself of the good he deserves, although he does not deserve as much as the great-souled man. This is a bad kind of humility. He does not appreciate himself, his capabilities, his deserts. He is slow to venture into noble actions and pursuits and to receive due recognition when he does because he considers himself unable and undeserving.

The vain man (vanity, chaunotēs), on the other hand, errs by excess. He thinks that he deserves great

75

honors. but he does not deserve them. He over-estimates
himself. Thus he does not know himself and his capabilities and his deserts. He may be aware of the weak
foundation of his claims for which he compensates by
showing off in his undertakings, attire and manners.
Aristotle would call him a foolish man.

Chapter 4

Pride and Lack of Ambition as Two Extremes of a Nameless
Virtue

As liberality is related to magnificence in
matters of dispensing money, the former on a modest
scale, the latter on a large scale, so does a nameless
virtue (we call it dignity or proper pride) stand to
greatness of soul in regard to honor. Whereas
greatness of soul pursues honor on a grand scale, dignity desires deserved honors on a modest scale. Some
men desire honor more than they deserve it; we call
them ambitious or proud (pride, philotimia). Others
desire honor less than they should according to their
deserts; we blame unambitious (lack of ambition,
aphilotimia) people for not desiring to be honored for
their noble deeds. The median between these two extremes is the virtue of dignity or the pride proper to
a man who pursues the honors he deserves.

Chapter 5

Gentleness, Irascibility, Spiritlessness

This chapter interrupts the study of moral virtues in the sphere of action by inserting a discussion of the moral virtue concerned with the moderation of anger. Aristotle had difficulty forging names for the mean and the two extremes in handling the passion of anger. He called the mean gentleness (praotēs) but he observed that this word tends to deficiency in our handling of anger. The gentle man is not led by emotion; he has a calm temper. When angry, he is less angry than he could and should be. He is more prone to forgive injuries than to seek retaliation for them. But, however deficient the word "gentleness" is in designating the proper mean for handling the feeling of anger, it is used here for this precise purpose. The gentle man becomes angry as his right reason dictates. Gentleness stands for the moral disposition of the man who is angry "on the right grounds and against the right persons, and also in the right manner at the right moment and for the right length of time." 6

The deficiency in the feeling of anger is called spiritlessness or apathy (aorgēsia), and it consists in not feeling anger or feeling it in a lesser degree than one should in special circumstances. We blame a man who does not get angry at things he should be angry at, and we blame a man who does not feel enough anger in the right manner, time and other circumstances. Such people seem deprived of feelings, even for pain inflicted; they do not seem to defend themselves; they act as slaves letting others offend them and those near and dear.

Excessive anger has no proper name--here it will be called irascibility (orgilotēs)--but there are several categories of people who are excessively angry. Before we classify them, it is necessary to say that all of them are excessively "angry with the wrong people, for the wrong things, or more violently or more quickly or longer than is right."7 First of all, there are short-tempered people. These people get angry quickly, but they do not brood over it for a long time; they do not keep anger within themselves; their anger is over as they retaliate. Choleric people react violently on every occasion. Bitter-tempered people remain angry for a long time. The resentment lingers on and on

in their souls. They are hard to placate until they
have a chance to retaliate against those making them
angry. But if the revenge does not take place,they continue to feel their resentment. Since no one knows that
they are angry, they are not helped to cope with it, and
digesting it internally takes time. Angry people are
hard on themselves and on those with whom they live.

At the end of Chapter V, Aristotle refers to what
he said in Book II.[8] In Book II he gave moral advice
on how to become virtuous. He recognized in both II and
IV, almost verbatim, how difficult it is to be angry for
the right reason, at the right person, to the right
extent, on the right occasion, and for the right length
of time. But this is the difficulty, he said, with all
moral virtues. What is correct between irascibility
and spiritlessness will depend upon particular circumstances,with the decision resting on our moral sense.

Chapter 6

Friendliness, Obsequiousness, Quarrelsomeness

Aristotle returns to the virtues concerned with action. The first refers to the pleasures and pains arising out of daily interpersonal relations. The man who wishes to please everybody and never objects to anything, never inflicts pain on anyone, is called the obsequious (areskos) man. The obsequious man has no personal stake in the matter. On the contrary, the flatterer (kolax) who acts similarly and even more so than the obsequious man aims at his own interests. On the opposite side, the quarrelsome (dyskolos) man objects to everything, quarrels with everyone and does not care at all if he hurts people. The middle position is that of the friendly (philos) man. His companionship pleases people because he is well-disposed to be agreeable at the right time and place and with the right person.

It must be noted that Aristotle referred to this virtue as nameless, although he regularly designated it, for lack of a better word, philia. He tells us however, that friendliness differs from friendship because it does not involve emotion or affection. The friendly man acts as he does because he is the kind of person he is and because it is the right thing to do. He behaves equally toward those he knows and those he does not know, although the degree of pleasantness will differ with regard to the persons he knows well or he does not know at all. His standard rule is do what is noble and beautiful to everyone, but it is not proper to show the same amity to the familiar and to the strange.

As a rule, the friendly man will choose to give pleasure to others and avoid giving them pain; yet with a view to important moral consequences in the future, he must occasionally inflict pain on others. He will do that when a) it may be ignoble for him to contribute to the pleasure of others, and b) it may be hurtful to some member with whom he associates. When such harm threatens the doer, even if opposition will give him a slight pain, the friendly man will not approve his deed but will show his disapproval. Such is the noble conduct of the friendly man. He is a gentleman to everyone. But he does behave differently toward prominent men and common men, toward the well known and less well known, toward the familiar and the strange.

Chapter 7

Truthfulness, Boastfulness, Self-Depreciation

A good deal of social intercourse is reflected in conversation. Here Aristotle looks for the virtuous mean in speech. If the speaker is truthful (truthfulness, aletheia) and sincere, he is a virtuous man. A liar, either by exaggeration or by understating the state of affairs, is a vicious man deserving blame. The blame, however, is more appropriate when directed to the boastful than to the otherwise modest man.

The boastful (boastfulness, alazoneia) man claims praiseworthy qualities that he does not possess or to a greater degree than he possesses them. The self-depreciator (eiron) is the opposite, as he disclaims or belittles his good qualities. The mean between these two extremes is found in the straightforward (authekastos) and truthful (aletheutikos) man who is sincere both in his life and in his speech. He admits to the qualities he possesses without either exaggeration or understatement. He is truthful and sincere because he is the kind of person he is and because that is the right thing to do. In other words, he is honest in speech without any hidden motives, interests or designs. Since he is sincere and honest when nothing is at stake, and he is that way for the love of truth, he will be even more so when something is at stake that depends upon his correct statement, such as his or other people's reputation.

The boastful man with no ulterior motive but sheer delight in spreading lies about his non-existent qualities is more foolish than the vicious man. Even when his ostentation has reputation and honor as its ulterior motive, he is not yet to be severely blamed as a vicious fellow. He pretends to qualities we all wish for and for which a man is praised and regarded as a happy, human being. However, when his boastfulness directly or indirectly aims at financial gain, he is to be blamed because of deliberately choosing bad means for his goal. As a rule, he pretends to have qualities benefitting others, but he does not have such qualifications; for example, when he claims to be qualified as physician and is only a quack.

The self-depreciator (self-depreciation, eironeia)

who plays down his real merits can be called a modest man, too modest, according to Aristotle. If he does it to avoid being ostentatious, he is not to be blamed. If he does it because he feels unworthy or inferior, he is to be pitied and helped. This kind of man does not seem purposely deceitful nor does he use subtle ways to gain profit (neither of these is totally excluded, though). When a man of this kind plays down even his most obvious good qualities, we would call his speech an affectation of humility. When he plays down his latent good qualities, he strikes us as educated. Finally, when he disclaims qualities highly valued by others, as Socrates would plead ignorance when the Sophists boasted of their knowledge, he shows a higher degree of wisdom.

In conclusion, the boastful man is more opposed to the truthful man than the self-depreciating man.

Chapter 8

Wittiness, Boorishness, Buffoonery

As a necessary part of human life, amusing conversation is a province of the virtue of wittiness
(eutrapeliā). There is a sphere of telling and hearing
the right jokes in the right way. The virtue of wittiness hits the median between two extremes in joking.
On the side of excess stands the buffoon (buffoonery,
bōmolochia) who stops at nothing to get laughs. He does
not care to keep his jokes within the bounds of decency.
He does not spare himself, and he offends others when
they become the targets of his jokes. The boorish man
(boorishness, agroikiā) is deficient in the realm of
pleasant and amusing talk. He cannot say anything funny,
and he does not appreciate it when others do. If he is
the target of jokes he will be easily offended. He contributes nothing to his peers' relaxation and amusement.

Those whose jokes remain in good taste are called
witty (eutrapeloi) and also tactful (epidexioi) because
they say and listen to things suitable for a virtuous
man and gentleman. There is a difference in joke making
between a free man and slave and between an educated
and uneducated man. This difference can be marked, for
example, in the old comedies (those of Aristophanes in
the fifth century) and in the new (those of Menander in
Aristotle's time). The jokes in old comedies are rather
obscene and rude; those in the new are more subtle;
their humor is more refined.

What, then, would be the standard for distinguishing a good from a bad jester? Aristotle leaves this
question without a specific answer, except to remark
that the witty man will do nothing unsuitable to a virtuous man and gentleman. His wise man, the model of conduct, is invoked again as the standard to look at and
imitate. But the wise man is led by right reason. As
a result, his jokes are reasonable, told with taste in
the right way, time, place and in front of the right
people. The educated man will be a law onto himself because he obeys his logos. He will take particular care
not to tell slanderous jokes at the expense of others.
The laws forbid slander. Perhaps they should also
forbid that any one make fun of others.

Aristotle did not here go into the definition of the witty or ridiculous (geloion). However, he offered definitions in two other places. In one place he calls wittiness a kind of educated arrogance, a 'cultured insolence.' [9] His definition of the ridiculous is found elsewhere: "The laughable consists in some blunder or ugliness that does not cause pain or disaster, an obvious example being the comic mask which is ugly and distorted but not painful."[10] The second book of the Poetics, unfortunately lost, had a full treatment of comedy and its object, the ridiculous, but even the above definition can help us understand the nature of the ridiculous.

Chapter 9

Modesty, Shamelessness, Bashfulness

The two remaining quasi-virtues, modesty (aidōs) and indignation (nemesis) are listed in Book II, vii, 14-15. Modesty is concerned with feelings of shame because of wrong deeds, indignation with pain and pleasure felt at the good fortune of others. This latter is totally omitted; the former only partially discussed. Shamelessness (anaischyntiā) and bashfulness (kataplēxis) are not even touched upon, and Book IV ends abruptly.

Modesty is a sense of shame, a fear of disrepute. Its bodily effect is similar to what is experienced in the fear of danger. People who are ashamed blush, and those who are in fear of death grow pale. Since both of these effects are physical, modesty seems to be more feeling than virtue.

Modesty is suitable to young people. They live as their emotions carry them; hence, it is understandable that they commit many mistakes for which they should be ashamed. We praise young people who have a sense of shame. On the other hand, it is not to be expected that shame can be found in older people. Since shame is a consequence of base and unreasonable actions and older people are supposedly masters of their emotions and live according to practical wisdom, they should not commit base actions and consequently there is no reason for them to be ashamed of such actions. Aristotle adds that mature people should avoid even those actions which are despised by public opinion although they are not base in reality.

Although other moral virtues are simply good, modesty is good only conditionally in the sense that a decent man would be ashamed if he were performing base actions. Thus, feeling shame is not yet, by itself, any virtue. But when one is ashamed for bad acts done knowingly and willfully, such shame has virtuous elements in it. Of course, one should not think that performing a shameless act for which he is later ashamed is a virtue credited to him. He should not have performed the shameful act in the first place.

A few words may be added here about the two extremes of modesty.[11] Whereas the modest person (aidēmōn) handles the feeling of shame rightly, the shameless (anaischyntos) man acts basely and is not ashamed of it. A bashful (kataplēx) man is excessively ashamed even for a small mistake. He looks as if he were terror-stricken; he is abashed at everything.

BOOK IV

Footnotes

1
Nicomachean Ethics, Book IV, 1, 19-1120b 10.

2
N.E., Book IV, 1, 27-1121a 5.

3
N.E., Book IV, ii, 5-1122a 35.

4
N.E., Book IV, iii, 16-1124a.

5
N.E., Book IV, iii, 22-1124b, 5.

6
N.E., Book IV, v, 3-1125b 30.

7
N.E., Book IV, v, 7-1126a 10.

8
N.E., Book II, ix, 7-9-1109b 14-25.

9
Rhetoric, Book II, xii, 16-1389b 10.

10
Poetics, v, 2 - 1449a 35.

11
N.E., Book II, vii, 14-1108a 30.

BOOK V

JUSTICE AND INJUSTICE

Aristotle discusses in Book V the objective and
subjective side of the just and unjust, justice and injustice. The act itself is examined from the objective
angle, and the disposition or character of the moral
agent is analyzed from the subjective viewpoint. The
two approaches together make justice a moral virtue and
injustice a moral vice. However, the subjective approach points to a deeper insight into the nature of
justice than its external performance alone could
suggest.

The following is an outline of the topics covered
in Book V.[1]

I. Objective Viewpoint: Just and Unjust

A. Just and unjust, abstractly considered:
    Two meanings of the terms 'just' and 'unjust'
    First meaning of the term 'just': The concept
        of legal and legal or general justice
        ...Chapter 1.
    Second meaning of the term 'just': The concept
        of equal and particular justice
        ...Chapter 2.
    Particular justice subdivided:
        ...Chapters 3 and 4.
    Distributive justice
        ...Chapter 3.
    Corrective justice
        ...Chapter 4.
    Reciprocity and justice
        ...Chapter 5.

B. The 'just' and 'unjust' considered concretely:
    Justice in the city-state:
        Definition of political justice
        Two species of political justice
        ...Chapter 6.
    Discussion on natural justice
        ...Chapter 7.

II. Subjective Viewpoint: The manner in which one must do just things to become just.

A. An unjust act becomes such when it is done by free choice
...Chapter 8.
Classification of unjust acts in view of the character of an agent
...Chapter 9.

B. Questions:
1. Can one suffer injustice voluntarily?
2. Who commits distributive injustice?
3. What is worse: to inflict or to suffer injustice?
...Chapter 9.
4. Could one commit injustice against oneself?
...Chapter 11.

Conclusion: Equity
...Chapter 10.

Chapter 1

Legal or General Justice

Aristotle starts his study of justice (dykaiosyne) by clarifying various meanings ascribed to it in his times. Following in Plato's footsteps, Aristotle examines first the kind of justice that is general virtue and is better translated by the word righteousness. As such, justice is the will to do what is lawful and fair. Its opposite, injustice (adikia), includes all unlawful and unfair deeds. Aristotle uses in this context the third characteristic of an unjust man which was in current usage in his time, namely pleonektes, a greedy, covetous, avaricious man looking everywhere for gain whether he deserves it or not. The term is later dropped because it is covered by the more general one, namely, anisos, unequal or unfair.[2] The 'lawful' or legal (to nomimon) refers to deeds done according to law. The 'fair' or equal (to ison) means taking one's right share of the good and bad, neither more nor less, but even or equal. The 'unfair' or unequal (to anison) means taking more than one's share of the good and taking less than one's share of the bad.

The law-abiding man is just, and the observer of fairness or equality in his dealings with other men is also just. Since laws cover all virtues--not their habits but their deeds--then legal justice is a general justice. The fair or equal is legal, but not all laws dictate equality in sharing society's goods and services. The brave and temperate and benevolent do not aim at equal shares of social goods but they are included under the laws. Hence the justice of fairness or equality has a narrower meaning; it is a subdivision of general or legal justice: it is a particular justice.

Strictly speaking, then, everything lawful belongs to justice as a legal or general virtue. We must remember that among the Greeks, law (nomos) was not a dry, legal formula, written decree, or even an unwritten but fixed custom. On the contrary, law in the Greek context was a principle or dictate of reason, a guardian of virtue: not only of justice, but also of bravery, temperance and gentleness. It was a guarantor of the republic's common good and a promotor of the citizen's social and political happiness. The law was a way of life, written or unwritten, expressing that which is right and just, and so embodying that moral public opinion which had developed from the experience and wisdom of ages. Aristotle defined law as follows: "[a rule of life] such that will make the citizens virtuous and just".[3] Otherwise, if law is nothing but a decree for external observance, the polis will be a pure alliance and not a community, and the law will be nothing but a covenant which aims to guarantee man's rights against another.[4]

Thus, in its general sense, justice includes every virtue; it is the 'whole of virtue', or, expressed in legal terms, justice is obedience to laws. Its opposite, injustice, is 'the whole of vice' or disobedience to laws. Justice, however, should not be simply combined with the other virtues. It adds to all of them, displaying and bringing into focus the social character of every virtue by implying an element of 'otherness'. A just man does for others what the wise, temperate, and brave do for themselves. "Justice alone of the virtues is 'the good of others', because it does what is for the advantage of another, either a ruler or an associate." [5]

Chapter 2

Particular Justice

Particular justice is a part of general justice and falls within its genus; particular justice is concerned with man's deeds toward others. However, particular justice has a specific meaning since it is concerned with that which is fair or equal, and of course, due to others. Whereas legal or general justice was defined as 'the whole of virtue' to be identified with every good deed done for others, particular justice is concerned with what is fair and equal for others. It focuses on the right share of goods and services in society and so points to the gains and losses in social conduct. Who ever takes more than his right share of goods and less than his right share of bad things does something solely ascribed to particular injustice.

Aristotle proves the existence of particular justice by using the ordinary language of his times which, if there were no particular justice, would have no meaning.

1. There are other-regarding bad acts which are assigned to injustice in a general sense but not in a particular sense. Each is assigned to its own particular vice: a man who drops his shield in battle and runs away is a coward; a man who uses abusive language is bad-tempered; a man who refuses to help his friend who is in need is a mean fellow. Not one of these men takes more than his share of goods: therefore, not one is unjust in a strict, particular sense.

2. There are other-regarding bad acts, such as adultery which is not ascribed to particular justice unless it is done in view of gains. Particular injustice alone takes more than man's right share out of the society. For example, adultery committed because of passion is self-indulgent vice and an intemperate act; adultery committed for a profit is an unjust act.

Aristotle assumed that men live freely and equally in a city-state (polis). The mean of justice as a particular moral virtue is that every citizen has a right to his equal share of goods and services both in public

and private life. The man who takes more than his due
share of wealth, honor, or security acts against distributive justice. Such a man contributes less than his
due share to the political community. The man who takes
more than his due share of goods and services in private transactions with other citizens acts against
corrective justice. Each one of two kinds of particular
justice must be discussed in more detail.

Chapter 3

Distributive Justice

Injustice amounts to inequality whereas justice
amounts to equality. The equal (ison) is the mean between two extremes, too much and too little, involving
two persons in a just deal. Thus, justice involves at
least four terms, two persons and two shares. When
people are totally equal in regard to their deserts,
their shares will be totally equal; but when people are
not equal, their shares will not be equal either.

Distributive justice (dianemētikon dikaion) is
"exercised in the distribution of honor, wealth and the
other divisible assets of the community, which may be
allotted among its members in equal or unequal shares."[6]
It operates between the state and its citizens. The
criterion for the state's distribution of goods and services is found in the merits and demerits of citizens.
If the citizens are of equal merit, there will be an
equal share for every citizen in the assets of the political community. But since not all citizens are of
equal merit, the distribution of assets will also be unequal. Citizens will receive proportionately equal rewards for proportionate contributions to the political
community. This does not, however, constitute actual
inequality or injustice. The mean of distributive justice is found in the equal proportion between merits and
rewards, demerits and punishments. Strictly speaking,
citizens are equal and free with respect to their basic
human constituents, body and soul, but they are unequal
in their bodily and mental abilities and in their contributions to the community. We must now know what sort
of merit we are talking about. Aristotle explains:

> All are agreed that justice in distributions must
> be based on desert of some sort, although they do
> not all mean the same sort of desert; democrats
> make the criterion free birth; those of oligarchi-
> cal sympathies wealth, or in other cases, birth;
> upholders of aristocracy make it virtue."[7]

Hence, distributive justice involves a proportion,
not an arithmetical one, but a proportion of merits; proportionately equal shares are justly assigned to citizens
equal in their merits and vice versa.

To present this graphically Aristotle used three
parallel lines of equal length. Two parts of one line,
A and B, represented two persons; two parts, c and d,
of another line, represented their shares. Now, if

A:B = c:d, then

A:c = B:d, and therefore

A+c : B+d which makes A equal to B, i.e., "if the shares
are proportioned to the persons, their relative condition after receiving them will be the same as it was
before."[8] Justice will have been done.

Accustomed as we are to look upon the citizen as
taxpayer, Sir David Ross has observed that this concept
of distributive justice in which the state is a distributor of goods and services to the citizens seems
strange to us.[9] However, the state was a distributor
of offices and land, of pay for attendance at assemblies
and law courts, of honors to the deserving and gifts of
money to the needy. In many respects our modern welfare
state resembles the Aristotelian type of state. Furthermore, the modern citizen enjoys public protection and
the use of many facilities made possible by a tax-
collecting government.

Chapter 4

Corrective Justice

Corrective justice (diorthōtikon dikaion) per-
tains to relationships between citizens, and it concerns
the fairness in their private transactions (synallagmata).
It is subdivided into the following categories:

1. That concerned with voluntary transactions
    (hekousia synallagmata) is based on a volun-
    tary contract between two parties in matters
    of selling, buying, lending with or without
    interest, and applies when one of the parties
    breaks the contract.

2. That concerned with involuntary transactions
    (akousia synallagmata) involves transactions
    independent of any consent, such as fraud or
    force. Cases of fraud are the following:
    theft, adultery, poisoning, assassination,
    false testimony and others. Cases of force
    or violence are assault, murder, robbery
    with violence, maiming, abusive language and
    others. In both types of cases there is the
    same problem: redressing or correcting the
    disturbed equality.

    What is this equality or equal mean of cor-
    rective justice? The emphasis here is not
    on the merits or personal qualities of the
    partners, but on the transaction itself and
    the corresponding injury. The damage in-
    flicted must be repaired and equality re-
    stored. To what condition? Not more nor
    less than the condition prevailing when the
    disturbance occurred. Hence, there is no
    proportion involved as in distributive jus-
    tice, but simply arithmetical mean. The
    judge will have the task of equalizing loss
    and gain. The excess (gain) will be taken
    from the wrongdoer. The loss of the one who
    suffered injustice will be corrected by re-
    storing his share, ". . . it follows that
    Justice in Rectification will be the mean
    between loss and gain." [10]

Graphically represented this redressing of damages and
their correction looks as follows:

A+C : B-C. When the injustice was done

A took C and so B became short of C; A+C results in B-C.

Each of the two persons, through the gains and losses,
must return to his former equality: A+C-C = B-C+C.
And justice will have been done.

Chapter 5

Reciprocity and Justice

Reciprocity (antipeponthos) means, according to the Pythagoreans, retaliation. One must suffer in return and in the same measure for injury committed against others. Thus, the judge shall do to A what A has done to B ("an eye for an eye"). Such definition of strict reciprocity fits neither distributive nor corrective justice; the former involves a proportionate distribution, the latter implies a correction proper to each case.

Reciprocity in terms of a proportion is the bond that keeps societies together. Not only must a judge do justice to a defendant and to an injured party, but the statesman must also deal justly with the citizens, and the producer with the consumer in selling a real value product and receiving a countervalue from the consumer. In order to emphasize the point of proportionate versus strict reciprocity as the cities' bond, Aristotle notes that in order to remind their citizens to promote reciprocal exchange, that is, to return not only what is strictly just, but that also which one owes in gratitude: favor for favor, good deed for good deed, service for service, several Greek cities have erected sanctuaries to the Graces (Charites), goddesses of love, grace, beauty, favors and gratitude.

The law of proportion regulates the exchange of goods and services. The proportionate exchange between the producer and the consumer may be represented by a square. Let A be an architect, B a shoemaker, c a house, and d a shoe.

Now the architect must take the shoemaker's product and give him a part of his own product. This reciprocal exchange will be represented by the diagonals of the square.

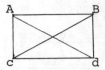

The product d(shoes) of the shoemaker goes to the architect (A), and the product c(house) goes to the shoemaker
(B). Thus, proportional equality is established between the goods and traders and so the reciprocity of
proportion is effected. Since society is composed of
different and unequal people and their products are
equally different and unequal, the reciprocity of proportion will keep them together. Otherwise, where there
is no reciprocal exchange, society is bound to dissolve.

Before the exchange is made, the respective value
of commodities must be determined. The value of a product is measured in terms of the amount of labor put into
it. But the law of supply and demand will ultimately
mediate in making possible fair exchange; namely, how
many pairs of shoes for a house, or how many bushels of
wheat for so many pairs of shoes.

In order to avoid barter, which is not always possible and often impractical, money has been invented as
a means of exchange of commodities and so a transition
from barter to trade and commerce effected. Money is a
useful invention because it is a measure or standard
against which the value of things can be measured. The
real equalizer of products are human needs and demands
and money services them. When need or demand arises,
money can be used to satisfy it. Of course money can
vary in value as products do; but the more stable the
value of money, the more fixed prices are and the more
stable economic life.

Ending this section, Aristotle shows how justice
is a moral virtue because it observes the mean which is
realized in the median amount. Injustice, on the contrary, is found in the extremes of deficiency and excess.

Aristotle then finds new distinctions in the virtue of justice. One is universal between man and man
regardless of political association; another is political
justice.

Chapter 6

Political Justice

Political justice (<u>politikon</u> <u>dikaion</u>) is the justice among fellow-citizens sharing a common life in a city-state in which they seek self-sufficiency. They are ruled by law and enjoy at least some equality either proportionately or arithmetically. Proportionate equality belongs to an aristocracy in which honor and privileges go to the deserving, the intellectually and morally virtuous who contribute goods and services to the state. The same quality is found in oligarchies in which benefits are distributed to the wealthy. Arithmetical or numerical equality is to be found in democracies, where every freeborn citizen may rule and be ruled by law.

Hence, between the unequal and unfree political justice cannot exist. Justice exists only among those who are ruled and live by law. If we look strictly at the origin of injustice, we may say that law exists where injustice or wrong-dealing may occur. The wrong-dealing here means that one is alloting to himself too much of intrinsically good things and too little of intrinsically evil things. That is the essence of injustice and its redress is justice. Although injustice is committed when the law is broken, justice, as the middle between two extremes, has already been broken in the mind and choice of the unjust man before he has come into conflict with the law. Justice therefore, is before and above state law.

According to Aristotle, this is why we do not allow man to rule in the state but instead allow the rule of law and reason. Power easily corrupts and man takes too large a share for himself and becomes a tyrant, a ruler who rules exclusively for his own selfish interests. On the contrary,

> "a just ruler seems to make nothing out of his office; for he does not allot to himself a larger share of things generally good, unless it be proportionate to his merits; so that he labors for others, which accounts for the saying mentioned above, that 'justice is the good of others'. Consequently some recompense has to be given him, in the shape of honor and dignity. It is those whom such rewards do not satisfy who make themselves tyrants." [11]

Since political justice is found among people
sharing equally in ruling and being ruled, where there
is no such equality there is no political justice. Such
is the case of <u>domestic justice</u> (<u>oikonomikon dikaion</u>)
between husband and wife, parent and child, master and
slave. Women, children and slaves are dependents; in
Greek terms, they are the property of the husband,
father and master. Of course, there are degrees in
these relations; the most similar to political justice
is justice between a husband and wife; to a lesser degree, is justice between parent and child, and the[12]
least similar is justice between master and slave.

Chapter 7

Natural and Conventional Justice

Political justice may be further divided on the
basis of its origin into natural (physikon) and conventional (nomikon). Natural justice includes rules that
are unchangeable and valid in all places and at all
times. Conventional justice is the product of local customs and traditions agreed upon and decreed by law; for
example, the ransom for a slave varies from one city-
state to another. Aristotle rejected the Sophist
teaching that all justice and all laws are merely
conventional and therefore changeable. Rules of justice
may vary from people to people, but the rules of natural
justice are not ordained by decree (taxei) but by nature
(physei). "A rule of justice is natural that has the
same validity everywhere, and does not depend on our
accepting it or not."[13] Aristotle refers in the Rhetoric
to the natural and thus unchangeable law and justice:

> By the two kinds of law I mean particular law
> and universal law. Particular law is that which
> each community lays down and applies to its
> own members: this is partly written and partly
> unwritten. Universal law is the law of
> nature. For there really is, as everyone to
> some extent divines, a natural justice and in-
> justice that is binding on all men, even on
> those who have no association or covenant with
> each other. It is this that Sophocles' Anti-
> gone clearly means when she says that the
> burial of Polineices was a just act in spite
> of the prohibition: she means that it was just
> by nature.[14]

It is interesting to note that Aristotle admits
that even in natural justice exceptions are possible in
our imperfect world. He says:

> That rules of justice vary is not absolutely
> true, but only with qualifications. Among the
> gods indeed it is perhaps not true at all; but
> in our world, although there is such a thing
> as Natural Justice, all rules of justice are
> variable.[15]

Aristotle may be looked upon as the father of the natural
law theory. He however, avoided the rigidity of certain
natural law advocates who have appeared through long
centuries of Western thought.

Chapter 8

Responsibility in Justice and Injustice

Before offering further distinctions on Justice,
Aristotle paused in Articles 8 and 9 to tell us that it
is wrong to consider justice as concerned only and exclusively with the external just mean or proportion.
Justice is a moral virtue, and therefore, involves
choice. It disposes a man to give to others what is
equal and due to them. Consequently, whenever the inner
control of one's act is impeded by the obstacles to
voluntary choice, ignorance, anger, fear, violence,
there is no justice or injustice done. Both justice and
injustice are evaluated in terms of the deliberate
choice that precedes them.

According to the amount of the choice accompanying
them there are different degrees of unjust wrongs.
Externally the same act might be a mistake (hamartēma)
if performed out of ignorance; a misfortune (atychēma),
when some external factor turns it against reasonable
expectation; a wrong act (adikēma) when done in full
knowledge but without previous deliberation. Similarly,
when an externally unjust act is done in a fit of anger,
responsibility, as a rule, will not rest upon the agent
but upon the provoker.

The wickedness and thus the full responsibility
for unjust acts results only

> if a man does an injury of set purpose, he is
> guilty of injustice, and injustice of the sort
> that renders the doer an unjust man, if it be
> an act that violates proportion or equality.
> Similarly, one who acts justly on purpose is a
> just man; but he acts justly only if he acts
> voluntarily.[16]

103

Chapter 9

Voluntariness and Involuntariness in Just and Unjust Actions

This chapter, by means of answering certain difficulties and objections with regard to the nature of justice and injustice, completes and deepens the conception so far given of them. These questions follow:

1. Can one suffer injustice voluntarily?

2. Who commits distributive injustice?

3. Which is worse: inflicting or suffering injustice?

4. Can one commit injustice against oneself?
   (The last two questions are answered in Chapter 11).

The first two questions are answered as follows. Our definition of acting unjustly is not complete if we say only that one harms another when he does so knowingly and willingly. An unjust act must also be against another person's wish. A person may voluntarily be harmed or suffer something unjust, but no one voluntarily receives unjust treatment. If and when someone wishes to submit to unjust treatment, it will be for another reason and not because such treatment is unjust. It is clear, therefore, that without a violation of the will, harm does not constitute injustice. The act of injustice implies a collision of two wills: a loss on one side and a gain on the other.

Similarly, the answer to the second question puts emphasis on the will of the distributor and the recipient. The distributor who knowingly and willingly assigns to someone else a larger share than to himself although he deserves more is acting unjustly towards himself. The distributor who assigns too large a share to another acts unjustly. The initiative for action is in him and not in the recipient.

The chapter ends by combating some of the popular errors about justice. Men believe that it is easy to be just because justice consists only in an external act. We have proven in Chapters 8 and 9 the falsehood of this position. People think that knowing what is just is easy. However, one must not only know the facts but

must also know and understand the principles of justice
in order to have a mind disposed to act justly. Some
thinkers (Plato?) believe that if justice is knowledge,
it must have a contrary; hence, the just man may easily
do unjust acts. The truth, though, is that a just man
could not at will act unjustly. His mind is habitually
turned to just acts. Finally, Aristotle points out that
justice is limited in a human condition. Things intrinsically good are beneficial to men up to a certain
point. There is a measure in everything and good things
are subject to that standard in our human life.

Chapter 10

Equity

The last important distinction that Aristotle makes is that between law (nomos) and equity (epieikeia). Equity is a rectification of justice which is applied to a literal interpretation of a law. No law can cover all cases. The most law can do is take into consideration the majority of cases. But since laws are the result of legislative wisdom and purport to make men good and righteous, when a case arises in which acting according to law results in injustice, equity steps in and "corrects" the law. Equity can be defined as "rectification of law where law is defective because of its generality."[17] The equitable is not legally just but by nature a corrective of legal justice. The equation that the lawful is the just or that law is justice is not true here. Equity is justice, but it is not a legal justice, i.e., according to the letter of the law. In fact, if the lawgiver were present in the case, the lawgiver who declares the laws according to his legislative practical wisdom, he would accept the equitable exception to the law.

Equity goes beyond the written law and reaches the natural law. It embraces a wide range of what is fair, decent, humane and good. An equitable man has a fair humane understanding and forgiving temper. He does by choice and habit what is fair and decent. Although the law is on his side, he does not stand on the written law when pressing for his rights. He is ready to receive a smaller share of goods and services than those to which he is entitled. It is fitting to add here the eloquent description of equity as a truly superior virtue from another of Aristotle's works.

> It is equitable to pardon human weaknesses, and to look, not to the law but to the legislator; not to the letter of the law but to the intention of the legislator; not to the action itself, but to the moral purpose; not to the part, but to the whole; not to what a man is now, but to what he has been, always or generally; to remember good rather than ill treatment, and benefits received rather than those conferred; to bear injury with patience; to be willing to appeal to the judgment of reason rather than to violence; to prefer arbitration to the law

court, for the arbitrator keeps equity in view,
whereas the dikast looks only to the law, and
the reason why arbitrators were appointed was
that equity might prevail."[18]

The treatise on justice would be truly defective without
an eye-opening study of equity.

Chapter 11

Could One Commit Injustice Toward Oneself?

As an after-thought, Aristotle ends the discussion on justice and injustice by taking a critical look at the Platonic concept of justice. According to Plato[19] there are three 'parts' of the soul: the rational and the irrational; the latter is subdivided into the spirited and the appetitive parts. Each part is regulated by its special virtue: the rational by wisdom, the spirited by bravery, the appetitive by temperance. The three parts together are ruled by the virtue of justice when the spirited and the appetitive obey the rational part, thereby establishing cooperation, coordination and harmony among them. Injustice is the discord and war between the parts of the soul. For Plato justice in the State occurs when the three classes: the rulers, the defenders (soldiers), and the producers of the material goods (farmers, craftsmen, husbandmen) live in mutual harmony, each doing his specific work. Injustice in the State occurs when the three classes interfere with one another's work, quarrel and fight and neglect to do their proper work. Plato sees justice in man as nothing but the reproduction of justice in the State on a smaller scale.

Aristotle has no objection to Plato's description of justice in the State. However, he does attack Plato's understanding of justice in the individual soul. The 'parts' or faculties of the soul do not meet the essential requirement of 'otherness' for justice. He says: "Justice and injustice always necessarily imply more than one person."[20] Hence even suicide, an injustice inflicted upon and suffered by the same person, really is injustice against the State. A suicide suffers voluntarily the injury inflicted but no one suffers injustice voluntarily as shown in Chapter 9. Therefore, only analogously can man act unjustly against himself. In this case, we take a man as composed of various rational and irrational faculties and understand that one faculty may frustrate another or take a greater share of pleasure, for instance, than belongs to it.

The last question, "What is worse: inflicting or suffering injustice", refers to Socrates' famous dictum that it is better to suffer than to inflict injustice. Here is one of the many places where Plato discusses the problem:

> Polus. Then you consider miserable and pitiable him who puts to death any man he pleases, and does so justly?
> Socrates. No, not that, but he is not to be envied either.
> Polus. Did you not call him miserable just now?
> Socrates. The man who puts to death unjustly, my friend, and he is pitiable too, but he who does so justly is not to be envied.
> Polus. Surely, it is the man unjustly put to death who is pitiable and wretched.
> Socrates. Less so than his slayer, Polus, and less than he who is put to death justly.
> Polus. How is that Socrates?
> Socrates. In view of the fact that to do wrong is the greatest of evils.
> Polus. Is that the greatest? Is it not a greater to suffer wrong?
> Socrates. Most certainly not.
> Polus. Then you would wish rather to suffer than to do wrong?
> Socrates. I would not wish either, but if I had either to do or to suffer wrong, I would choose rather to suffer than to do it.[21]

Aristotle agrees with Plato (Socrates) that it is worse to inflict injustice than to suffer it at the hands of others. Why? Acting unjustly against others involves bad intention, premeditation, free choice, and thus, full injustice, the vicious and malicious disposition of the wrongdoer's soul. On the contrary, the suffering of injustice does not imply any such vice and least injustice. Morally speaking, the unjust aggressor is inferior, and hence pitiable and miserable whereas the one suffering injustice is superior because of the absence of a bad disposition. He is a victim of human weakedness. Only physically speaking, one may say that suffering injustice is a greater evil than inflicting injustice.

BOOK V. FOOTNOTES

1
René Antoine Gauthier and Jean Yve Jolif.
L'Éthique à Nicomaque. Introduction, Traduction et Commentaire. Vol. II, Part I, p. 328-29.

2
N.E. V. i, 9-11 - 1129b 1-10.

3
Politics, III, v, 11 - 1280b 10.

4
Politics, ibid.

5
N.E. V, i, 17 - 1130a 3-5.

6
N.E. V, ii, 12 - 1130b 30.

7
N.E. V, iii, 7 - 1131a 25.

8
H. Rackham, op. cit., ft. c p. 270-1.

9
W. D. Ross, op. cit., p. 210.

10
N.E. V, iv, 6 - 1132a 15.

11
N.E. V, vi, 6-7 - 1134b 1-8.

12
Aristotle treats these relations, as well as the
problem of slavery, in the Politics, Book I, chapters
3-13.

13
N.E. V, vii,1-1134b 18.

14
The Rhetoric I, xiii - 1374b 18.

15
N.E. V, vii, 3 - 1134b 25.

16
N.E. V, viii, 11 - 1136a.

17
N.E. V, x, 6 - 1137b 25.

18
Rhetoric I, xiii - 1374b 17-19.

19
Republic IV, xi-xix - 434-445.

20
N.E. V, xi, 4 - 1138 20.

21
Gorgias 469, b. See also ibid. 473, 509 c.

Book VI

INTELLECTUAL VIRTUES

Aristotle considered intellectual virtues not only a fitting subject for ethics but also the essence of ethical knowledge. Why?

a. Moral virtue is a choice of the mean between excess and deficiency, but that virtuous mean is what right reason (<u>logos</u>) dictates.[1]

b. Moral virtue implies a practical wisdom which is its very form . A man may be inclined by nature towards doing good deeds; but if he lacks prudence to guide him, his natural, virtuous inclination will never develop into a proper moral virtue and a good moral character.

c. Finally, Aristotle teaches that intellectual virtues are formal causes of human happiness as well as of moral conduct. If we want to know what happiness is, we must study moral as well as intellectual virtues to discover which of the two is better.

There was no doubt in the mind of Aristotle, Plato's most famous disciple, that primacy goes to the intellectual virtues, and among these to wisdom. Wisdom is the formal cause of happiness. We recall that happiness has been defined as an activity in accordance with virtue, indeed,in accordance with the best virtue,[2] which refers to theoretical wisdom, as will be seen in Book X.

It is not surprising, then, that Aristotle dedicated all of Book VI to the intellectual virtues.

Chapter 1

Right Reason

Aristotle, in his analysis of moral virtue,[3] gave a full definition of moral virtue by collecting all of the elements indispensable for both understanding and practicing moral virtue. Those elements were the following: the choice of a virtuous mean relative to us, determined by right reason, which is preceded by deliberation and right desire, and applied to each individual person by his practical wisdom with the aid of the example of a wise man. Hence, the very essence of moral virtue, its mean, is determined by right reason (orthos logos), and then applied to an individual case by practical wisdom (phronēsis) with the example of a wise man (phronimos). What, then, is right reason, practical wisdom, and the vision of moral values in the wise man? Although the answer was necessary for grasping and practicing moral virtue, it was not given in Book II. As a result, Book VI will be dedicated precisely to the study of the intellectual element in moral virtue.

Reason is right (sound, correct) when it hits the mean between two extremes. Embodied in the virtuous man, right reason avoids excessive and defective feelings and actions by choosing the mean between the extremes of feeling and acting. The wise or virtuous man does this by establishing a personal mean in his moral life. What is his standard for setting this mean? He has a proper vision of human goals, of moral values, and can, therefore, set the proper mean in his own life. His right reason is the rule or standard or norm of right moral conduct.

Instead of his usual distinction of theoretical from practical reason, Aristotle here follows Plato's distinction of the two intellectual faculties according to their objects. The scientific reason (epistēmonikon) contemplates invariable, necessary, and eternal things: essences and their transcendental properties. The deliberative or calculative (logistikon) reason considers variable, contingent, and temporal things in their relation to right reason and desire, and works out the rules of moral conduct.

Chapter 2

The Intellectual Faculty at Work in All Human Action

There are three elements in the soul that are rele-
vant to moral action, namely, sense perception (aisthe-
sis), desire (orexis), and intellect (nous). The latter
is considered in its all-encompassing activity theoretical, discursive and practical. Sense perception does
not move to action (praxis), by which Aristotle meant
distinctly human or moral action. This involves Aristotle's distinction between man and animals: animals
react; they do not act. They respond to stimuli but
lack reason which leads to genuine, deliberate and
responsible action. Animals are moved by sense perception and emotion. Desire alone cannot move to action
because it is the irrational part of the soul. Only
when desire is deliberate, when it has been determined
by   choice and reason, can it influence human action.

We see, then, that the most important factor in
human conduct is the intellect presiding over the process of deliberation. It is true, though, that thought
alone does not move us to act,whereasthought motivated
by right desire does. The result of this combination of
true thought and correct desire is moral choice.

> Hence inasmuch as moral virtue is a disposition
> of the mind in regard to choice, and choice is
> a deliberate desire, it follows that, if the
> choice is to be good, both the principle (logos)
> must be true and the desire right, and that
> desire must pursue the same things as principle
> affirms.[4]

This principle (logos) is the practical, deliberative or
calculative reason seeking   practical truth in order
to guide action.

Both rational parts of the soul, the scientific and
the deliberative, seek the truth the former for its own
sake, and the latter for the direction of action.
"Therefore, their respective virtues are those dispositions which will best qualify them to attain truth."[5]

114

Chapter 3

Individual Intellectual Virtues

Virtues of Scientific Intellect

There are five intellectual virtues. Three are
found in the scientific intellect and are concerned with
knowledge that cannot be other than it is, i.e. necessary knowledge: a) science (epistēmē) reaches necessary
conclusions about reality through the deductive method
of demonstration; b) intelligence (nous) grasps first
principles of simple reality directly or immediately;
c) wisdom (sophia) combines science and intelligence in
order to judge reality from the standpoint of ultimate
causes or reasons. Two intellectual virtues are found
in the deliberative intellect (logos). These are concerned with what can be other than it is, i.e. contingent knowledge; a) practical wisdom or prudence (phronēsis) applies moral knowledge of the virtuous mean to
human individual acts; b) art (technē), as skill and
fine art, applies productive knowledge (know how) to
shaping matter to make it both useful and beautiful.

Let us begin with scientific knowledge or science
(epistēmē). Science can be described as follows:

a) it is concerned with the necessary, invariable and
    eternal truths;

b) it is "the quality whereby we demonstrate"[6] i.e. prove
    by deduction;

c) it can be communicated by teaching. Teaching always
    starts with the known and proceeds by induction or
    deduction. First principles are reached by induc-
    tion which leads from particular instances to uni-
    versalities. Deduction works in reverse. It leads
    from universal principles and definitions to
    necessary conclusions.[7]

In Aristotle's view only deduction leads to demonstration and hence to scientific knowledge.

Chapter 4

The Virtues of the Deliberative Intellect: Art

The second virtue of deliberative intellect is art
(technē). There are three basic types of human activity,
each perfected by corresponding intellectual virtues:

a. Thinking, or contemplating the truth (theorein).
    This is perfected by the three virtues of the sci-
    entific intellect: wisdom, science and intelligence.

b. Acting or doing (prattein), i.e. conducting oneself
    according to right principle (logos). This is the
    task of practical wisdom (phronēsis) in cooperation
    with moral virtue.

c. Making or producing things (poiein). Man shapes or
    molds the world around him by mastering its matter
    and channeling its energies, making for himself a
    better place in which to live.

    Through artistry man is able to embellish his
    surroundings and refine, enhance and enrich his life.
    This enhancement of life is the subject of art in
    its broad Aristotelian sense. It involves all
    skills, applied science or technology, fine arts,
    music, dance and literature.

    Art is concerned with a product (ergon) which is
neither necessary nor natural. While practical wisdom
is concerned with man and his conduct, as an intellectual virtue, art is directed exclusively to the product. Aristotle thus defines art as follows: "An art
is the same thing as a rational quality, concerned with
making, that reasons truly"[8] how to apply productive
knowledge to the product.

Chapter 5

Practical Wisdom

Practical wisdom or prudence (phronēsis) is the ability to deliberate well about what is good for oneself and for others. The deliberation is not about particular states such as health and strength, but is about what is useful as a means to man's good life. Prudence is therefore a"..truth-attaining rational quality, concerned with action in relation to things that are good or bad for human beings."[9]

Man must first know where his happiness lies (it will be shown that happiness lies in a contemplative life), and then must choose the means for attaining it. What is the nature of those means? Since no one deliberates about unvarying things nor about things beyond one's power to accomplish, practical wisdom differs in this sense from science. It is different from wisdom as well because its primary realm is that of particular facts, things and events.

> Nor is prudence a knowledge of general principles only; it must also take account of particular facts, since it is concerned with action, and action deals with particular things."[10]

Prudence is different from art because its aim is immanent, the good of a moral agent, while the aim of art is transient, the perfection of a product. In prudence, motives are of first importance; in art, motives are of secondary importance because it is the product that counts. Art can be forgotten while prudence cannot. Mistakes in art reflect upon the product; mistakes in prudence are harmful and may even be fatal to humans.

Chapter 6

Intellect or Intuitive Reason

Intellect (<u>nous</u>) is the faculty of rational intuition whereby we grasp the ultimate principles of being, knowing and becoming. No other intellectual virtue could have these primary principles for its own object. Epistēmē involves demonstration, but those principles are not demonstrable; they are self-evident. They are to science the primary, immediate premises from which all scientific reasoning begins. Sophiā (wisdom) includes ultimate principles but requires demonstration as well. Both <u>phronēsis</u> and <u>technē</u> deal with human affairs that may be other than they are. Therefore, by elimination of other intellectual virtues, Aristotle finds that <u>nous</u> and only <u>nous</u> is fit to grasp immediately those first undemonstrable principles.

Intellect (<u>nous</u>) proceeds in this task of grasping first principles by 'induction'. For Aristotle, induction means that after experiencing a certain number of particular instances of the same object, the mind grasps a universal truth. Such truth is then fixed in the mind as a self-evident, universal principle.

> As soon as one individual percept has "come to a halt" in the soul, this is the first beginning of the presence there of a universal (because although it is the particular that we perceive, the act of perception involves the universal, e.g., 'man', not 'a man, Callias'). Then other 'halts' occur among these [proximate] universals, until the indivisible genera or [ultimate] universals are established. E.g., a particular species of animal leads to the genus of 'animal', and so on. Clearly, then, it must be by induction that we acquire knowledge of the primary premises, because this is also the way in which general concepts are conveyed to us by sense-perception.[11]

Chapter 7

Wisdom

Wisdom (<u>sophiā</u>) comprises two types of knowledge: that of the intuitive intellect (<u>nous</u>) and that of scientific knowledge (<u>epistēmē</u>). It is directed to the most exalted objects, the most valued, perfect and absolute truths: namely, those of metaphysics, mathematics, and the philosophy of nature. Wisdom aims not only at a comprehensive vision (<u>theoriā</u>) of these truths as <u>nous</u> does, but also at the explanation of them as <u>epistēmē</u> does. However, this explanation is not any explanation but the one aiming at the ultimate, deepest, or highest reason of things and events.

> The wise man therefore must not only know the conclusions that follow from his first principles, but also have a true conception of those principles themselves. Hence Wisdom must be a combination of Intelligence and Scientific Knowledge: it must be a consummated knowledge of the most exalted objects.[12]

Although politics is the 'architectonic' virtue, first among the various species of practical wisdom, <u>sophiā</u> is above it. It is the highest intellectual virtue, having as its object the highest philosophical knowledge of which the human mind is capable. "For it is absurd to think that Political Science or Prudence is the loftiest kind of knowledge, inasmuch as man is not the highest thing in the world."[13] To Aristotle the sun and stars are of divine nature, and therefore higher than men. But we also have to remember that the objects of <u>sophiā</u> are unchangeable and eternal truths, whereas the object of political, or any other prudence is changeable human action, i.e. contingent, temporary, particular event.

Chapter 8

Practical Wisdom in Politics

In Chapters 8 through 11, Aristotle further develops and explains the concept of phronēsis by comparing and contrasting it with closely related virtues. As elaborated in this chapter, the first such virtue is political wisdom. Phronēsis in its primary meaning is concerned with the personal affairs of the individual. However, that is not the exclusive realm of phronēsis; it is also concerned with the affairs of the family (oikonomikē) and of the state (politikē). Just as Aristotle calls ethics a political science because he believes that no man can develop normally, and especially not morally and intellectually outside his family and his city-state (polis), so phronesis also serves political life. Statesmanship is exercised first through the supreme and directive, architectonic, legislative science (nomothētikē) and then through political science (politikē). The latter is subdivided into deliberative (bouleutikē) and judicial (dikastikē) types of practical sciences.

Phronēsis is necessary in each of these. Why? Political knowledge is directed to securing the public good for the state. This knowledge is acquired by the practical intuiting of general moral principles (one of the tasks of phronēsis) from which moral premises are fashioned and conclusions deduced covering all similar cases. Such are the laws of the state. On the other hand, the deliberative conclusions of an assembly-man or a judge about the particular facts in particular circumstances are indispensable precedents for the wise exercise of both deliberative (in assemblies and councils) and judicial (in courts) functions. Phronēsis is necessary in both cases.

120

Chapter 9

Excellence in Deliberation

Aristotle has analyzed the nature of deliberation (bouleusis) in Book III, Chapter 3. His analysis clearly shows that deliberation is a search for a particular kind of object or means used for reaching some end. . Here the study turns around the question: in what consists the excellence of deliberation? An answer develops as the result of a process of elimination. Thus the excellence of deliberation does not consist:

1) in epistēmē, because people do not investigate matters already known. But when a person deliberates, he is engaged in investigating things known but not yet decided upon;

2) in shrewd guessing (eustochiā), because shrewd guessing involves no reasoning and proceeds quickly. On the contrary, deliberation is a mulling over means and takes time;

3) in opinion (doxa), because a person who deliberates well, deliberates correctly. Opinion is an uncertain state of mind which, if correct, has become the truth and ceased to be a simple opinion. Furthermore, opinion is no longer an object of investigation but has reached the point of affirmation, i.e. an object of opinion is already fixed and determined as far as the one entertaining the opinion is concerned. Deliberation, on the other hand, deals with objects remaining to be determined.

From this one may conclude that the excellence of deliberation consists in correctness. However, not every kind of correctness constitutes the excellence of deliberation. Deliberative activity is not:

1) that of a morally weak man who, as a result of correct calculation, sets and reaches wrong life goals;

2) that of a man who reaches right conclusions by a false syllogism or right goals by bad means;

3) that of a man who deliberates a long time and hence believes that he must have reached a right conclusion;

4) that of a man who deliberates correctly regarding human goals or the good life in general but is unable to deliberate about particular ends in his life or in the lives of others.

In conclusion, let us say that the excellence of deliberation consists in assessing correctly what is conducive to the end.

Chapter 10

Phronēsis and Understanding

Understanding (synesis) is the ability to make judgments about practical problems in human life. Phronēsis adds commands to the judgments of synesis. Furthermore, understanding of the practical problems of conduct adds to phronēsis the quality of correctly judging others' actions and learning from what they say.

Chapter 11

Phronēsis and Good Sense

Good sense (gnōmē) is that aspect of phronēsis which judges rightly what is equitable. Equity is a general term covering all virtuous conduct towards others. Because of the demands of equity men are said to be considerate, or to show consideration to others.

Chapter 12

The Use of Scientific and Practical Wisdom

Both sophia and phronēsis contribute to human happiness. Sophia in action is happiness for possession of sophia and its exercise in contemplative life makes man happy.[14] Phronēsis ensures the right means for attaining happiness. It is operative in determining what is just, noble and good for man. There is no doubt in Aristotle's mind that the primacy belongs to sophia, whereas the role of phronēsis throughout human life is to guide man in the choice of good means towards his life's goal. It disposes man to become truly wise and happy by ordering his feelings and actions.

Chapter 13

Phronesis and Moral Virtue

Moral virtue implies prudence (phronēsis) and prudence, as we have said, implies moral virtue. A man may be naturally inclined to do good deeds; but if he lacks prudence to guide him, his natural, virtuous inclination will never develop into virtue proper and good character. In addition, prudence without the moral virtues of justice, courage and temperance will not produce good character. The fact that we know what is good does not guarantee that we will do it. The role of the moral virtues is to dispose the various faculties to cooperate with phronēsis.

Book VI's conclusion should clearly answer the question raised at the beginning: What is the right reason, rule or norm of moral conduct? The answer is given in an indirect way. By analyzing each one of the five intellectual virtues, all of which contribute to the formation of right rules of moral conduct, Aristotle has given his answer. He has, however, paid particular attention to prudence and its mode of operation in man's private and public life. His answer could be summarized as follows:

> The right rule is a rule reached by the deliberative analysis of the practically wise man, telling him that the end of human life is to be best attained by certain actions which are intermediate between extremes. Obedience to such a rule is a moral virtue.[15]

THE ANALYSIS OF PRUDENTIAL REASONING

A complete prudential judgment is a complex act; its principal ingredient is an act of deliberation. Deliberation is an act by which one arrives through correct practical thinking at means which expediently lead him to an end. Deliberation can be considered thinking through the practical syllogism. [16]

Let us consider the pattern of the practical syllogism.

The <u>major premise</u> is always a universal or general rule of conduct. It contains a general moral principle flowing immediately from the first ethical principle. This principle can be expressed in many ways, but in Aristotelian ethics, one expresses it by saying: "Live in accord with right reason (and right desire)." The general moral rules which derive from the first moral principle cover the basic needs of human nature satisfied in moderation. The major premise expresses human ends or ideals.

An example of the universal major of the practical syllogism:

Such and such a goal is good for man. Example:

<u>One has to take care of his health</u>.

<u>Each minor premise is particular</u>. The general moral rule in the major premise is <u>applied to a special kind of action or thing</u>. We may distinguish several minor premises, each of them subsumed under a major premise and descending more and more to a practical conclusion. Let us take as our first <u>minor premise</u> the following:

<u>One takes care of his health by eating wholesome food</u>. In general terms, this minor premise means that such an action (eating wholesome food) is compatible with the moral principle (rule) of the major premise.

The principal difference between the practical and demonstrative syllogism is that no particular term can enter the demonstrative syllogism. The universal major and the universal minor(s) end in a universal conclusion. On the contrary, the practical syllogism must have a singular term (the predicate of the minor premise), and therefore a particular minor premise. For it has to end in a particular conclusion in order to influence a here-and-now decision about particular action.

However, this first minor premise has a certain universal character because "such and such kind of action fits into the moral principle of the major premise" covers all similar cases of that kind of action. Hence, a second, more particular minor is needed in the practical syllogism. For instance,

Light meat is a wholesome food (because it is easily digestible).

The third particular minor precedes the conclusion:

This chicken on my table here and now is light meat. Or, this action of mine here and now (eating this prepared chicken) happens to be of such a kind. This is an application of the less particular to the concrete minor, and it is a necessary step to a particular conclusion.

Conclusion: I must eat chicken meat here and now.

The above conclusion expresses a particular judgment about a particular act and tells us what to do here and now, in this or that case. In general terms, it may be expressed as follows:

This action of mine, here and now, is good and should be done.

Thus, the following will be the general formulation of the particular moral conclusion:

This action of mine, here and now, is good for me. (Affirmative conclusion)
Consequently: This action of mine, here and now, must be done by me. (normative conclusion)

In our example:

It is good for me to eat chicken meat.
I ought to eat chicken meat.

If someone (like Hume) raises the objection that the conclusion coming from "is-premises" must be an "is-conclusion" and nothing else, one may say that the moral value-judgment built into major and minor premises brings in itself not only an affirmation of what is good for the moral agent but also an obligation to do it. Moral truth and moral action go together. The meaning of moral truth is to direct action. Aristotle says:

> In a practical syllogism, the major premise is an opinion, while the minor premise deals with particular things, which are the province of perception. Now when the two premises are combined, just as in theoretical reasoning the mind is compelled to affirm the resulting conclusion, so in the case of practical premises (which involve action) you are forced at once to do it" [17]

Sir David Ross comments upon this text as follows: "When both premises of the practical syllogism are present...you must do the act to which the syllogism points: this is as certain as it is that if you grasp in their connection the premises of a theoretical syllogism you must draw the conclusion".[18] This is obviously the case in which moral knowledge is fully realized and therefore fully effective.

126

The question arises: By which faculty do we grasp
these various parts of the practical syllogism? The
major premise which contains general moral principles is
grasped by the practical intuitive intellect (nous).
The practical deliberative intellect extends the general
moral principles to all cases included in its minor premise. The second and third particular minors are a sequence of applications of the less particular to more
and more particular minors. The conclusion, which is
completely particular, is grasped again by the practical
intuitive intellect through some kind of direct perception. The principal characteristic of intuitive knowledge is its immediacy or direct contact with the truth
of things. Such is the case with both the major premise
and the conclusion. The former is self-evident, whereas
the latter refers to the immediate fact of experience.
However, the perception in this latter case is not one
of sense but of intellect. Aristotle says:

> Also intelligence (nous) apprehends the ultimates
> in both aspects--since ultimates as well as pri-
> mary definitions are grasped by intelligence
> (nous) and not reached by reasoning (logos): in
> demonstrations intelligence apprehends the im-
> mutable and primary definitions, in practical
> inferences it apprehends the ultimate and con-
> tingent fact, and the minor premise, since these
> are the first principles from which the end is
> inferred, as general rules are based on parti-
> cular cases; hence we must have perception
> (aisthesis) of particulars, and this immediate
> perception is Intelligence (nous)." [19]

This immediacy, however, does not imply intuition-
ism. The crucial role of practical reasoning consists in
linking the middle term of the minor to both the major
premise and the conclusion of practical syllogism. Thus,
strictly speaking, the conclusion is a kind of judgment
about a particular action, an intuitive kind of judgment.
Not all men will be able to follow the practical syllogism throughout. In fact, most people will reach the
right conclusion without consciously passing through a
fixed pattern of reasoning. They will do that from long
experience and good character. On the whole, their moral
knowledge is derived from virtuous experience rather
than from any deliberative reasoning.

1
N.E.   II, vi, 15 - 1107a 2.

2
N.E.   I, vii, 15 - 1098a 15.

3
N.E.   II, vi.

4
N.E.   VI, ii, 2 - 1139a 25.

5
N.E.   VI, ii, 6 - 1139b 10.

6
N.E.   VI, iii, 4 - 1139b 30.

7
For deduction see Aristotle. Prior Analytics
I, i and for induction Aristotle, Posterior Analytics
II, xix.

8
N.E.   VI, iv, 3 - 1140a 5.

9
N.E.   VI, v, 4 - 1140b 5 and 20.

10
N.E.   VI, vii, 7 - 1141b 15.

11
Posterior Analytics II, xix - 100a 15 - 100b 1-5.

12
N.E.   VI, vii, 3 - 1141a 15.

13
N.E.   VI, vii, 3 - 1141a 20.

14
As is clear from Book X, chapters 6, 7, and 8.

15
Sir David Ross. Aristotle, ch. 7, p. 221.

16.
Though Aristotle does not use this term, the texts
of Book VI, chs.8-11, and Book VII, ch 3,
suggest it.

17.
N.E. VII, iii, 9 - 1147a 25-30.

18.
Sir David Ross, Aristotle, p. 223.

19.
N.E. VI, xi, 4-5 - 1143b 1-5.

BOOK VII

CONTINENCE AND INCONTINENCE. PLEASURE

Book VII is divided into two parts: the first
part studies continence and incontinence (Chapters 1-10)
and the second part examines the problem of pleasure
(Chapters 11-14). The subject of the first part is the
important psychological and ethical fact of the interplay between human reason and desire (logos and orexis).
Books II-VI could give the reader the impression that
in morality there are only two states, virtue and vice.
Aristotle thoroughly examines the gray area of human
weakness between these, thus enriching his moral teaching with a deep insight into the human condition. As a
consequence of this insight into moral weakness or incontinence, Socrates' position that no man is evil willingly and knowlingly is challenged. Since Aristotle's
ethics is as intellectualist as that of Socrates, the
weakness of will will be explained as a lack of knowledge
of the premises of the practical syllogism.

In Book VII Aristotle employs the method of inquiry used in the preceding ethical investigations.
First he examines the opinions of his predecessors and
contemporaries; then he raises questions and objections
in order to cast light on their arguments. When other
thinkers deserve credit, he gives it to them. But in
order to resolve a problem under discussion, he finally
makes his own decisions and offers his own solutions,
together with definitions and proofs. His dialectical
method is strengthened by his penetrating analysis of
continence and incontinence, which goes deeper and farther than the description of moral virtues offered in
Book IV.

Part 1.   CONTINENCE AND INCONTINENCE

Chapter 1

Moral Strength(Continence) and Moral Weakness(Incontinence)

Current Opinions

Beside virtue and vice there are two other moral states deserving special attention. There are three degrees of goodness and three degrees of badness. The latter are the following: vice (kakiā), moral weakness or incontinence (akrasiā), and bestiality (theriotēs). Moral weakness is less than vice, and bestiality is more than vice. The three degrees of goodness are: virtue (aretē), moral strength or continence (enkrateia) and superhuman virtue (aretē heroikē).

Neither superhuman virtue nor bestiality (the latter is only mentioned in Chapters five and six) are studied by Aristotle. By definition, Superhuman virtue is divine or heroic and, properly speaking, the gods have no virtues. They are perfect, and perfection is beyond and above men. On the other hand, bestiality is beneath men and is found mostly among barbarians and seldom among civilized people. Hence Aristotle's ethics of virtue, built upon the reasonable mean between the extremes of too little and too much, has room for neither heroic virtue nor bestiality. Therefore, his main interest in Book VII is concentrated on a discussion of continence and incontinence.

Opinions about continence and incontinence current in Aristotle's day may be reduced to six:

1.   Continence is good and incontinence is bad; the former deserves praise, the latter blame.

2.   The continent man is the one who abides by the results of his reflection; the incontinent man readily abandons his reason's moral conclusions.

3.   The incontinent man acts under the influence of passion knowing that what he does is bad; the continent man, knowing that his desires are bad, accepts the guidance of his reason and refuses to follow his desires.

4. The temperate man is always continent. The converse, that the continent man is always temperate, is accepted as universally true by some and denied by others. Similarly, the intemperate (self-indulgent) man is always incontinent. However, not all agree that the incontinent man is always intemperate.

5. Some say that the prudent man cannot be incontinent; others say that sometimes he is incontinent.

6. Men are said to be incontinent even in anger and in the pursuit of honor and profit.

Chapter 2

Difficulties Involved in the Current Opinions

About Continence and Incontinence

Among the above-mentioned opinions about continence and incontinence, the third represents the main
problem: how can a man who judges rightly what he ought
to do behave incontinently? Socrates maintained that
no man did wrong knowingly (fully aware that what he was
doing was bad); he did wrong through ignorance of the
fact that what he did was bad.[1] Hence, Socrates did not
believe that moral weakness existed.

Aristotle states that this theory contradicts
facts. The important element of incontinence is to act
from passion in spite of knowing that one's action is
bad. The morally weak man knows what he should do but
he does not act accordingly.

Plato's followers in the Academy accepted the
Socratic theory but explained it in their own way. They
maintained that one can act contrary to what seemed the
better course of action. Therefore, when the incontinent
man is mastered by his passion, he has an opinion (doxa)
instead of knowledge (epistēmē). Consequently, if one
only has an opinion and is uncertain, he cannot be
blamed for adandoning his opinion in the face of a strong
appetite for pleasure.

But for Aristotle the fact is that we do blame
the incontinent man. Therefore there must be something
stronger than an opinion behind incontinence. Is it
practical wisdom (prudence)? It cannot be the prudence
which is the strongest conviction resisting the appetite
of immoderate pleasures, for it is impossible that a man
be prudent and incontinent at the same time. It has been
shown already that a prudent man possesses the other moral
virtues as well as continence.[2]

Other opinions about continence and incontinence
also involve difficulties. With regard to #4, if continence involves having strong and bad appetites, the temperate man will not be continent nor the continent man
temperate. A temperate man will have neither excessive
nor bad appetites while the continent man must. The
temperate man is a well-balanced personality; he seems
to control his appetites without special effort

Though the continent man has a passionate temper, he manages with a struggle to control it.

The following difficulty arises with regard to opinions #1 and #2. If continence makes a man obstinate in his opinions, it may be bad if it makes him persist in a faulty opinion. If incontinence makes a man abandon all opinions, in some cases incontinence will be good, namely, when it leads to the abandonment of a bad opinion. For example, Neoptolemus[3] refused to follow Odysseus' entreaty to lie because it caused him pain and regret.

Concerning opinions #1 and #3, Sophists entertained the fallacy that folly combined with incontinence is a virtue. Their reasoning was as follows: If a man is both foolish and incontinent, his incontinence makes him do the opposite of what he believes he should do. But being foolish, he believes that good things are bad and that he should not do them. Therefore, by acting contrary to his conviction, he will do what is good and not what is bad.

With regard to #2 and #4, it would appear that the intemperate man acting from his convictions and calculations is better than the incontinent man acting from moral weakness. The former may be persuaded to change his mind and be cured. The latter, however, when persuaded that he should do one thing nevertheless does another.

Concerning opinion #6, if the subject matter of incontinence is so broad, how far will the incontinent man go? Even though no one is incontinent in every way, still we do call some people unqualifiedly incontinent.

These are some of the difficulties involved in various opinions about continence and incontinence. Aristotle will discard some and embrace others for whatever truth they contain.

Chapter 3

The Nature of Moral Weakness

This chapter discusses an important question concerning incontinence and moral will, namely, how is it possible to know what is right and yet do wrong? The chapter begins with the three following questions:

1. Does a morally weak (incontinent) man act with knowledge, and, if so, in what sense?

2. What are the objects of incontinence? What kinds of pleasures tempt the incontinent man?

3. Is continence the same as endurance (tenacity)?

The second question is answered briefly by stating that the subject matter of incontinence is the same as the subject matter of self-indulgence (intemperance), i.e, pleasure. However, there is a difference in an agent's attitude. A self-indulgent man is involved in pleasure by choice, thinking that he ought always to pursue momentary pleasure, whereas the morally weak man does not think so but pursues it nevertheless. This problem will be further discussed in Chapters 4 and 8.

The third question will be answered in Chapter 7.

The first question is the most important. Aristotle proposed to solve this problem in Part One of Book VII. Platonists contended that a morally weak man acts against opinion (doxa) rather than knowledge (epistēmē). However, this answer will not help solve our difficulty, for opinion might be accompanied by as great a feeling of certainty as knowledge.

Aristotle offered his own solution to the Socratic problem. He tells us that there are four possible ways of knowing (exercising knowledge) and having knowledge (without using it):

1. Knowledge, actually exercised or not, may be present in our mind actually and potentially. If one actually knows here and now that such and such an action is wrong, it would be surprising if he does it anyway. But it is possible to act wrongly if one has the knowledge of what is right without realizing it, that is, when one is not fully aware of it. Various elements of knowledge are involved in knowing what we ought to

do. Let us turn to these.

2.   A practical syllogism has two kinds of minor pre-
     mise, universal or particular. One may actually
     know not only the universal major premise, for
     example, "dry food is good for all men", but also
     the universal minor "all cereals are dry foods."
     Yet if he does not actually know the final and par-
     ticular minor "this food (dry wheat) is of that
     kind", which is typical and necessary in the prac-
     tical syllogism in which the conclusion is always
     particular, he may act incontinently, that is,
     he may be drawn to act by instincts and desires.

    Furthermore, two kinds of universal term must be
distinguished in the universal major of the practical
syllogism, one applying to the agent and the other to
a thing.

           <u>Dry</u> <u>food</u> is good for <u>all</u> <u>men</u>.

This is a universal statement about men and dry food.
Therefore, two syllogisms can be developed from the
major premise. In the first, the personal term 'men'
of the major premise is predicated in the minor of the
particular person concerned:

           Dry food is good for all <u>men</u>.
           I am a man.
           Therefore, dry food is good for me.

In the second, the universal term referring to things is
predicated in the minor of a particular thing about
which the person is concerned.

           <u>Dry</u> <u>food</u> is good for all men.
           This kind of food is dry.
           Therefore, this kind of food is good for me.

    In the first syllogism, the minor is obvious and
known, but the conclusion is general without pointing to
a particular food. In the second syllogism, the minor
premise is the application of the general rule not to the
agent but to the particular thing. The incontinent man
seems not to know that minor premise when he is attracted by a bowl of porridge instead of a bowl of cereal.

    If the incontinent man acts out of ignorance of the
practical syllogism's minor premise, such ignorance
would turn his act into an involuntary act. However, his

act is voluntary and thus the ignorance involved must be of the major premise, something for which only he is responsible. In this case, he acts in but not through ignorance. Aristotle adopts this position in his ensuing discussion.

3. Another distinction between potential and actual knowledge is possible. A man both has and yet does not have knowledge when he is asleep, mad or drunk. He has knowledge but it is not exercised. Similarly, the incontinent man's passion changes his bodily state just as sleep, madness or drunkenness change his mind. The incontinent man thus has knowledge in the way that man who is sleeping, mad or drunk has. At times, he may utter sound moral statements. However, such statements do not indicate his actual knowledge of them.

4. Aristotle considers the three preceding arguments as logical or dialectical. In the fourth, he will try to consider moral weakness from the viewpoint of human nature. But first he feels the need to return to the practical syllogism. When both premises are present and logically combined, a particular minor falls within the universal rule of its major or the universal major is realized in a particular minor. One must then do the act to which the syllogism's conclusion points. This is the case when moral knowledge is fully realized and therefore fully effective. However, we often face cases where knowledge is present yet one still does not act accordingly. In this instance, we need to have in mind the condition of human nature or the psychology of moral weakness.

Suppose the practical syllogism has two majors and two minors. There will also be two conclusions. Desire dictates the first, and right reason the second syllogism as follows:

> Everything sweet is pleasant; not everything sweet is good for everyone.

> This cake is sweet and pleasant; this cake is not good for me.

> Therefore, I should eat it; therefore, I should not eat it.

When the incontinent man eats too many sweets, he is acting under the influence of reasoning and rule, a rule which is incidentally rather than intrinsically opposed

to right reason, It is not the opinion that everything
sweet is pleasant, but the desire for a particular sweet
thing that is opposed to right reason which says that
not everything sweet should be tasted by everyone. An
appetite for pleasure latches onto the opinion that
everything sweet is pleasant and transforms this opinion into the action of tasting sweet cake. This is the
known psychology of forbidden fruit: it pleases the imagination, the appetite and the senses. It attracts us
both to take and to taste.

The Socratic theory that no man knowingly does
wrong except through ignorance is verified to a certain
extent. In the grip of passion a morally weak man does
not reject a true and universal major premise, but he
either does not know the minor particular premise or he
utters it as an actor may utter the verses of Empedocles.
He lacks the universal knowledge that not all sweets
must be tasted and his sensory knowledge of particular
sweets is dragged about like a slave by his appetite, an
irrational part of the soul. Moral weakness is therefore
to be looked for in the appetite or desire that drags
sensory knowledge astray.[4]

Chapter 4

The Field of Incontinence

The second problem raised in the preceding chapter must be answered: What is the field or subject matter of incontinence?

According to his attitude to pleasure and pain, man is called either continent or incontinent. We must, therefore, distinguish between the various kinds of pleasure. Some pleasures are necessary to the body's life--eating and drinking. Other pleasures are unnecessary but desirable in themselves--victory, honor, wealth; all are naturally sought.

A person violating right reason by excessive indulgence in the latter type of pleasure is not called incontinent (morally weak) in an unqualified sense. Only with qualification is he called morally weak with regard to profit, honor, or anger, but not simply morally weak.

On the contrary, when someone pursues to excess things pleasant to the body--those which excite by touch or taste--and avoids excesses of things painful to the body (hunger, thirst, heat, cold), and does so against his choice, he is called morally weak but without the addition of 'in regard to such-and-such', e.g. in regard to feelings of anger. Without qualification, he is simply morally weak.

Let us repeat that the field of incontinence is the same as the field of self-indulgence (intemperance). The morally weak man is the same as the self-indulgent man, and the morally strong man is the same as the temperate man, but with a difference. The self-indulgent man pursues excessive pleasures by choice, thinking that he should pursue bodily pleasures. However, the morally weak man does not so choose or think but pursues pleasure nonetheless.

Aristotle observes that men are not blamed for pursuing honor, wealth, victory--all desirable pleasures. They are blamed only for the manner in which they do so, or when they do so to excess. To him honor, wealth and victory are noble things. Though necessary, the pleasures of the body are not looked upon as noble but as animal-like and base. Strictly speaking, there cannot be moral weakness in the pursuit of noble and naturally desirable things. Nevertheless, due to a similarity in attachment to necessary pleasures, we call the pursuers of the desirable, not-necessary pleasures morally weak in regard to such-and such a thing (honor, profit, victory) when excess is involved.

Chapter 5

Moral Weakness and Bestiality

Chapter 5 discusses briefly and unclearly both the
bestial and morbid states.

1. Some things are pleasant by nature, either absolu-
   tely--life and health--or relatively to the different races of animals and men, i.e. living on
   water or land, in mountains or valleys. 'By
   nature', in the former, absolute sense, means that
   which is in accord with the constitution of
   animals and men as they ought to be. In the latter,
   relative sense, 'by nature' means that which is in
   accord with the constitution of animals and men
   as it is formed by environment.

2. There are things which by nature are not pleasant
   but which come to be pleasant:

   a. through physical disability;

   b. through habit;

   c. through an innate depravity of nature. Unnatural
      depravity is shown in examples like canniba-
      lism.

   All of these states produce bestiality (theriotēs)

   Bestiality should be distinguished from the morbid
states of insanity and homosexuality. These states are
due either to a perverted constitution (nature) or to
habit and upbringing. Should we call these people incontinent and blame them for their practices? To possess
any of these vices is beyond the limits of vice. If a
person possessing them subdues them or is subdued by
them, we call him continent or incontinent in an extended
sense. Why? Morality requires for its operation certain natural conditions of mind and body. In morbid
states, whether constitutional or induced by habit,
the distinctions of right and wrong are not applicable.

Chapter 6

The Incontinence of Anger

The Incontinence of anger is less base than the incontinence of lust.

1. An angry man seems to listen to reason but draws hasty conclusions. When reason and imagination suggest that an insult has been suffered, an angry man before hearing the order of reason, rushes off to take revenge. Conversely, an appetite of pleasure does not listen to reason at all. As soon as pleasure is perceived, one rushes off to enjoy it. Desire for pleasure is selfish, while anger is less so. In the long run, anger is less debasing to a man's personality. One may say that an angry man pursues some kind of justice though not necessarily what is right.

2. Anger is a moral, natural, almost constitutional emotion, and therefore it is more excusable to follow it; in contrast, desire for pleasure often aims at unnecessary, excessive and thus unnatural pleasures.

3. The more one plots against others, the more unjust he is. However, the man of lust is more crafty, and therefore, more unjust than an angry man. For example, Aphrodite, the goddess of love, is called "the weaver of guile on Cyprus born." The angry man, on the other hand, does not plot against others; he is openly hostile.

4. One feels pleasure rather than pain when insulting another without being provoked; an angry man, on the other hand, feels pain when reacting to provocation. Therefore, he is less unjust, and the victim feels less injured by an angry man than by a lustful man who inflicts an unprovoked insult on his victim.

Therefore, incontinence caused by desire for lust is more unjust than incontinence caused by anger.

We must distinguish, however, between human and brutish pleasures which are due to physical disability and sickness. The word brutality is derived from similar behavior in animals. We do not call beasts either temperate or intemperate except metaphorically because

142

animals have no reasonable choice. Even when some animals are called extremely wanton (asses), destructive
(wild boars) or voracious (pigs or sharks), again, this
is metaphorical language because animals have no choice.
Among other animals they are extravagant as mad men are
among humans. But that is their nature.

Brutality is less evil than vice, for in it principle or logos does not exist, whereas in a vicious man,
logos is corrupted or even perverted. Evil is definitely
less harmful when a guiding principle is not involved
in its behavior. Guided by his twisted mind, a bad man
can cause enormous harm to others and to himself as well.
"For a bad man can do ten thousand times more harm
than an animal." 5

Chapter 7

Is Continence the Same as Endurance

and Incontinence the Same as Softness?

Chapter Seven first compares temperance and intemperance with continence and incontinence; secondly, it compares endurance and softness with continence and incontinence, and concludes by distinguishing two kinds of incontinence springing either from impetuosity or from weakness of character.

The pleasures and pains of touch and taste, and the corresponding acts of desire and avoidance are the domain of temperance and intemperance.[6] A continent man (enkratēs) is one who struggles with pleasures yet masters them whereas most people are defeated. If he is defeated by pleasures, he is incontinent (akratēs). If a man struggles with pains and succeeds, he is an enduring or tenacious man (karterikos). If he cannot cope with pain, he is soft (malakos).

The disposition characterizing the majority of men lies (though leaning toward the worse extreme), between the incontinent who are mastered by pleasure and who are soft in regard to pain, and the continent who master pleasure and the strong who endure pain.

Some pleasures are necessary and others unnecessary, but neither excesses nor deficiencies of pleasure are necessary. The same is true of desires and pains. A man pursuing excessive or necessary pleasures by deliberate choice and only for their own sake, is called intemperate and thus incorrigible (akolastos). He is incorrigible because he does not feel any regret for what he does; without repentance there is no correction of conduct. Opposed to the intemperate is the man deliberately indulging too little in pleasures while the temperate man occupies the middle position. There is also the man who avoids bodily pains; he is also intemperate provided that he deliberately avoids pain. If he avoids pain, not by choice, but because he is easily overcome by pain, he is called soft.

Those who do not act by deliberate choice are to be distinguished as those driven by pleasure, and those who avoid the pain of an unsatisfied appetite for pleasure. The man who does something wrong without or with the slightest influence of desire is worse than the man who does it.

in anger. Hence the intemperate is worse than the incontinent.

Endurance (karteriā) is constituted by resistance
and is compared to remaining undefeated in battle: continence or moral strength is constituted by mastery and
is compared to winning a victory in battle. Thus, continence is more desirable than endurance because it is
better to win than simply to hold one's ground. The
opposite of endurance is softness (malakiā); the opposite
of continence, incontinence. A soft man does not offer
resistance to pains withstood by most people and may be
called effeminate. A man loving amusement is soft and
effeminate rather than incontinent because amusement consists in an avoidance of work's pain. A soft man avoids
work's pain and indulges in relaxation to excess. A man
may be pardoned when overcome by powerful pleasures or
pains in spite of his resistance. We still call him a
morally strong man. But there is no excuse for a man who,
without constitutional or morbid weakness, cannot withstand pleasures resisted by most people. He is morally
weak.

Finally, Aristotle finds two kinds of incontinence,
one born out of impetuosity (propeteia) and another out
of a weakness of character (astheneia). The impetuous
man does not deliberate and is driven by emotion; the
weak man deliberates, but lacking moral strength and
under passion's influence does not abide by the results
of his deliberation. If the impetuous man would deliberate by preparing himself and his reasoning power when
the emotion emerging is felt and seen, he would not be
easily driven by emotion. Usually the keen (oxys) and
the excitable (melancholikos) are prone to impetuous
kinds of incontinence. Neither the keen nor the excitable wait for reason to guide them: the former because
of his quick intellect and lively imagination, the latter
because of his warm and passionate temper.

Chapter 8

Incontinence and Intemperance

Chapter Eight continues Chapter Seven by comparing incontinence and intemperance. Two questions are
discussed: Is intemperance more curable than incontinence? Is incontinence absolutely bad? Both are answered in the negative. As a result, the intemperate are
worse than the incontinent.

First, the intemperate man, as often stated, chooses
pleasure over reason and feels no regret. He is aware
that his choice is evil and thus he may be likened to
the chronically sick man. The incontinent man always
feels pain while seeking unreasonable pleasures. Keenly
aware of his weakness, he is only intermittently sick.
Due to this difference, the incontinent man is more curable than the intemperate.

Among the incontinent, the impetuous are better:
that is, those acting from passion in contrast to those
aware of rational rule yet do not obey it.

Incontinence, as we said,[7] is less than vice, because incontinent's _logos_ is not as perverted or corrupted as it is in a vicious man who acts by choice against
his reason. Thus vice destroys the major premise of the
practical syllogism whereas virtue preserves it. Incontinence is in the middle. The incontinent preserves the
moral goals stated in the major premise but does not act
accordingly. He knows that he should not do what he is
doing. He is not corrupted but out of weakness acts
wrongly.

Finally, the incontinent is a victim of his passions. They overcome him to the point that he acts against
right reason despite the fact that he is convinced he is
doing what he should not do. On the other hand, the intemperate is convinced that what he does is what he should
do. Therefore, the incontinent man is better than the
intemperate.

The answer to the second question, "Is incontinence
absolutely bad?" is clear. It is not. It is, however,
relatively bad when compared to its opposite, continence,
a habit of great moral worth.

Chapter 9

The Continent and the Obstinate Man

Once again[8] the question is raised, "Does the continent follow the dictate of any reason and choice or true reason and right choice?" Is it any reason and choice or is it the right reason and right choice that the incontinent fails to hearken to? The answer is that it may incidentally be any reason and choice when they seem right, but essentially it is the true reason and the right choice that the continent pursues and the incontinent fails to pursue.

Some people with strong views hold obstinately to their opinions and are very hard to convince of error. They resemble the continent but the resemblance is superficial. The continent do not change their minds under the influence of emotion, and on occasion they can be persuaded by rational arguments. Obstinate people, on the other hand, are driven by pleasure and are not easily persuaded by rational arguments.

Obstinate people are opinionated, ignorant and boorish. They feel pleasure when those trying to persuade them to change their minds do not overcome them by argument. When their views are disproved, they feel pain. They are unwilling to be taught by anyone, want always to follow their own views and seek the pleasure of victory for their views and not the victory of the better reason. They definitely resemble more the incontinent than the continent.

There are those who do not persist in the things they decide to do for pleasure but not because of incontinence. Such was the previously mentioned case[9] of Neoptolemus who did not, as Odysseus wanted, lie but told the truth. For that reason, he is continent rather than incontinent because he told the truth solely for the noble pleasure derived. For not everyone is incontinent and intemperate who acts for pleasure. Only he who acts for evil pleasure is incontinent and intemperate.

There is a rare type of man who desire to seek pleasure is overpowered by his disinclination toward pleasure. He acts against right reason on the side of too little; the incontinent man on the side of too much. The former feels less pleasure and joy in life than he

should whereas the latter feels pleasure and joy more
than he should. In the middle between the two extremes
stands the continent man. The continent man adheres to
right reason and stands undiverted by either extreme.
Since few, practically speaking , are reluctant to engage
in bodily pleasures, the only extreme to continence is
incontinence.

Finally, there is a similarity between continence
and temperance. Since language is often used in metaphorical sense, we speak of the temperate man's continence (moral strength). Indeed, both the continent and
the temperate have the same ability to do nothing against
right reason for the sake of bodily pleasures. However,
they differ in one very important aspect: the continent
man's desires are bad while the temperate man's are good.
Furthermore, the temperate man does not find pleasure in
violating the dictates of reason, whereas the continent
man finds pleasure in such things but does not allow
these pleasures to distract him. A similarity also exists
between the incontinent and the intemperate. Both indulge in bodily pleasures but differ insofar as the intemperate thinks that he should seek pleasure whereas the
incontinent thinks he should not. The intemperate man
has a perverted judgment about his human goals.

Chapter 10

The Prudent and the Incontinent Man

Aristotle answers the question "Can prudence co-exist with incontinence" negatively. One man cannot be both prudent and incontinent because prudence implies goodness of character and is not only a knowledge of what here and now should be done, but also the ability to act accordingly. Although the incontinent man knows what he should do, he does not do it.

The clever (shrewd) person who looks like the prudent is not prudent because he has no moral choice[10] and may be incontinent. The incontinent is so far from the prudent that the former is compared to a man who is asleep or drunk. He is only half wicked because he acts voluntarily and is conscious of his goals. Nor is he unjust because he does not deliberately do evil. He is either a weak person who fails to abide by the results of his deliberation or a highly excitable person who does not deliberate at all.

The impetuous man's incontinence is more easily cured than the irresolute man's. Furthermore, incontinence acquired through habit is more curable than inborn incontinence. Changing a habit, is obviously, easier than changing a nature. However, it must be said that habit may become a kind of second nature, and thus hard to change as well.

PART II

PLEASURE

Aristotle discusses the problem of pleasure
(hedonē) twice: in Book VII, chapters 11-14, and in
Book X, chs. 1-5.[11] The study of pleasure in Book X
was written during the years of Aristotle's teaching
in the Lyceum in Athens. The latter study is Aristotle's
definitive position on the subject. [12]

Ethics (politics for Aristotle) is concerned with
the problem of pleasure for several reasons:

1) Many claim that pleasure and happiness are
one human end. We expect the master sciences of human
ends--Ethics and Politics-- to tell us whether or not
pleasure is the end of human life.

2) It was said earlier,[13] that pleasure and pain
are tests of virtue and vice.

3) The preceding discussion on incontinence indicates that incontinence is bad because it involves an
excessive appetite for pleasure. This conclusion raises
the question: Are all pleasures bad?

Chapter 11

Differing Views on the Nature of Pleasure

Book VII, Part II, discusses bodily pleasures in the abstract, an abstraction which is due to the opinions that Aristotle disproves or partially accepts. As we shall see later, Aristotle's position in Part II differs from that in Book X.

Three views of pleasure, two hostile and one favorable, follow.

1. Pleasures are not at all good. This opinion, ascribed to Speusippus, Plato's successor as head of the Academy, is supported by several arguments:

    1) Pleasure is a process or movement toward natural perfection, and therefore, is imperfect in itself.

    2) The temperate man avoids pleasures, which proves that pleasures are not good.

    3) The prudent man seeks an absence of pain and not pleasure as such.

    4) Pleasures hinder thinking; for example, the greater the joy in sexual intercourse, the less one's capability for rational insight.

    5) There is no art of pleasure. If pleasure were good, there would be an art of pleasure.

    6) Children and animals pursue pleasure because they do not know what is good.

2. Some pleasures are good but most are bad. This opinion is discussed in Plato's Philebus and supported by the fact that some pleasures are disgraceful and others are harmful.

3. Pleasures are good, but they cannot be the supreme good. The proof adduced is that pleasure is not an end but a process or a movement towards an end. For Plato, pleasure is a movement parallel to that of human activity. Consequently, we enjoy it imperfectly, a little at a time.

151

Chapter 12

The First View Discussed: Are All Pleasures Bad?

Aristotle refuted the view that all pleasures are bad as follows:

1. "Good" in the first place has two meanings: a good may be either absolutely good or relatively good, i.e., for certain people and under certain circumstances. Consequently, although some pleasures are generally bad for human nature, they may be good for particular people or for a person in particular circumstances. Pleasurable things can also be relatively bad, harmful to one person's health and salutary to another's.

Furthermore, pleasure is not a process but a function (energeia) and state (hexis), an activity and end. Pleasure aims at restoring an impaired state or condition. An unimpaired state, function or activity does not involve pain or a dissatisfied desire such as thinking or contemplating. Bodily pleasures aimed at satisfying the natural desire of an impaired state such as hunger and thirst, are pleasant only partially or incidentally because they are subject to pain until the satisfaction has reached fulfillment.

Finally, it is not necessary to suppose that there is something better than pleasure since the end is better than the process which leads to it. Pleasure is not a process toward, but is a function (energeia) proceeding from a state (hexis). It is also an end realized by a subject doing something not undergoing a process. Pleasure is defined not as a process of which one is conscious, but as an unimpeded function of our natural state.

2. The temperate man avoids only excessive bodily pleasures; however, he does not avoid all pleasures because even the temperate man enjoys pleasures in moderation.

3. The prudent man moderately satisfies his natural desire for bodily pleasures and trains himself to ignore their absence. However, he does not do both for the sake of pleasure but to be free from the pain arising from the want of those pleasures.

4. To argue that pleasures are bad because some pleasant things are detrimental to health is nonsense. Both pleasant and healthy things can be only relatively, not absolutely bad. All pleasure qua pleasure is in some sense good. The intellect or any other power or (faculty) is hindered only by alien pleasures not by its own pleasure. If any pleasure appears bad, it is not really pleasure.

5. It is to be expected that there is no art of pleasure because art deals with the capacity (ability) for activity, never with the production of the activity and consequent pleasure.

5. Children and animals pursue bodily pleasures that are relatively not absolutely good.

Chapter 13

The Third View Discussed: Is Pleasure the Highest Good?

Some pains are evil in themselves whereas others are evil because they impede the natural function of our faculties. Therefore pain must be avoided. Since pleasure is the opposite of pain, it must be good and sought. Speusippus who claimed that pleasures are not at all good tried to disprove this argument by saying that pleasure may be the opposite of pain without being good. Pleasure is opposed, he said, to both pain and the good, as the greater is opposed to both the less and the equal. Aristotle deemed this answer incorrect. Pleasures qua pleasures cannot be evil.

The third view stated that whereas pleasures are good, they can not be the supreme good. Although some pleasures are bad, the highest good can still be some sort of pleasure. The proof depends on Aristotle's former assertion that pleasure is an activity, more specifically, an unimpeded activity of our faculties. Why, however, is it not the best unobstructed activity? The unobstructed activity of either one or all states, depending on which constitutes happiness, is the most desirable. Since this activity entails pleasure, the highest good is some sort of pleasure. This is why all people associate pleasure with happiness.

It is necessary to add that prosperity, including goods of fortune, external goods, and the goods of the body, are necessary for the unimpeded function of our faculties. Those thinking that the poor and the unfortunate may be happy are talking nonsense. Nevertheless, in spite of the fact that happiness needs fortune, it is mistaken to identify happiness with good fortune. Too much prosperity may easily impede our faculties' natural function.

The fact that all men and animals pursue pleasure indicates in some way that pleasure is in a sense the highest good.

All men pursue different pleasures. However, they all pursue bodily pleasures. But to suppose that bodily pleasures are the only existing pleasures is mistaken.

Finally, since pleasure is necessary for happiness, obviously pleasure is good. It should be found in a morally good man's life more than in others' lives.

"And if the good man's activities are not pleasanter than those of others, his life will not be pleasanter either." [14]

Aristotle is not a hedonist because he made pleasure the highest good. He identified pleasure with happiness--an unimpeded activity, with which pleasure is inextricably united as its indispensable ingredient. His position that the greatest happiness equals the greatest pleasure must be understood in this component meaning. Later on [15] Aristotle will distinguish between an unimpeded activity and the pleasure which is understood as an accompaniment and reward of the activity.

Chapter 14

The Second View Discussed: Are Most Pleasures Bad?

The second view stated that some pleasures are good--for instance, noble pleasures, but pleasures of the body are bad. Evidently, the second opinion is based primarily upon a consideration of bodily pleasures--food, drink, and sex--because most people experience only this kind of pleasure. Aristotle argues, however, that since bodily pleasures are opposed to bodily pains, they must be good. Admittedly, we do find that bodily pleasures may be evil, but that does not result from the fact that they are pleasures but that they are excessively pursued.

Now why is it that excessive bodily pleasures seem more desirable than other pleasures? The answer to this question reveals the origin of the mistaken view that all or most pleasures are bad. Aristotle tried to explore the psychology of a man seeking bodily pleasure, often to excess. Why does man seek pleasure? He seeks pleasure for three reasons:

1.   Pleasures of the body drive pain out. These remedial pleasures are pursued because in contrast to pain they are intensely experienced.

2.   Intense bodily pleasures are sought by those incapable of enjoying other pleasures, for it is painful to feel neither pleasure nor pain. The objects of pleasures unattended by pain are what is pleasant by nature in contrast to remedial pleasures which are only incidentally pleasant.

3.   The opinion that bodily pleasures, and illogically all pleasures, are bad is further supported by the fact that some are indicative of evil habits, and others indicative of a person's defective state. Both of these groups are bad (although the second may be incidentally good) and this explains why pleasure is considered bad.

This however, is an exaggeration. Bodily pleasure is not evil--everyone needs bodily pleasure--but its abuse or excess is evil. The need for bodily pleasure and for their variety and increasing complexity is the result of our composite human nature. No object is pleasant forever because of our divided nature, one element being the intellectual (soul), the other the material (body). Our human potentiality strives for maximum human development

156

and ultimate actualization; thus activity or motion is pleasant to us because of the imperfect state of our nature, which needs change in order to be actualized. If we had simple natures, we could find enjoyment in the same unchanging activity and its indispensable ingredient, pleasure. This is the case with a being of simple nature for whom the same action will always be most pleasant. He is pure act and his activity is one of immobility. Consequently his pleasure consists in rest rather than in motion.

> Since if any man had a simple nature, the same activity would afford him the greatest pleasure always. Hence, God enjoys a single simple pleasure perpetually. For there is not only an activity of motion, but also an activity of immobility, and there is essentially a truer pleasure in rest than in motion .[16]

"An activity of immobility" implies that the end has been reached; there is no further need of forward movement. However, being at the source of all striving, the activity of immobility is the highest and most intense activity. Such an activity, we will see, is a contemplative life.

FOOTNOTES

1
Plato. Protagoras 352 b-c.

2
N.E., VI, xiii, 6-1144b 30-1145a.

3
Sophocles, Philoctetes 54-122.

4
N.E., VII, iii, 14 -1147b 15.

5
N.E., Vii, vi, 7 - 1150a 5.

6
N.E., III, x.

7
N.E., VII, chs. i and vi

8
N.E., VII, ii - 1146a 16-31.

9
N.E., VII, ii - 1146a 16-21.

10
N.E., VI, xii - 1144a 25-35.

11
The discussion in Book VII is earlier, dating pro-
bably from the years Aristotle spent in Asia Minor after
Plato's death.

12
A.J. Festugière. Aristotle. Le Plaisir (Paris,
1936). Reprinted without changes in 1960, pp.xx-xxiv.

13
N.E., II, iii - 1104b8- 1105a 15.

14
N.E., VII, xiii, 7 - 1154a 5.

15
N.E., X, i-v.

16
N.E., VII, xiv, 8 - 1154b 25.

BOOK VIII

FRIENDSHIP

Introduction

Aristotelian ethics extols the wise man who embodies
all virtues and who is truly happy. The wise man is both
a prudent--phronimos--and true philosopher--sophos. The
former lives a good moral life; the latter exercises his
intellect in contemplation of the most exalted part of
reality, its essences. The former needs external goods
and friends to live a full life of temperance, courage,
justice, and continence. The latter needs very little
external goods and even friends are not necessary for him
to indulge in his god-like contemplation.[1] Aristotle
has built up a long and convincing picture of the phronimos who realizes his obligations of justice to others,
who knows the value of emotions and who cultivates them
through the series of moral virtues. Nevertheless, he
seems to extol the sophos and his life of theoria to the
point of declaring the whole moral life and happiness of
the phronimos to be only secondary.[2] He recognizes, however, that the life of the sophos is more divine than human[3]
and that the sophos being a man will need at least some
external goods and some company of friends. "...though
it is true that, being a man and living in the society of
others, he choses to engage in virtuous action, and will
need external goods to carry on his life as a human
being."[4] Even the sophos is a political animal and needs
friends.

> People say that the supremely happy are self
> sufficing, and so have no need of friends....
> But it seems strange that if we attribute all
> good things to the happy man we should not
> assign him friends, which we consider the
> greatest of external goods...also perhaps it
> would be strange to represent the supremely
> happy man as a recluse. Nobody would chose to
> have all possible good things on the condition
> that he must enjoy them alone; for man is a
> social being, and designed by nature to live
> with others; accordingly the happy man must have
> society, for he has everything that is naturally
> good... Therefore the happy man requires friends.[5]

Hence, even sophos cannot live in a splendid isolation and give to the intellect such absolute primacy that
he will have only contempt for others. The true link between the phronimos and the sophos is the philia.

Is Aristotle's Nicomachean Ethics primarily an ethics of friendship rather than solely an ethics of courage, temperance, continence and justice? As to justice Aristotle points out that society needs another social virtue--friendship--which is not only a necessary complement of justice but also its superior. Justice allows us an enjoyment of our possessions, but it also divides things and their owners. Friendship unites humans in their common endeavor to live a happy life. Furthermore, if genuine friendships in society prevailed, justice would not be needed. Two reasons could be mentioned for that assertion. First of all, in the case of friendship among citizens, friends should have all things in common, and, secondly, a friend is another self, and there is no justice towards oneself. In fact, the more just men are, the friendlier they become. "And if men are friends, there is no need of justice between them; whereas merely to be just is not enough--a feeling of friendship is also necessary. Indeed the highest form of justice seems to have an element of friendly feeling in it."[6] Therefore, while justice may go so far as to remove injuries, friendship goes further by binding citizens into many forms of individual, domestic and political communities.

The study of friendship was an integral part of moral and political philosophy in antiquity. Plato developed the theory of friendship in his dialogues Lysis and Symposion, and among Romans, Cicero in his treatise De amicitia. The same study has all but disappeared from contemporary studies of moral and social philosophy. Because it is a necessary moral and social factor, it should be restored again to its rightful honorable place.

Book VIII is divided into three parts: Part I discusses the need, nature and kinds of friendships (chs. 2-8); Part II brings in the social aspects of friendship (chs. 9-12); and part III studies the obligations toward one's friend (chs. 13-14). The last topic is continued in Book IX (chs. 1-3).

Chapter 1

The Need for Friendship

For Aristotle friendship (<u>philia</u>) is necessary for a good and happy life. It is either itself a virtue or implies a virtue. Friendship plays an indispensable role in social and political life. Friends particularly are needed when we have everything that makes life good and happy. What good is it for a rich man to have wealth and the ruler to have power if they have no friends to help them and bring them good and to share their possessions with them? On the other hand, the poor need friends to help them. Friends help the young avoid errors, and they help the old overcome their infirmities and illnesses. When adults perform noble actions, friends are at their sides.

The affection of friendship is natural to people. Parents naturally love their offspring, and children love their parents. Even animals love their young ones. Friendship is natural among those of the same species, so that every human feels a natural affinity towards all his fellow men. Friendship is a particularly necessary bond among citizens of the same state. Statesmen work hard to achieve concord among citizens without which even the best laws do not hold, and commonwealths are bound to dissolve through civil war and strife.

Friendship is not only the means to a good and happy life, but it is also something sought for its own sake, a noble feeling of love for others.

At the end of Chapter One, Aristotle itemizes three difficulties in the discussion of the nature and kinds of friendship. The first difficulty is the question of whether friendship involves an attraction based upon similarities or upon differences among friends. The second is that of the possibility of friendship between the unvirtuous, and the third, is the question of whether there is more than one kind of friendship.

Chapter 2

The Nature of Friendship

The solution to the second and third questions
raised at the end of Chapter I is given in Chapters 2-6.
The similarities and differences are treated in Chapters
7-8. According to the goods that are lovable, there are
three types of friendships: the noble (kalon) sought for
its own sake, the pleasant (hēdy), that which appeals to
the senses, and the useful (hrēsimon), that which is a
means to something else. Since all men seek the good,
friends do the same. Friendship cannot exist among the
wicked. However, one may ask: Does each man love that
which is universally good for everyone, or that which is
good only for himself? Furthermore, since each man loves
that which is good for himself, does he love that which
is really good for him or only that which appears to him
to be good? It seems that the latter is more likely the
fact. Aristotle dismisses the difficulty by saying that
in our discussion 'lovable' will mean 'what appears to
be lovable.' Each man, however, is responsible for his
moral vision, his wishes and choices.[7]

We may now proceed to define friendship. Several
important elements are to be taken into consideration.
First, friendship is not any kind of love, but is a
mutual or reciprocal love between two or more human
beings. It cannot be only the love-gift (agape), or
love-desire (eros), or exclusive self-love (philautia),
or simple benevolence (eunoia), a one-dimensional love
towards others. When men feel goodwill for one another,
are aware of one another's goodwill, and base their own
goodwill on a friend's noble, pleasant, or useful qualities, the love between two human beings is called friendship. While Plato in the Lysis develops his theory of
friendship in such a way that friends fall in love with
the Good-in-Itself or the Form of Good, Aristotle dis-
covers, on the other hand, that friendships are based
upon a friend's good qualities--his physical, moral and
intellectual excellences, or, at least, his usefulness.
Friendship, then, is a conscious, reciprocal well-wishing
which is based upon the good qualities of friends.

Chapter 3

The Kinds of Friendships

Since acts are different according to their objects and love is an act of friendship, according to the three lovable objects which are the honorable good, the pleasant good, and the useful good, there will be three kinds of love. Therefore, there are three kinds of friendships: the virtuous, the pleasant and the useful.

The friendship of usefulness is based on a mutual exchange of benefits. The friendship of pleasure is based on agreeable feelings that friends derive from one another's company. The friendship of virtue is based on the moral and intellectual qualities possessed and shared by friends. In each kind of friendship, friends wish each other good and growth in good, and as the case may be, to become more virtuous, more pleasant and more useful. The goodwill (eunoia), an essential element in the concept of friendship is different essentially in each case.

Without excluding the positive side of the others, Aristotle considered the third type-virtuous friendship-to be the best. It is the only one that pursues the excellence of friends for what they are, not for what they have. The friendship of usefulness, however, points to the benefits derived from it by friends, and the friendship of pleasure seeks satisfaction and joy in the company of friends. Hence, these two friendships are incidental because they are based upon accidents of fortune, beauty, wittiness, and others.

> Hence in a friendship based on utility or on pleasure men love their friend for their own good or their own pleasure, and not as being the person loved, but as useful or agreeable. And therefore these friendships are based on an accident, since the friend is not loved for being what he is, but as affording some benefit or pleasure as the case may be.[8]

Utility and pleasure change as fortunes and beauty change. Virtue, however, is a deeply-rooted habit. As a result, utilitarian and hedonistic types of friendships change easily while virtuous friendship is lasting. One may wonder why Aristotle shows great optimism for the permanence of virtue. It is part of his intellectualist approach to see the virtuous or the happy man enjoy the serene and permanent state of virtue and happiness.

Changes of fortune will not destroy his peace of mind or his virtuous style of life.

> ...no supremely happy man can ever become
> miserable. For he will never do hateful or base
> actions, since we hold that the truly good and
> wise man will bear all kinds of fortune in a
> seemly way, and will always act in the noblest
> manner that the circumstances allow.[9]

We are told that the wise, virtuous man will <u>never</u> do base actions throughout his life and will <u>always</u> act nobly. But what about the possibility that he may neglect the exercise of virtue, acquire some vicious habit contrary to his virtue, or simply let his weakness of will overcome his best convictions? Aristotle seems to identify the established virtue with the person embodying it and makes it durable for the duration of earthly human life.

Let us return to the useful and pleasurable friendships. Age also plays an important role in them. Old people, as well as many mature adults and a few young adults, look first of all for profit. A friendship of pleasure is found mostly among the young because they pursue emotions, and pleasures and beauty and wit that stir their emotions. They easily fall in love and wish to live together with their friends whose company is agreeable to them.

In a virtuous friendship, however, age is unimportant. Friends are bound by their goodness regardless of age. Each wishes the other to be good in himself, to be richly endowed with good physical, moral, and intellectual qualities. Hence, mutual goodwill or reciprocal benevolence is perfect only in virtuous friendships. Friendships of utility or pleasure reach only an imperfect degree of mutual benevolence, which is obvious, since they are based upon possessions of fortune and transitory beauty, while a virtuous friendship rests upon lasting personal qualities.

A virtuous friendship contains the good characteristics of utilitarian and hedonistic friendships. Good friends are useful to each other in their personal growth. They are pleased in each other's company because each finds himself in his friend's person. As we know already, friends love the moral and intellectual qualities of each other as part of their persons. Hence, in a virtuous friendship utility, pleasure and virtue are not something external, such as good things or events that happen to friends: all three refer to the personality and character of friends; three of them, in this context, are found within the innermost being of friends.

> Now this kind of friendship [virtuous] has all the requisite qualities we have mentioned and has them _per se_, that is, as an essential part of the characters of the friends.[10]

Aristotle ends this chapter with a wise remark. Since fully virtuous men are few, virtuous friendships are rare, and utilitarian and hedonistic friendships are more prevalent. This fact of life will not, however, move him to proclaim virtuous friendships good only in theory. They continue to be the best in practice and theory in spite of their small numbers. After all, whatever is the best cannot but be rare. Aristotle is a moral aristocrat; full morality will never become mass morality.

Furthermore, virtuous friendships are slow to make because time is needed for future friends to know each other. By conversing often and sharing their activities, a degree of familiarity and intimacy is attained--another requirement for virtuous and personal friendships. In such a relationship friends discover each other's inner ego, are impressed by the other's good qualities of mind and body, grow fond and confident of each other, look at each other with respect because they see each other as subjects worthy of admiration and affection. More than simple liking is needed for finding a human being worthy of admiration: friendship needs affection and imitation for a mutual, intimate relationship benefitting both friends and making both aware of the valuable companionship they have found. True friends are rare. Virtuous friendships are delicate human affairs; they should be carefully built up, and, once established, diligently cultivated.

Chapter 4

Useful and Pleasant Friendships Compared

As has been said, virtuous friendship is similar to pleasant and useful friendships. Although good men are pleased in each other's company and useful to each other, pleasant and useful friendships are less durable than virtuous ones. However, a friendship of pleasure is more durable than a friendship of usefulness because the lover is attracted by the beauty and youth of the beloved, and the beloved is attracted by the attention received from the lover. With the passing of years, the bloom of youth passes away and pleasurable friendship may easily dissolve, but friends who enjoy each other's company may have discovered each other's good characters and continued their friendship now based upon more permanent qualities. Useful friendships, on the other hand, do not have personal attachments but only profit in view; as a result, when advantages cease, such friendships are also dissolved.

Strictly speaking, friendships based exclusively upon pleasure and profit are also found among bad people, but this is not so in the case of noble friendship; only good people can have friends on the grounds of their good characters.

Virtuous friendship is the only guarantee against mistrust and slander. The long and intimate companionship of two friends makes for a deep mutual acquaintance, and a good friend will never believe the word of a third person against his friend. However, useful and pleasurable friendships do not guarantee such trust.

In reality, we say 'friends' of pleasure and profit only by analogy. A prime analogate of true friendship is, of course, virtuous friendship; useful and pleasurable friendships are only approximations. Thus, pleasure is a pleasant good, utility a useful good. Both share in the virtuous good which is pleasant and useful too. Pleasure and profit make friends only incidentally, but nobility of character is essential to a good and permanent friendship.

Chapter 5

Active and Habitual Friendships

After carefully describing the three kinds of
friendships Aristotle now distinguishes them by reason
of habit and act. He says that in moral virtues, although not actually engaged in a brave or generous
action, some men are called brave and generous by reason
of habit, while other men are called temperate and just
only when performing virtuous deeds. So in friendship,
friends are those who live together, exchange mutual
favors, please each other and profit from each other's
company. This is an active friendship. But those
friends who are separated by geographical distance, unable to engage in active friendship, may still be
habitual friends through their good mutual disposition.
However, long absences may easily break a friendship--
one would say "out of sight, out of mind."

Distance and absence are not the only obstacles
to active friendship. The lack of friendly actions by
those who do not cultivate friendships or associate with
their friends indicates that they are more men of goodwill than true friends. Friendship must grow and
flourish in the community of life. It is not so much an
exchange of material gifts or the pleasure friends derive
from each other's company that makes friendships last and
deepen, but the companionship enriching the characters
of both friends. The poor look for friends in order to
ask for help; the rich seek friends for the company that
would break their isolation. Real friends, however, are
equal, equally sharing their nobility of mind and heart.
Next, the old and the sour often find it hard to open
themselves to friendly mutual companionship and, consequently, have difficulty forming friendships.

Finally, unless friends are pleasant in each other's
eyes and have common tastes, it is impossible for them to
be companions. Athenian hetairoi, at least during Aristotle's time, are good examples of friendships based upon
mutual affection and common tastes because of their being
companions from childhood--of the same age and of the
same tribe, social standing and similar fortune.

In conclusion, the best active friendships can be
developed between good people. What is truly worthy of
affection and choice is noble and pleasant without qualification. For each individual what is worthy of love and
choice is that which is good and pleasant to him. On

both grounds good men make excellent candidates for friends. They are good and pleasant, worthy of affection and choice absolutely (they have worth in themselves), and they are good and pleasant, worthy of affection and choice to their friends. These are the conditions for developing the best active friendship among human beings.

Aristotle returns to prove what he has only stated previously--that besides active there are also habitual friendships. First of all, affection and choice are indispensable ingredients in friendship. Now affection seems to be nothing more than emotion or passion. In fact, we may like inanimate things--food and gold, for instance--out of pure passion. The same can be said also of passionate love for animals and humans. However, mutual affection or love between friends is accompanied by deliberate mutual choice. Passion or lust is one-sided, selfish and self-centered. Mutual love, on the other hand, is reciprocal, hence, chosen. What is done by choice is not done by passion but by habit or habitual disposition. Therefore, friendship is a habit.

Secondly, friends wish each other good for their friend's sake. This attitude cannot spring from passion, which is individual and selfish, but from habit. Thus, friendship is a habit.

Thirdly, if one objects to the idea of loving a friend for his own sake, by stating that such love goes against the rule that each loves what is good for him, the answer is given that when a good man loves his friend, he loves his own good and equally returns to his partner his nobility, pleasantness and benefit. This is particularly true in friendships between equals.

Chapter 6

Friends in Three Kinds of Friendships

The three kinds of friendships being compared to
the love and lovable qualities in friends are now compared to the friends themselves. The type of man likely
or unlikely to become a good friend is discussed. As
was stated before, the elderly and the sour do not make
good friends because the old are self-centered, sus-
picious and stubborn; the sour are quarrelsome, grouchy,
and critical of others. The elderly and the morose can
be benevolent and helpful to each other, but they are not
true friends because they do not look for each other's
company nor do they enjoy social life. Good temper and
sociability, however, are the most important and indispensable dispositions needed for making friendships. For
instance, young men become friends easily because they
have good tempers, are not yet hurt by unpleasant experiences, and they love to mingle socially.

Next, the number of friends is discussed, and
virtuous friendship is first explored. For several
reasons, one cannot have many good friends. Being in
love with many people at once is impossible because love
is an extreme emotion and naturally felt only for one
person at a time. This is true for both sexual love and
friendly love. Pleasing many people at once is not easy
because everyone has an unpleasant side to his personality. A true friend will put up with that unpleasant
side in his friend, but not in many friends. It also
must be noted that there are not many good men to make
virtuous friendships work. Finally, friendship implies
experience and intimate relationships with friends, but
such familiarity takes time, and consequently, is hard to
establish with many people.

If we have in view both utilitarian and pleasurable
friendships then it is possible to have several friends
because many people can be useful and pleasant to us at
the same time. Furthermore, a long period of familiarity
is not required in these friendships: the pleasure and
profit can be enjoyed at once.

Let us now compare the two lower kinds of friendship. It seems that pleasurable friendship is closer to
the virtuous than the useful. Pleasure and delight in the
company of another is more related to that person than are
profits. Such a person is supposed to be sociable and of

good temper, possessing extra endowments such as beauty and personal charm. Since friendship implies mutual exchange, it is, however, necessary that friends of pleasure find delight in one another and in the same things. Furthermore, a friendship of pleasure seems to be more generous than a friendship of utility which is for gain. Pleasant friends are loved for their own sake. Also, rich people do not need useful friends, but instead seek pleasant friends because they need the company of others. Consequently, people look for pleasant friends in the first place. Even those who are our friends for their virtue's sake must be pleasant as well as good.

However, many people do not seek in the same person goodness, pleasantness and utility, but instead differentiate among them. Thus, men in power do not look for pleasant friends who are equally good and useful for noble purposes, but they look for the witty to entertain them and for the clever and aggressive to execute their profitable orders. These two qualities are rarely found in the same person, yet we have stated that the good man is noble, pleasant and useful. But a virtuous man does not become a friend to a man in power unless his superior in rank is also superior in virtue.[11] But princes of superior virtue are a rare breed.

Friendships discussed in the chapters covered so far are all based upon equality. Both partners render the same benefits, wish the other good and exchange an equivalent amount of two different things, for instance, pleasure and profit.

Utilitarian and pleasurable friendships resemble the virtuous friendship because one is pleasant and the other useful, and both qualities are inherent in the virtuous friendship as well. However, the two former friendships differ from the virtuous friendship because the latter's is unchanging and lasting while the others change easily. Because of this difference, they are not genuine friendships.

Chapter 7

Friendship Between Unequals

In previous chapters Aristotle maintained that equality is a necessary ingredient of friendship. He now examines the possibility of friendships between unequals.

Friendships of a superior for a subordinate, such as between father and son, husband and wife, ruler and subject, or, in general, between the older and the younger person are, evidently, not based upon equality, but upon differences. Furthermore, those friendships are different from one another. The friendship of a father for his son is different from that of a husband for his wife, and both of these friendships are different from that of a ruler for his subjects.

The above friendships are also different within themselves for two reasons. First, in each case, the partners have different virtues or habits and different functions to perform. Father and son show different habitual dispositions towards their mutual friendship, as husband and wife, ruler and subject must. Next, all of them perform differently in their friendships.

The motives of the partners are also different. A father loves his child and a child loves his father for different reasons, and the same is true for husband and wife and ruler and subject. Hence, their affection and friendship are different too.

How is friendship possible between unequals? They mutually offer each other what is proper to each one. Parents render their children what is due them; namely, protection, food, clothes, education, and children render their parents what is due them; namely, respect, love and obedience. In such a mutual exchange of proper affection and cooperation, lasting friendship could be established. However, the inequality of partners is still there, and must be overcome for friendship to begin and to last.

The exchanges of unequal friends must be proportionately equal. Whenever there are friendships involving the superiority of one of the partners, the superior partner must receive more affection than he gives. This is also true for the more useful, more pleasant and more virtuous partner. The love due to the superior partner is proportionate to his worth. When such a proportionate love is given, friendship may be established because inequality is being bridged by a proportionate reciprocation of love.

Proportionate equality is applicable to justice and friendship, but in a different manner. In matters of distributive justice, the equal is primarily proportionate to personal merits of a citizen and its quantitative sense (i.e. strict equality) is secondary. In friendship, on the other hand, the quantitative meaning of strict equality--two persons rendering love to each other--is primary, and the equality proportionate to merit is secondary. Friendship starts with equality between friends; justice ends in equality between humans.

In fact, when there is a wide disparity between friends with regard to their virtue, wealth or social standing, friendship is not possible. This can be illustrated in three examples: gods immeasurably exceed mortal man in virtue, kings and humble people cannot be friends because of the disparity in social position and wealth, and the wisest cannot be friends with people of ordinary virtue because of the gap between them.

Kings and wise men, however, may be befriended with the love proportionate to their worth, but what about man's friendship with god? Aristotle cannot find strict equality or even proportionate equality between gods and man. Friendship between gods and mortal men is impossible because they are simply too far apart in virtue.

An interesting question is raised here: should we wish our friends the greatest good so that they become gods? Not at all, Aristotle promptly answers, for we would lose the great good of their friendship, affection and mutual completion, and for that reason, our friends should remain humans. Yet, aren't we depriving them of their greatest good--that is, to become gods if that is possible? The answer is given that a friend wishes good to his friend for his own sake, i.e., for what he is as a human being . Consequently, "he will really wish him only the greatest goods compatible with his remaining a human being."[12]

172

Chapter 8

Giving and Receiving Love in Friendship

After Aristotle has determined that friendship between unequals is maintained by a proportionality of loving and being loved, he shows how loving and being loved are related to friendship. For Aristotle, to love is more characteristic of friendship than to be loved. Why then do many people wish to be loved rather than to love? The Key to this answer is a deep human desire to be honored. It is more befitting the worthy, to whom honor is due, to be loved than to love, and for this reason, most men are fond of flattery. A flatterer is, or pretends to be, a friend of lower status who receives favors he knows he does not deserve and returns, or pretends to return, more love than he receives. Thus, he pretends to love more than to be loved; however, being loved seems closely connected with being honored which many people desire. Honor is a mark of goodness in him who is honored; and anything that is good or apparently good is loved.

Let us now analyze the comparison of being loved with being honored. First, we must inquire why people wish to be honored. Men apparently desire honor not for itself but incidentally. They seek to be honored especially by men of two classes: the powerful and the wise. Many are glad to be honored by the powerful, not for honor itself but because they expect to obtain something they need from those who honor them. Others desire to be honored by the virtuous and wise because in this way they seek to confirm their personal opinion about their own goodness and excellence. In fact, they rejoice in the fact that they are virtuous, accepting the judgement of good men who by the very fact of honoring them seem to say that they are good.

Nevertheless, men delight in being loved more than in being honored, because love, unlike honor, is sought for its own sake. The very possession of friends seems to be the principal external sign of honor. Therefore, being loved is better than being honored inasmuch as friendship is in itself desirable.

We come now to the main point of this chapter: loving (giving love) is more proper to friendship than being loved (receiving love). Friendship is a habit, but, more importantly, it is also an act. To love is an act of friendship: to be loved is a state of reception or

173

passivity of love. For example, mothers who have a
strong affection for their children truly take more
pleasure in loving them than in being loved by them. If
for various reasons those mothers give their children to
others to rear them, they continue to love their children
and are happy to see their children grow and excel even
when they know that their children will not return them
love because they do not know their mothers. Therefore,
friendship consists more properly in giving than in receiving love.

One final point remains to be discussed. Friendship consists in equality and similarity of friends'
qualities.[13] This is the answer to the question raised
before in chapter 1.   Likeness is the basis of true
friendship. We said earlier that the cure for inequality
in friendship is that an inferior loves more in proportion to his friend's worth. In this way the abundance
of love makes up for the inadequacy of excellence.

But likeness will determine how lasting friendships
will be. The likeness of virtue makes friendship enduring because virtuous friends remain like-minded both
in themselves and in friendship with one another. This
is so because they do not change easily to the worse by
committing evil, nor do they ask their friends to do anything evil; and, when there is a possibility of evil
coming between good friends, they will try to prevent it.

The least enduring friendship is that between evil
men. Evil men possess unsteady characters. The reason
is that wickedness, to which they adhere, is in itself
hateful even to them. Furthermore, since they find nothing
in which their will can be satisfied, their love varies.
Thus, they do not remain like-minded. But yet they
desire things contrary to what they previously wanted.
Hence, they are friends for a short time, as long as they
enjoy the evil in which they agree.

There are two kinds of friendships that hold a
middle ground. Friendships of utility and pleasure last
longer than friendships between evil men whose friendship
lasts only as long as pleasure and profit are mutually
provided.

At the end of this chapter, Aristotle discusses
friendship between persons of disparate condition. He
shows that this friendship is formed for the sake of utility, inasmuch as one friend seeks from the other what he
himself needs and gives something in return to the other.

For example, the poor man desires to obtain money from the rich man in return for his service.

The friendship of opposites also may be character-istic of the pleasurable friendship. Sexual love may be asked for and given by the partners who are the ugly and the beautiful.

One may infer here the following corollary. Since lovers may be very different in worth, beauty and virtue, it is unreasonable to demand that the less worthy partner be equally loved as he loves.

At the conclusion of this chapter Aristotle suggests that the supposed attraction of opposites may only seem to be that. Rather, what they actually desire is the mean between them, for the mean is the good sought essentially, and it seems achievable through striving for the opposite of oneself. That the desire is for the opposite is thus only an accidental adjct to the essential goal, reaching the mean, and contrariety is not an attraction in and for itself. However, after this brief comment, Aristotle leaves the subject of the attraction of opposites as foreign to his concerns.

PART II.   SOCIAL ASPECTS OF FRIENDSHIP

Chapter 9

Friendship Accompanies All Social Relations

Friendship and justice are both found in some kind of association or community (koinōniā). Justice and friendship deal with the same subject--people united in associations or communities, and both justice and friendship have the same objective--to make people equal. Since justice is essentially an other-oriented virtue, friendship is as well.

We find that in day-to-day life, men united in common undertakings call each other friend. Sailors, for example, are attracted by sea-faring and the gains associated with it, soldiers by victory and its advantages, and so too all others sharing in common ventures. Both friendship and justice are found between these men.

Friendship obviously consists in the mutual sharing of goods, according to the known proverb that "friends' goods are common property" (koina ta philōn).[14] There are different associations, and so there must be different friendships. Brothers and relatives (hetairoi) have all things in common: homes, meals, work and play, while other associates have particular things in common, some more and some less. Accordingly, their friendships vary in degree. Friendship is greater when friends have much in common, and lesser when friends have little in common. However, when there is no community of life, friendship cannot exist.

Similarly, justice also differs in different associations. The right, the object of justice, is different in diverse associations. It is obvious, for example, that the same right does not exist between father and son as between brother and brother, and justice between the people of the same age, education, status and tribe (hetairoi) is different from the justice between citizens who have no close connection.

In fact, justice and injustice increase in proportion as they are done to closer friends. The reason is that it is greater justice to render dues to a close friend, and greater injustice to injure him. So it is more unjust to rob or to steal money from one's hetairos than from a fellow citizen, to refuse help to a brother

176

than to a stranger or to strike one's father than to
strike someone else. Thus, we may say that justice naturally increases with the closeness of friendship since
justice and friendship exist in the same persons and
are equally extensive.

In the second part of this chapter, Aristotle
relates every association to the civic or political association which is the state. Friendship accompanies every
association, but each association aims at the state; thus,
the state will be the model association upon which friendship should be built up and kept. The difference between
so many associations among citizens and the all-inclusive
state is that all of them aim at particular goals while
the state aims at the common, comprehensive good of all.
Particular associations aim at meeting some needs of the
partners. For example, the family meets daily needs, the
village meets more than daily needs.[15] Other particular
associations are similar--for instance, sailors unite for
seafaring, and soldiers unite for victory. Furthermore,
men of the same tribe (phylē) and commune (dēmos) unite
not only for political advantages but also for religious
and social ones: they offer sacrifices to gods and gather
in temples to pray together, and they socialize with each
other.

Other associations seem to be formed for the sake
of pleasure exclusively, but even these serve a useful
purpose. Such associations are religious choirs and
social clubs which were established to perform at sacrifices and feasts and especially weddings.

Now, then, all previous associations are contained
under and subordinate to civic association (hē politikē).
The former aim at their partners' private good, the latter
at the common good of all citizens: the good that is not
only present but also enduring throughout their lives.
For associations which perform sacrifices and prayers and
those which play at festivals, there is an element of
'here and now', and not of 'everywhere and all the time'.
Thus, the ancient sacrifices and festive gatherings take
place after the harvest as a kind of offering of first
fruits to god and as an occasion for the harvesters to
repose after their hard labor and enjoy dancing, eating
and drinking. But all these things aim ultimately at the
wellbeing of citizens, and hence, are subordinated to the
state. In conclusion, friendship and justice are to be
understood and determined according to the model and ultimate association which is the state (polis).

Chapter 10

Classification of Constitutions and Analogous

Household Rules

Since all kinds of friendships are reducible to political association, let us study the kinds of states or constitutions. The constitution (politeia) determines the distribution of offices in the state, designates the subject of the supreme or sovereign authority in the state, and fixes the end to be pursued by the citizens of the state. Thus, the constitution not only organizes the exercise of and appoints the subject of the supreme power in the state, but also becomes the way of life typical for each state, the norm of moral conduct in political life, the whole system of political and social ethics for the citizens of an individual state.

> ...for a constitution is the regulation of the offices of the state in regard to the mode of their distribution and to the question what is the sovereign power in the state and what is the object /telos/ of each community...[16]

The end (telos) of the state is the promotion of the good human life in all sectors--bodily, intellectual, economic, social, political--and, above all, ethical. The state was conceived in Aristotle's politics as existing to help men become better human beings, to promote justice and friendship among men, and to educate citizens and help them unleash their creative capacities for good and restrain their propensities to evil. That was the purpose of politeia. "The good life then is the chief aim of society both collectively for all its members and individually..."[17] Consequently, those constitutions are good which aim at the good human life of all citizens; those which aim at the private interest of the rulers are bad or corrupted. Thus, Aristotle classifies right constitutions as follows:

Kingship (basileia) is ideally the rule over citizens by a man superior in virtue and wisdom, self-sufficient, and hence able to look after his citizens' interest. Aristocracy (aristokratia) is the next best rule of the best few men over the majority of citizens with their excellence consisting primarily in virtue and wisdom. Plato named the third legitimate constitution timocracy (timokratia). Aristotle, however, does not derive it from the word time (honor) as Plato does,[18] but from the word

timema (property qualification), thus making the claim of
timocratic rulers to power depend upon their wealth.
Later, Aristotle will use the general term polity
(politeia) or constitutional government for the third
legitimate political rule inasmuch as the people rule
themselves by themselves in view of the common good life
for all citizens.[19]

Perverted constitutions spoil the best in the
legitimate. Tyranny (tyrannis) is totally opposed to
kingship. It is a single person government aimed at the
tyrant's own private interests and exercised despotically.
That means that the tyrant treats his subjects as a master
treats his slaves. There is no doubt in Aristotle's mind
that tyranny is the worst kind of government "for the
opposite of the best (kingship) must be the worst."[20]
Perverted aristocracy is called oligarchy (oligarchia).
It exists where those who have wealth are the sovereign
authority in the state and distribute public offices not
according to merit or personal moral and intellectual
value but according to wealth. While ruling the state,
they look after their private interests. Finally, a corrupted form of constitutional government is democracy
(demokratia) in which the sovereign authority is in the
hands of the poor. They serve only the interests of the
poor.

If we take a look at domestic rule, we will find
there a resemblance to, not identity[21] with the mentioned
forms of government. The relationship between father and
son is compared to the royal government, because the father takes care of his son's interests. It must be mentioned here that among barbarians the father is likened
to a tyrant who has absolute power of life and death over
his son. The former is right; the latter is wrong, for
each kind of person should be ruled differently: sons and
slaves must not be ruled in the same way.

The relationship of husband and wife is likened to
an aristocracy because the husband rules on account of his
virtue, and he leaves to his wife the affairs that are
proper to a woman. If the husband or the wife rules not
because of virtue but because of the will to rule or the
wealth he or she brought to the marriage, that rule is
similar to the oligarchical.

179

The relationship between brothers is similar to
timocratic rule because brothers are equal in everything
except age. If their ages are too close their timocratic
relationship could not be maintained. They would slip
into what is called democracy. Democracy is found in
those households where there is no master and all are
equal. Furthermore, democracy is at work in those households where the head of the family is too weak, and
hence, everyone is free to do what he likes.

Chapter II

Friendship and Justice in the

Different Political Systems

Each legitimate form of government--kingship, aristocracy, timocracy--involves some kind of friendship because in each there is a goodwill towards justice. Justice and friendship are not far from each other; they are concerned with the same persons and are expressed in communication with others.

There is friendship between a king and his subjects which consists in the king's superior virtue by which he bestows benefits upon his subjects. The subjects return honor, respect and obedience to their king.

By analogy, the father-son friendship is likened to that of a king toward his people. The merits of the father for his son are superior even to those of a king for his people. A father is his son's source of life and the provider of his son's nourishment and education. In return, the father is honored, respected and obeyed by his son. Hence, it is as natural for a father to rule his children as it is for a king to rule his people. There is justice between father and son and between a king and his subjects set in terms of the merits of father and king. And there is friendship between benefactors and beneficiaries in the family and in the state, based upon the same ground--the excellence of virtue of kings and fathers who bestow benefits upon their dependents.

Friendship between husband and wife is likened to that between aristocratic rulers and their subjects. Here again the partner superior in excellence gives more and is, in turn, given more. The husband as his wife's superior is supposed to lead, give to and support his wife. However, the wife excels in the domestic tasks which are proper to her. Her husband accepts and honors such division of labor and authority. This way, both justice and friendship between husband and wife endure.

Brothers are friends like hetairoi in Athenian society. For they are almost of the same fortune and upbringing. The common upbringing results in similar feelings and characters of brothers. As to the political system, brothers, like timocrats, are friends. The citizens who are in control in timocracy are equal, just and virtuous. They rule in turn so that each may have

an equal share in power. Their friendship is based upon
equality and virtue. The friendship of brothers also
should be based upon equality and virtue.

In this context, Aristotle does not mention
oligarchy; however, we may assume that there could be
some friendship and justice limited to wealthy rulers
and wealthy citizens. Democracy allows for some friendship and justice since where the citizens are equal they
have many things in common to share.

There is very little friendship as there is very
little justice found in the bad systems of government.
Friendship in tyranny is minimal if any. There is
nothing in common between a tyrant and his subjects: he
looks solely for his own interests and not for theirs.
There is also no justice between them. Whenever a des-
potic relation between humans exists, there is no justice,
no friendship. As long as a man's relationship to something or someone is based on the consideration of that
other thing or person as a tool, either lifeless (thing)
or alive (animal, slave), to be used for the exclusive
benefit of the user, neither friendship can develop for
the lack of mutual goodwill, benevolence, and love, nor
justice because a tool as a tool is not a person, and
therefore, cannot participate in law, contracts,rights
and duties.

Aristotle remarks that friendship can be established
between master and slave when a slave is looked upon as a
human being. Then and only then can equality be established, things in common are found and communication may
develop.[22]

Chapter 12

Friendship Within the Family

After distinguishing civic and domestic friendships
Aristotle now subdivides both kinds of friendships. All
friendships, it was said in Chapter 9 involve some
kind of community or association. Now, the friendship
between blood relatives and <u>hetairoi</u> seem to have less
of the consciously agreed upon community of interests
than civic friendships of fellow citizens, fellow tribesmen, fellow travellers and others. The latter ground
their friendship upon some kind of agreement to do and
enjoy things in common , and to these we may add the
friendship between a host and his guest.

The main thrust of this chapter is, however, an
analysis of the various friendships and their characteristics within the family.

All friendships between relatives derive from
<u>parental friendship</u>. Parents love their children as a
part of themselves. The son is, so to say, a separated
part of his father. Consequently, this friendship is
nearest to the love of man for himself which is the
source of all friendships. 23 Children, on the other
hand, love their parents because they owe them their
lives.

However, parental love is stronger than filial
love for three reasons: (1) Parents know the identity
of their children better than children know the identity
of their parents. Parents know the generative act
which brought children to life but children do not, for
they were not alive yet when the generative act took
place. The more a man knows the causes for love, the
more reasonable it is that he loves more. Hence, it is
reasonable for parents to love their children more than
children love their parents. (2) That which has sprung
from a thing belongs to its source whereas the thing from
which it springs does not belong to a thing which has
sprung from it, or, if it does in the sense of its bed-
rock, it does to a lesser degree. Such is the case of
a progenitor as compared to its progeny. Parents, then,
love their offspring more than their children love them.
(3) Friendships are strengthened by the passage of time.
Parents love their children for a longer time than their
children could love them. Parents love their children
from the birth of each one of their children. Children love
their parents only after they begin to distinguish them

183

from other adults and especially after they reach a sufficient use of reason to be able to understand their relationship to their parents.

The three reasons just mentioned--closeness, generation, length of loving--point to the fact that maternal love is stronger than paternal. Mothers know better than fathers who their children are. Mothers are more deeply the sources of their childrens' lives than are their fathers, for mothers carry and nourish their children with their own blood and food even before they are born. However, Aristotle's theory of sexual generation states that a male is an active principle (form) of his child and the female only a passive factor offering matter to the father's form. "If, then, the male stands for the effective and active [sex], and the female, considered as female, for the passive [sex], it follows that what the female would contribute to the semen of the male would not be semen but material for the semen to work upon."[24]

In concluding the section on parental friendship, Aristotle summarizes it in the following way: "Parents then love their children as themselves (one's offspring being as it were another self--or a second self produced by separation of oneself); children love their parents as the source of their being"[25]

The ground for _fraternal_ friendship is their origin from the same parents. Being thus identified with their parents they are identified among themselves. Hence, the saying goes that brothers are the same by blood or coming from the same stock. Brothers share, therefore, the same being although they are individual persons, separate from their parents and from each other.

Fraternal friendship is strengthened by common upbringing and by their closeness in age. On the broader level these characteristics are found among the members of the same _hetaireia_ or fraternity. _Hetairoi_ enjoy each other's company due to their closeness in age and common upbringing.

Cousins and other blood relations derive their friendship from the fraternal one insofar as they derive their origin from brothers, who are sons of the same parents. They are more or less related as they are closer to or farther from the common ancestors.

Before opening discussion on conjugal friendship Aristotle examines the characteristics of the friendships mentioned above. With regard to parental friendship, he says that children love their parents as those who are superior in goodness and excellence, for their parents gave them life, upbringing and education. Friendships between parents and their children contain more pleasure and utility than an outsider's friendship since parents and children live life together.

Brothers resemble each other in age, upbringing, education and character. Furthermore, brothers have loved each other from birth so that the test of time for their friendship has been the longest and most reliable.

Friendship between cousins is also similar to the brotherly inasmuch as cousins are close to the common ancestors and resemble each other in age, upbringing, education and character.

It remains to analyze the friendship between husband and wife or conjugal friendship. There exists a natural friendship between husband and wife since man is by nature inclined more to conjugal than to political society. "The family is an earlier and more fundamental institution than the State and the procreation of offspring is a more general characteristic of the animal creation.:"[26] But while other animals couple to continue their species, humans cohabit in couples to secure the needs of human life. Husband and wife divide their labor and each contributes, according to their inclinations and capacities, to the common good life. The husband works outside of the home while the wife is busy with household occupations. Thus, conjugal friendship is not only natural due to the generative instinct but also is the result of the concerted domestic efforts of husband and wife to provide for the needs of the family.

Conjugal friendship involves all three factors making up every friendship: utility, pleasure, and virtue. It is useful because it provides for family life; it is pleasant because it brings pleasure not only in the generative act, but also in the company of the two people who love each other. Conjugal friendship is virtuous, and this characteristic should be the couple's most enduring bond.

Children are regarded as the bond uniting husband and wife more than anything else because they are common to both. This common factor attracts and ties husband and wife together. Childless couples separate more easily precisely because of the lack of children who would bind them more effectively and more deeply.

At the end of this chapter Aristotle raises the question: which rules of conduct should govern the friendship of husband and wife, and, for that matter, any friendship? His answer is that basically one should first be able to understand the rules of justice between friends. Various friendships in various degrees meet justice and thus prepare the ground for engagement in friendly relations.

PART III.   OBLIGATIONS TOWARD ONE'S FRIENDS

Chapter 13

The Claims of Friendship Between Equals

There are, as we know, three kinds of friendships based upon virtue, pleasure and utility. Each of these friendships may be established between equals or unequals. Those friends who are equal in virtue, pleasure, and usefulness must give equal affection and help to their friends. Those friends who are unequal in merit have to render love and respect to their friends which are proportionate to their superior or inferior merits. We will study in this place possible quarrels that may arise between equal friends.

Complaints between equal friends are most likely to occur between them when they are united for utility or interest. Before we prove it, let us take a look at virtuous and pleasant friendships. Complaints do not occur between virtuous friends. Friends united in virtue usually give more than they receive because doing good for a friend is the proper function of the virtuous friendship. In this situation no one complains against the friend who is giving love and help. But, on the other hand, if he is a truly noble man he will try to return it. And if one gives more than one receives, he will not complain because he does what he set out to do, i.e., to do good. Here, then, "the measure of the benefit seems to be the intention or choice of the giver; for choice is the predominant factor in virtue and character."[27]

As long as friends for pleasure find joy in each other's company--and that is what each one of the two desires--there is no reason for mutual complaints. After all, it would be ridiculous for a "pleasure" friend to complain about the unpleasant company of his friend, for he is free not to spend his time in his friend's company.

Utilitarian friendships suffer more than other kinds of friendships from complaints and quarrels. Since a friendly relationship is based in this case upon material advantages, friends easily complain that they do not receive enough. What is the reason for the complaint? Material things do not satisfy deeply or permanently: the more one possesses them the more one wants them. It is, then, unsatisfied wants which come through in complaints between utilitarian friends.

Let us look further into the reasons for complaints between friends of utility. There are two
kinds of utilitarian friendships: one is moral and the
other legal. When friendships, based upon utility,
are formed on fixed conditions, they are legal. When
friends give and take gifts, in fact, loans which are
expected to be returned, without any fixed conditions
but on trust alone, according to moral practice, such
friendship is called moral. Quarrels usually occur
when friendship is established upon one kind of condition and ends in another kind of condition.

Legal utility is expressed in agreements. These
are of two types: the first, purely commercial, for example,
in buying and selling done from hand to hand when one
receives immediately what he expects from the agreement.
The second type of legal agreement is more liberal, al-
lowing time to return a loan or service although the
quid pro quo must necessarily be determined. The debt
is clear, but the postponement of repayment is a kind
of friendly gesture. For this reason, this second type
of friendly arrangement is not, in several states, subject to the formal judicial exercise of justice, but it
is assumed that friends dealing in good faith should
honor their word.

Moral utilitarian friendship is established when
gifts or favors are given without any fixed conditions.
They are given to a partner as a friend, although the
giver expects to receive as much or more on the assumption that he has not given but lent. If the recipient
does not repay an equal or greater amount, the giver will
complain.

The reason for the complaints and quarrels in this
case is that people wish for or approve what is noble--to
give without asking for return--but actually choose to
receive benefits for their gifts. They may even pretend
to be great givers because that is socially quite accep-
table, but in fact, they choose what is profitable.

How can such quarrels be avoided? The recipient
of a benefit should, when he can, make a return worthy of
the gift he has received. This he should do of his own
accord because we cannot make a man our friend against
his will. Since our friend expects an equivalent or
greater return of his gift or favor, we should give
exactly that. It was our mistake not to examine what

kind of person was giving us a gift and under which conditions. We took the benefactor for a friend, but he was not motivated by friendly feelings toward us. We should have broken the so-called friendship and should have established our relationship with the benefactor on fixed, legally defined terms. If we were able to repay a gift, we would bind ourselves to do so under specific conditions; if not, either the giver would not expect us to return, at least not the whole of it, or we should not accept the gift.

At the end of this discussion Aristotle raises a difficulty: Should the repayment be measured according to the material advantage of the recipient or by the beneficence of the giver? Why should such a question be raised at all? Because the recipients of benefits will easily belittle the gifts they accept saying that those gifts are small for their benefactors, that they can get the same from other people. The benefactors, on the other hand, insist that they have given the best they have, that the same was not available from any other source, that it was given in a time of emergency and so on.

Aristotle offers the following solution to the problem raised. In utilitarian friendships the measure is the utility of the receiver. For he needs help and the help is given to him on the assumption of an equal return. The value of assistance is measured in terms of material advantage received. The receiver must repay the equal amount of benefit received; if he does it in greater amount, that would be an even more noble gesture. The difficulty, however, hardly exists in virtuous friendship in which the giver gives out of his choice and goodwill without asking for a return.

Chapter 14

What Unequal Friends Owe Each Other

After discussing the reasons why complaints occur between equal friends, Aristotle proceeds to discuss the reasons why possible disagreements take place between unequal friends. As a matter of fact, here disagreements are even more likely to occur. Why? Each of the two unequal friends may think that he gets less than he deserves and friendship is easily broken. Let us explain this fact of life.

First, the superior party who gives more thinks that he deserves more benefit, for if good is due to the good man, then more good is due to the better man. Similarly, in useful friendships, the more useful should get more benefit out of friendship. It is fitting, they claim, that the less useful should not receive equal benefits with the more useful, because if he does, that kind of giving and receiving would be public service (leitourgia), [28] rather than friendship. Useful friendships should be like a business partnership: those who invest more should receive more.

Second, the needy in useful friendships and the less worthy in virtuous ones argue that the friend who excels in virtue or in fortune naturally provides for the needy friend. In fact, they say, what good would it be for a needy man to have a friend of high moral standards and of good fortune if he gets nothing out of friendship with such a man?

Aristotle looks for a solution to the problem by first asserting that both the superior and the inferior friend seem to estimate correctly what is just. Something, though not the same thing, ought to be given equally to each: to the superior, greater honor, to the needy, greater gain. Why? Because the reward of virtue and beneficence is honor, whereas the needy receives the aid in financial benefits.

To illustrate this point, Aristotle refers to what happens in political life. The man who does not contribute anything to the common good is not honored, but he who contributes to the common good receives honors from the community. It is not likely that one and the same deserving person will get both honor and money from the community at the same time. But each deserving person rightly expects to be given either honor or money by the community. The one who loses money serving his community deserves honor from the state, and the person who expects gifts for his service to the community is given money.

Therefore, in unequal friendships, each one receives a reward proportionate to his contribution. This way equality is established between friends and their friendship preserved.

To confirm the above reasoning, Aristotle tells us that friendship demands only the possible. Each friend returns what is possible to him. The needy returns honor, the virtuous gives out of his moral excellence and beneficence. The needy or the inferior in virtue cannot, as a rule, repay as much as a giver deserves such as parents and Gods do. All he can do is repay in honor and service.

At the end, Aristotle draws a corollary from the father-son relationship. No son, unless excessively wicked, would disown his father, but the father may disown his son. Why? First, let it be clear that a debt ought to be paid. But the son cannot repay what his father has done for him. Therefore, he will always be in debt. Now creditors have the power to remit debts and so does the father to his son.

Second, let us assume that no son would forsake his father and disown him unless the son is an excessively wicked man. Due to the natural friendship between father and son, it is human that no son should dismiss or expel his father who has supported him. But if the son is wicked, the father should disown him or not provide for everything he wishes because he would become worse in his wickedness. One final remark: most people would be willing recipients of benefits, but would like to avoid giving benefits because such action is unprofitable.

BOOK VIII

FOOTNOTES

1. N.E. X, vii, 4 - 1177a 25.

2. N.E. X, viii, 1 - 1178a 9.

3. N.E. X, vii, 8 - 1177b 25.

4. N.E. X, viii, 6 - 1178b 5.

5. N.E. IX, ix, 1-3 - 1169b 5-10.

6. N.E. VIII, i, 4 - 1155a 25.

7. N.E. III, 5.

8. N.E. VIII, iii, 2 - 1156a 15.

9. N. E. I, x, 13 - 1100b 30-1101a.

10. N.E. VIII, iii, 7 - 1156b 20. Trans. by Martin Ostwald, Aristotle, _Nicomachean Ethics_, p. 220.

11. This seems to be an unequal friendship. But, in fact, there is a proportionate equality which Aristotle discusses in the next chapter. Thus, friendship between the subject and the ruler can be based not upon absolute but upon proportionate equality. The man in power bestows upon rather than receives benefits from his subjects; but his subjects love and respect him more than he does them. Thus, proportion is established.

   The good man can love his prince more than the prince loves him when the prince surpasses him in virtue. In that case, the good man loves the worth of his prince, and with this love, he makes a return for the benefits he receives from the prince. The prince offers both material benefits and moral excellence; the good man, for the benefits he receives from the prince, offers greater love and esteem because of the prince's virtuous character. In this way, a proportionate equality is established between them.

12. N.E. VIII, vii, 6 - 1159 a 10.

13. N.E. VIII, viii, 5 - 1159b: hē d'isotes kai homoiotes philotēs.

14. N.E. VIII, ix, 1 - 1159b 30.

15. Politics, I, i, 6-7 - 1252b 16-28.

16. Politics, IV, i, 5 - 1289a 15.

17. Politics, III, iv, 3 - 1278b 20; see also Ibid. v,
     10-11 - 1280a 30 - 1280b 1-15.

18. Republic, VIII, 545a-b.

19. Politics III, v, 2 - 1279a 35.

20. N.E., VIII, x, 2 - 1160b 5.

21. Domestic rule is similar and not identical to poli-
     tical rule. Aristotle rejects the opinion of those
     who identify domestic and political rule. He says:
     "Those [Socrates and Plato] then who think that the
     nature of the statesman, the royal ruler, the head
     of an estate and the master of the family are the
     same are mistaken." Politics, I, 1, 2 - 1951b 5.

22. It is not easy to see how there could be a friend-
     ship between master and slave, even when a slave is
     understood to preserve basic human nature. "...
     for the slave even has not got the deliberative part
     at all..." he must be guided and directed by his
     master. (Politics I, v, 6 - 1260a 10) But the lack
     of deliberative intellectual power to make
     choices and decisions will make it impossible for
     a slave to grow in virtue, share in contracts and
     obey law as a free, law-abiding citizen.

     Aristotle tries to introduce more light into this
     question a little further in his Politics. The
     slave, he says, is the partner in his master's life.
     They have a community of interests in the common
     enterprise of building up a good household. Thus,
     at least a useful friendship can develop between
     them. But even here, the little virtue the slave
     must possess to be the living instrument of the good
     household is supplied by the master's admonition
     and guidance. "It is manifest, therefore, that the
     master ought to be the cause to the slave of the vir-
     tue proper to a slave. . . " (Politics I, v, 11 -
     1260b 4.)

23. N.E. IX, iv.

24. On the Generation of Animals I, xviii - 729a 30.
     Oxford Translation.

25. N.E. VIII, xii, 3 - 1161b 25.

26. N.E. VIII, xii, 7 - 1162a 15. Aristotle seems to
     contradict this assertion in Politics I, i, 11 -
     1253a 19. He says there: "Thus also the city-state
     is prior in nature to the household and to each of
     us individually." The natural primacy of polis over
     the family and individuals is justified by its telos
     i.e., the highest human good that can be reached in
     the city-state only, by the fact that polis is a
     self-sufficient political community, and that it is
     an all-inclusive organization for the good human
     life. Neither the family nor individual citizens
     have the opportunity to realize such a universal
     and comprehensive human goal. Thus, the family and
     individual men and women are temporally prior to the
     state--there is no state without families; in fact,
     the family is ontologically a more natural community
     than the state. However, the state has teleological
     primacy over the family and individuals. And in
     matters of life and action, telos (goal) is the
     most noble cause. The family and individuals attain
     their full development and well being only in the
     polis.

27. N.E. VIII, xiii, 11 - 1163a 20.

28. See Glossary.

BOOK IX

<u>PROPERTIES OF FRIENDSHIP</u>

Book IX continues the discussion on friendship and is
divided into three parts:

Part I in Chapters 1 and 2 continues and closes the third
part of Book VIII on the obligations toward one's friend.
The third chapter discusses the dissolution of friendship when obligations are not met.

Part II studies self-love as the basis of friendship as
well as other properties of friendship (chs. 4-8).

Part III studies the connection between friendship and
happiness (chs. 8-12).

PART I

OBLIGATIONS TOWARD ONE'S FRIEND

Chapter 1

How to Measure What Friends Owe Each Other

Aristotle discussed in Book VIII the nature and kinds of friendship and their relation to justice. He will discuss in Book IX the properties of friendship. First, however, he winds up Part III of Book VIII which deals with the obligations toward one's friends. In view of that he considers at the beginning of Book IX the problems involved both in the preservation and in the dissolution of friendship. In Chs. 1 and 2, Aristotle deals with the preservation of friendship.

Friendship between equals is preserved by a fair return of things and services made by the friend. Friendship between unequals, such as father and son, king and subject, is preserved by something proportionate to each partner,[1] For example, in political society, as we have said,[2] a return is made according to proportion, not equality in voluntary transactions. Thus, the proportionate return made to the shoemaker for his shoes is mostly in money, the measure of exchange. This way disturbances are avoided.

In friendships, however, the things exchanged, such as affection and services, cannot be measured by money. Friendship can be easily disturbed by the lack of return in a proportionate measure. Friends quarrel because the repayment was not what was deserved. When affection is given and sought, the lover sometimes complains that the beloved does not return the love given. When externals, either gifts or services, are given, the beneficiary often complains that he has received more promises than gifts.

Complaints regarding the reciprocity of gifts and services happen when friends have different motives. When a lover seeks pleasure, the beloved, utility, and neither is equipped to meet his partner's expectations, their friendship is on the brink of dissolution. The reason is simple: since the things sought for in friendship do not exist, friendship also no longer exists. The partners did not love each other for one another's sake, but for expected pleasure and utility; however, the expectation was not realized. May we add here that, in any case, neither hedonistic nor utilitarian friendships last very long. Only friendships based upon virtue and the

196

partner's character are enduring, as we have said,[3] because in such friendships friends love each other for the sake of virtue, a lasting habit.

Friends quarrel also when each partner gets something in friendship that he did not expect. One, for example, wishes love and receives a gift, another wants a gift and instead receives affection. Or, one has what the other wants and is ready to give it, but the other lacks what his partner wants and cannot give it to him. In both cases, friendship is in danger of being dissolved. A dissatisfied friend is hard to deal with, "for it is the thing that a man happens to need that he sets his heart on, and only to get that is he ready to give what he does."[4]

In the rest of this chapter Aristotle offers remedies for preserving peace in friendships dissimilar in the expectations of partners. First he suggests who should determine the return and then how the return is to be made.

Who will fix the amount due to both the giver and the receiver? Generally speaking, both should mutually fix the return. But it seems that the giver expects the receiver to do that. For instance, Protagoras had his students estimate the value of the knowledge they received from his teaching and then repay him accordingly.[5] He was satisfied to receive the reward according to the judgment of the recipients. What happens in this case is that the fee is measured with respect to man who gives a service or a gift and not with respect to the service itself. If the giver accepts that arrangement, the friendship is not in danger.

It may happen, however, that the giver will accept the money from the receiver before he renders his services. Then, either he renders poor service or he renders none at all. For example, Sophists accept money before they even start to teach, and when they do teach, Aristotle believes that their knowledge is so shallow that no one would pay for it afterwards. Naturally, these men are accused of not performing the services for which they are paid.

Now, let us see how the return of services and favors is to be made. In the case of virtuous friendship, difficulties are not expected. When a friend bestows a service for the receiver's sake and not in view of repayment, no complaints are expected. It is evident from what we said[6] that such a giver is a friend according to his virtue. Thus, in virtuous friendships the return is made according to the choice and love of the giver.

What is said about the virtuous giver may also be said about the teacher of philosophy. No price can be set for the imparting of philosophical knowledge. The intent of the philosopher giver is the only worthy repayment--to share mutually in philosophy. Nevertheless, as we do in the case of our parents and gods, we should repay as much as we can.

If the gift or service was made by a friend in view of recompense, as is the case in friendships for utility and pleasure, a return which seems just to both parties must be made. When this is not possible, then the beneficiary ought to determine a compensation that seems reasonable. This seems not only necessary but also just. Why?

A fair repayment will be determined according to the benefit or pleasure a person receives in useful or pleasurable friendships respectively. Buying too is done in this way: a buyer will pay what the thing is worth to him. But the amount of help or pleasure can best be known by the person who receives it. Consequently, it is necessary and just to make the repayment according to the judgment of the beneficiary.

The same is proven by the authority of the law. There are laws in some states which provide that no legal action can be taken to enforce voluntary contracts when one party claims to be deceived. When a man has dealings with a man in good faith, one should settle with him in good faith. The recipient of the benefit should settle the just payment at the outset. The giver and the receiver rarely agree on the value of the service or gift given, because the giver is inclined to overestimation, the recipient to underestimation. The latter's appraisal, however, should be the standard for repayment. Of course, the recipient should not estimate the benefit at the price that he considers fair after he receives it, but at the value he attached to it before he received it.

Chapter 2

Conflicting Obligations

The conflicting claims of different friends are discussed next. Several questions are raised in that context. First, should a man obey and respect his father
in all matters, or should he, when ill, obey his physician, and when electing his general in the army look
for the best soldier? Second, should a man aid his friend
rather than a virtuous person? Third, should a man repay
his benefactor before giving gifts to his <u>hetairos</u>
when he cannot do both?

Each case should be carefully examined in all its
moral circumstances. However, one may state the general
rule: no one person has an absolute claim to all defer-
ences.

To be more specific, Aristotle answers the above
questions. He solves first the third question. Generally
speaking, if he cannot do both, one must return a favor
or a thing to his benefactor before giving gifts to his
friend. This is a matter of justice just as one has
to pay back a loan to a creditor rather than give a
present to a friend, if he cannot do both.

Now, even the above general rule is not always to be
followed--for instance, in the case of someone who has been
ransomed from robbers, such a person faces three choices:
if the person who ransomed him fell himself into the
hands of robbers, should the man ransom his ransomer first
and before anybody else? Or, should he repay his benefactor who is not a captive but asks at the same time for
repayment? Or, should he ransom his father who fell into
the hands of robbers before anybody else?

The third choice must be made, because it seems that
a man is bound to ransom his father even in preference
to himself and more so in preference to others.

Aristotle delves further in exceptions to the general
rule that a debt should be paid first. In a situation in
which giving gifts is nobler--for instance, a virtuous man
needs assistance, and more necessary--for instance, someone is in a position to ransom his father--we must
abandon the general rule and make a gift. On the other
hand, the return of favors or benefits would be actually
unfair in some cases when, for instance, the benefactor

bestowed the benefit on a man known to be virtuous, and the return was made to a benefactor who has become wicked. There are also occasions on which one should not make a loan to a person who has previously made a loan. An example would be a man who does a favor to a good man in view of getting it back because he is an honest man; a good man, however, does not expect a return of a loan from a bad man because he is not honest. In the latter case, the demand for a loan in return of a loan previously given is unreasonable. It would still be reasonable for the recipient to refuse to give the benefactor a loan even when the benefactor is not wicked yet the recipient believes him to be bad.

The above exceptions to the general rule remind us that we can expect only so much precision and definiteness in questions concerning human emotions and actions. Aristotle has pointed out in previous discussions that there is no absolute certainty in moral questions.[7]

The answer to the first question raised at the beginning of this chapter will now be given. Not all honors are to be given to one's father just as all sacrifices are not offered to Zeus. Furthermore, one owes one's father a different respect and obedience than that he owes his mother. Finally, one's brothers, friends, benefactors are due different obligations, each that which is proper and fitting to him. Thus, people invite to weddings and funerals relatives who are related to the family and who will enjoy the increase of the family and mourn the loss of a family member.

Let us now be more specific about honors to be given to different people. In the first place, it seems natural that children should provide their parents with food if needed. They owe their life to their parents, and hence, ought to preserve their parents' lives even before their own lives. Similarly we owe our parents honor. However, a man does not have to render his parents every kind of honor. There is an honor we owe to a wise man, to a general or statesman, that we do not owe to our parents. Even the honor rendered to the father and to the mother is different.

We owe honor to every elderly person by rising and bowing to him. Besides, one ought to converse and share what he has with his brothers and hetairoi. Furthermore, one ought to honor his kinsmen, fellow tribesmen and fellow citizens, comparing their several claims with respect to their closeness to us, or their virtue, or usefulness.

The final answer to the second question: Should a man aid his friend rather than a virtuous person, is not easy. It is easy to compare and judge the various claims when the persons belong to the same group--for example, of two relations we must help the closer; of two wise men, the wiser. However, it is difficult to judge various claims when the claimants belong to different groups. For instance, should we help the wiser or the relations. In spite of the difficult decision involved in such a matter, we should not give up the task, but we must differentiate as best we possibly can between the various obligations.

Chapter 3

Doubts on the Dissolution of Friendship

The problem is raised, should friendship be dissolved when the friend does not remain the same as he
was when friendship was established.

It is to be expected that friendships based upon
utility and pleasure are broken when the partners are no
longer useful or pleasant. For these friends were
friends in view of the benefits rendered and the pleasure
procured. When the benefits and pleasures are gone,
friendship ceases.

There will, however, be reason for complaint if
someone loves another for his usefulness or pleasantness,
but pretends to love him for his good character. Many
complaints arise among friends when one partner is not
the kind of friend the other believed him to be.[8] There
is no reasonable complaint if one friend deceives himself
by thinking that he is loved for his good character
whereas his friend does not give him any such recognition.
In that case he is to blame for his self-delusion. But
there is a place for a reasonable complaint if he is deceived by the open pretense of his friend who hypocriti-
cally shows affection for the character of a friend while
in fact he cares for his friend's possessions or simply
takes pleasure in his company. Such a friend is worse
than a counterfeiter of money because his offense goes
against something more precious than money; he counter-
feits virtue--hence, he is worse than those who forge
money.

What about the breaking of the virtuous friendship?
If we make a friend assuming that he is a good person but
he becomes or we believe that he becomes wicked, should
we still love such a friend? Not at all. Only good is
the object of love. Neither man should become the lover
of evil nor should he become like an evil friend because
as we have said,[9] like is a friend of like.

Aristotle raises a specific question: how is the
former virtuous friendship to be broken? Immediately?
Not always, not with all friends, but only with those
whose wickedness is incurable. In fact, if there is a
chance that we may help our friend in reforming his
character or returning him to the path of virtue, we
should do that. It is more noble to help a friend regain his virtue than to help him regain his lost

possessions. If a person cannot be reformed, no one should blame a man for breaking a friendship, because he was a friend to a virtuous man and not to a wicked man.

Another question may be raised: If both friends remain good, yet one becomes considerably better than the other, can the former dissolve the friendship? Yes, he can. This is particularly evident among childhood friends. For, if one remains a child mentally and emotionally, and one grows into a fully mature man, they can no longer be friends. Why? They are too different; they do not enjoy the same things and have different tastes and talents. Without a common sharing in things, friendship is impossible as we have already said.[10]

In conclusion, the last question is asked: After dissolving a friendship, should a person behave toward his former friend as if he were never his friend? Not at all. A man should remember the past common life spent with his friend. He should act more kindly with him than he would with a stranger. An exception is allowed when the dissolution of friendship was due to the excessive wickedness of a former friend. Then a man has no obligation to show friendliness to the former friend with whom he has terminated his friendship of which the wicked friend was unworthy.

PART II

SELF-LOVE AND OTHER PROPERTIES OF FRIENDSHIP

The concept of friendship has been defined in
Chapter 2 of Book VIII. Aristotle, however, finds it to
be important to delve deeper into that concept and its
elements, namely, goodwill (eunoia), concord or community of ideas and feelings (homonoia), beneficence
(euergesiā) or voluntary offering of benefits to one's
friend, virtue (aretē), and friendly affection
(philēsis). Aristotle deepens his analysis of friendship in Chapters 5, 6 and 7 of this book. This careful analysis of the concept of friendship has led
Aristotle to the fundamental insight that self-love
(to philauton) is the standard, model, and real basis
of every true friendship. He dwells on this idea in
Chapters 4 and 8 of this book.

Chapter 4

Self-Love is a Standard of Friendship

A careful analysis of the concept of friendship shows that all the sentiments found in the true friendship have their prototype in genuine self-love (to philauton). Such a conclusion can be justified,

a) metaphysically, because one has to be first constituted in himself in order to be able to turn to others and benefit them as his friends. Furthermore, one is closest to himself in oneness of his being. This first union will be a pattern of the union with others.

b) psychologically, because one takes best care of himself first, and, if he loves others as he loves himself, we know that his love is strong and permanent.

c) morally, because only a virtuous man loves himself in an orderly manner: he loves his body and soul, in particular his mind or intellect, the highest faculty of the soul which makes him distinctly human. His love for others also will be virtuous.

Let us see which friendly feelings are found among friends.

A true friend is one who[11]

1) wishes for good and does real or apparent good to his friend, for his friend's sake. He not only wishes but voluntarily offers benefits to his friend. He sometimes offers benefits that are not really good for his friend, but he thinks they are. One thing is certain, everything he does for his friend, he does for his friend's well-being.

2) wishes his friend a full life for his friend's sake. This sentiment is the real proof of true friendship. Friends desire that their friends live and enjoy the fullness of life for their own sake. A mother's love for her child is a good example of this unselfish love.

205

3) lives in peace and harmony with others because

   a. He lives in close contact or association
       with others;

   b. He has the same tastes and desires as those
       of his friends;

   c. He shares in the joys and sorrows of his friends.

Again, a mother's love for her child is a good example of
a true friendly love.

   Taking into consideration the above friendly sentiments, Aristotle finds that the virtuous man first refers those basic friendly sentiments properly to himself,
and then to others. He takes the virtuous man, the wise
and morally integral man to be the general standard or
measure of human conduct, and in friendship the particular
standard or measure. Thus, he finds that only a virtuous
man

1) wishes good, real or apparent, for himself and
   works for it by practicing virtues and virtuous
   deeds.

2) takes best care of his life, that is of his body
   and mind, but particularly of his intellect
   which makes him a human being. Hence, a virtuous man wishes and acts reasonably. It is a
   human condition that makes every man, and
   particularly a virtuous man wish for and live a
   fulfilled life. God needs no such wish for
   growth: he is perfect for eternity. On the
   contrary, man grows, develops and perfects himself each day. The wise or virtuous man aims
   primarily at the full intellectual life. By
   intellect man is closer to god: he is living
   the life of that part of the soul, the active
   intellect, which is immortal. Such life is
   above change, time and place. It is by its
   nature permanent. This is why a man who wishes
   to live his life in terms of his body only,
   does not wish really to live a full life, because the body is changeable and corruptible.

3) lives at peace with himself, because

   a. he enjoys living by himself. He has good
       memories of the achievements of the past and

good hopes for success in the future.
He has great thoughts to contemplate in
his peace of mind.

    b.   he is at peace with his desires and passions
which are moderated by reason. His faculties act in mutual harmony. Even when he
has not yet succeeded in subduing his
passions totally, which is hardly possible,
at least his passions do not resist his
reason's guidance.

    c.   he is aware and shares in his sorrows and
joys with his whole being, sensitive and
rational. There would be war, not peace in
his soul if one part of him enjoyed what was
distasteful to another part. One may also
say that the virtuous man has few regrets
and many joys because he tries to do what is
reasonable.

In summary, our good man feels deeply all the
friendly sentiments toward himself. He feels similarly
all those sentiments toward his friends. His friend is
another self, an extension of his own self. He loves
his friend for his friend's sake, but according to the
model of legitimate self-love. The more he properly
loves himself, the more he imparts true love to his
friends.

This is not the place to discuss the problem: can
one be a friend to himself. This was not implied in the
above description of one's friendly sentiments towards
oneself. We have tried to discover the proper source of
friendly sentiments. Friendship, however, being mutual
goodwill, beneficience, and love requires two or more
persons.

In the third part of this chapter, Aristotle
explicitly points out that an evil man cannot have friendly
feelings towards himself. Of course, most people do have
friendly feelings toward themselves, either because they
are good or because they think they are good. However,
truly bad people, who are aware of their wickedness, cannot have friendly sentiments toward themselves because
evil men,

    1)   neither wish real good to themselves nor work
for it. They do not practice virtue, either
out of cowardice or out of idleness.

    2)   having committed many crimes and being hated for

their wickedness, they actually run away from their life and from their best interests. They have become a threat to society, object of hatred for many, burden to themselves. They have nothing to love about themselves.

3) do not live in peace with themselves as is clear from the fact that

a) they cannot converse with themselves, because when they are alone, they remember unpleasant deeds from the past and know that the same will happen in the future. Thus, they avoid being alone and seek the company of others in order to forget their deeds.

b) their tastes and desires are fighting each other. They see better but follow worse. They know what is reasonable and noble, but follow only that which is pleasant and actually harmful to their humanity just as do morally weak men.

c) they do not share their joys and sorrows with themselves. One part of their soul, the sensitive, feels sorrow for not having indulged in wicked pleasures and deeds, and another part, the rational, feels joy for the same reason. The whole being of a wicked man is torn apart. Indeed, bad people are full of regrets.

In conclusion, it is clear that evil men are not friendly to themselves because there is nothing worthy to love and enjoy in their character. Those who want to to get rid of such and inhuman state have to change their lives, become virtuous, and then, and only then, they will be able to have friendly sentiments towards themselves and others.

Chapter 5

Goodwill

The basic sentiments of friendly love (<u>philia</u>)
have been described in the preceding chapter. Those
sentiments are the following: beneficence when one
works for his friend's good and for his friend's sake;
goodwill, when one wishes a full life and existence
for his friend's sake; and concord, when one lives in
peace and harmony with his friend. In the following
chapters--five, six, and seven--the three basic friendly
sentiments are described individually.

Let us first see what is and what is not goodwill
(<u>eunoia</u>). Goodwill involves wishing well to the person
of the friend. Hence, goodwill resembles friendship
because all friends must have good will. But goodwill
is only the beginning in the making of a friendship.
Good will is not friendship in its full sense. Why is
that? In the first place, goodwill may be felt towards
total strangers and toward those unaware of it. But we
have said that friends must be aware of their good will
for each other.[12] Furthermore, goodwill is not even
love (<u>philĕsis</u>) in its fullest sense. Love implies both
intensity and familiarity; an intense desire to unite
with the beloved and a familiarity or intimate acquaintance which requires time in order to mature into a
deep, mutual friendship. Neither can be said for goodwill because it lacks the intensity of desire for union
with the friend--it is still a one-sided good wish.
Good will also lacks familiarity because it can happen
at any moment. For example, sport spectators wish their
favorite player, whom they know only from the playground
and not from personal acquaintance, well. Hence, good
will is only a superficial, initial love. Friendly
love implies an element of reciprocity which is missing
in goodwill.

Goodwill is only the beginning sentiment of
friendship. It can be compared to the love which starts
with visual pleasure. For example, a young man feels
a delight at the sight of a beautiful girl. However,
that is only the beginning. True, he will not fall in
love with her unless he is first charmed with her appear-
ance, but Aristotle says that love takes more than that:
"one is in love only if one longs for the beloved when
absent, and eagerly desires his presence."[13]

Similarly, unless people first have goodwill for each other, they cannot become friends. Because the well-wishers do not necessarily work for the good of their beloved ones or trouble themselves in their behalf, goodwill is an inactive sentiment. Time, instensity, and familiarity are needed to turn goodwill into mutual and active love for one's friend.

Goodwill, it should be said here, is a necessary sentiment for building a virtuous friendship between friends. There are at least two reasons why goodwill does not exist either in a friendship of utility or in that of pleasure. First, if the person has been a recipient of a gift or good deed and thus feels a goodwill toward his benefactor, he is returning what is just; he is paying his due. Second, the goodwill which springs from a hope of receiving favors from others is, truly speaking, goodwill for oneself. Nor is goodwill the beginning of a friendship of pleasure because each lover desires his own enjoyment even if sometimes it is accompanied by   harm caused to the other. In both kinds of lower friendships, a person has no goodwill for those he uses for his own advantage and wishes good for his own sake rather than for his friend's.

Therefore, a true goodwill is aroused only at the sight of some moral excellence of human character. In other words, goodwill is based upon a friend's good qualities of mind and body. When we discover the brave, the generous, the wise, we are inclined to esteem them, to praise them, to admire them, and to conceive a goodwill towards them.

Chapter 6

Concord

Concord (<u>homonoia</u>) is the next basic feeling of friendship. It should be noted here that Aristotle does not elaborate on the concept of concord as a mutual feeling and thinking between individuals; he is concerned with analyzing the concord among citizens within their state. In other words, he stresses the social and political context of concord. However, his principal aim is to find the ethical side of friendly concord.

In his analysis of the concept of concord which enters into the make up of friendship, Aristotle tells us first what concord is not.

Concord is not an identity of opinion among citizens. Even total strangers may have the same opinions on particular subjects.

Concord is not an agreement on reasoned or scientific answers found in astronomy, mathematics and other sciences. Scientific answers come from sense and reason's evidence and not, for example, from a feeling of solidarity among astronomers. If these answers are not yet established, nothing prevents friends from holding different views on them.

Which matters, then, do belong to friendly concord? A general answer involves three elements. Concord includes the citizens' consent on what is useful; voting on the measures to be taken in view of these advantages; and their working which puts in practice what they voted upon. "Concord is said to prevail in a state, when the citizens agree as to their interests, adopt the same policy, and carry their common resolve into execution."[14]

In summary, concord is referred to the practical matters of a citizen's life. Its realm is the realm of action--what is to be done, what is important for citizens and that about which they can agree to act unanimously. Purely speculative matters, minor issues, and impossible projects are not of concern to those who need friendly concord.

Looking for specific cases of concord among citizens, Aristotle mentions the following:

When citizens agree that rulers should be elected and not chosen by lot or installed by succession; when Athenian citizens agree that they should have a military alliance with Spartans, or when the citizens of Mytilene agree that Pittakos should rule them while he himself is willing to do so,[15] there is a citizen's concord.

A few examples of civic discord are now presented in order to illustrate more accurately where civic concord is missing.

Discord and even civil war results when each of two candidates for power wants to be the sole ruler. Such was the case of the two sons of Oedipus, Eteocles and Polyneices, when each brother wanted to be the sole king of Thebes.[16]

Men are not living in concord when each wishes good for himself because, although there seems to be a similarity among men each of whom wishes his own well being, when each thinks about himself exclusively of others, that is the source of discord. Therefore, in order to have civic concord, citizens must feel and think about the issues in reference to the persons who will be able to put in practice those new policies. For example, when both the common people and the upper classes are in agreement that the best people should rule, all agree on the same persons, and everyone gets what he is striving for.

At the end of this chapter Aristotle turns to the ethical side of civic concord. Citizens establish among themselves a political friendship by concord. This political friendship is utilitarian, i.e., it refers to the interests and concerns of a citizen's life. In spite of that fact, Aristotle tells us that civic concord can be found among good or, more specifically, equitable (epiekēs) citizens, for they are of one mind with themselves and with one another. Moreover, they always stand on the same ground since virtue is a permanent habit, and does not change easily in their thoughts and feelings as does the Strait of Euripos.[17] They strive and work together to attain what is just and useful. Since the virtuous naturally strive for these goals, concord among the equitable is easy to achieve.

On the other hand, bad citizens do not live in concord either with themselves or with one another. They try to get more than their share of advantages and less than their share of public responsibilities. While each one of them is trying to get these profits, he spies on his neighbor to prevent him from obtaining the same. They are in discord among themselves, forcing each other to do their civic duty but unwilling to do it themselves.

Chapter 7

Beneficence

After goodwill and concord have been analyzed, beneficence (_euergesia_) must be studied. The proposition that benefactors love those they have benefitted more than their beneficiaries love them, if proven, will uncover the real nature of beneficence, i.e., the voluntary offering of benefits to others.

Several reasons are listed to prove the value of beneficence.

The relation of creditor and debtor may give us a start for understanding the nature of beneficence. The creditor who gives a loan wishes his debtor well so that he may live, prosper and return the loan. The debtor, on the other hand, may wish the creditor dead so that he does not have to pay back the loan. This may seem to look at beneficence from the wrong side as Epicharmus would say.[18] But the fact is that most men have short memories of benefits received and like to receive more than give.

Since the creditor-debtor relation is purely utilitarian, Aristotle is ready to abandon that comparison and give us a real reason for the apparent paradox that benefactors love their beneficiaries more than the latter love their benefactors. Moreover, benefactors love their beneficiaries and feel affection for them even when the beneficiaries give the benefactor nothing now and will not in the future.

There are several reasons for such an attitude of benefactor toward beneficiary.

1. Every artist loves his product more than his product would love him if it were alive. This especially is true for poets and other creative artists whose products are embodiments of their minds. Artists love in their products the best part of themselves, the hidden creativity which is actualized in their work, because "what a thing is potentially, that its work reveals in actuality."[19] They love themselves more for their actual works than for their potential capacities.

214

The following argument may condense Aristotle's teaching here.

> Being (i.e. life or actuality) is the object of love.

> But the activity is the actuality of the maker.

> But to make a product is an activity (second minor which is implied here).

> Therefore the product must be loved by its maker (as he loves his activity)

Similarly, a benefactor views his beneficiary as the embodiment of his better self. He gives of his abundant self and loves his friend as his product.

> 2. For the benefactor there is an element of nobility in the action of benefitting. Such action in itself is desirable or valuable.

Hence, the benefactor loves his beneficiary in whom his action is embodied. On the other hand, both the action and the person of benefactor are at most something useful to the person benefitted. But the useful (to hresimon) is something which is a means to something else; hence, it is not valuable in itself as the noble (to kalon) is. The feeling of utility is a less powerful and meaningful experience than that of the noble act done by the benefactor.

> 3. The benefactor's action of benefitting gives him joy, which is most pleasant while it is being performed.

When it has been done, it leaves pleasant memories in his mind. Those memories are long lasting since what is noble lasts for a long time. That is not so in the case of a beneficiary. The use of a gift or service rendered is transitory and the memory of it equally so.

> 4. The benefactor has a deep affection for the person he benefits.

Now affection is an active principle[20] and reception of it is a passive state. Affection makes the benefactor share his superior endowments. Beneficiaries receiving his gifts and services are in need of them. Hence, the love of recipients turns easily to the gifts and services and not to the person of their benefactor who loves them for their own sake.

5. Love for people and things is always intensified when labor and trouble is involved in doing things for them.

For example, those who have made money by their own efforts love it more and are more attached to it than those who inherit money. To do involves more effort than to receive. Hence, the love of a benefactor for his beneficiary is stronger than the love of a beneficiary for his benefactor

Chapter 8

Is Self-Love Right or Wrong?

The self-love of the virtuous man has been de-[21]
scribed as the standard for the love between friends.
However, doubts persist in mens' minds, as to whether a
person should love himself or someone else most of all.

The two alternatives point to the problem of the
relationship between egoism and altruism. How can the
gap between egoism and altruism be overcome? Let us
first see popular opinion.

On the one hand, men criticize those who love
themselves most and call them self-centered egoists,
that is, self-lovers (philautoi) in a pejorative sense.
They point out that the evil man does everything for his own
interest, and the worse he is the more selfishly he acts.

On the other hand, the virtuous man does what is
noble both for himself and for others, and the better he
is the more nobly he acts. Now people believe that the
good man is the one who neglects his own good for the
sake of his friend's good.

However, the facts are not in harmony with the
latter view. Our best friend should be the most loved.
But the best friend is he who wishes to his friend good
for his friend's sake. Now, this condition is met in
the most perfect way in man's love for himself. In
fact, as has been said, all the basic sentiments which
are found in friendship are found first and most in
legitimate self-love; others are extensions of our self,
our second selves.

Many proverbs confirm our assertion, such as
"Friends have one soul between them", "Friends' goods are
common property," "Friendship is equality", Friends are
akin as "the knee is nearer than the shin".[22] All these
proverbs point to the closeness of friends. They therefore apply most fully to oneself, for a man is closest to
himself and his own best friend. Therefore, he ought to
love himself most.

The two popular opinions: that only a bad man is a
self-lover, and that the good man should not be a self-
lover should be carefully examined. Clear distinctions

between true and false self love, and true and false
self will help us find the solution to the problem. As
will be seen, Aristotle's intellectualism is strongly
pursued in the following discussion.

A man is called a self-lover (<u>philautos</u>) in a
blameworthy sense when he assigns himself a share larger
than his due of material goods, honors and bodily
pleasures, such as eating, drinking and sex. Most people
zealously pursue these goods and set their hearts on them
as being the greatest goods. It is no wonder that people
censure that kind of self-love. Also, most people unfortunately express their self-love precisely in the manner
described. They try to appropriate more goods than they
deserve. They aim to satisfy their sense appetites,
their passions and their souls' irrational or sensitive
part. Such a "lover of self" is rightly condemned.

On the contrary, if a man dedicates himself to
doing always what is just, temperate, courageous and
wise, in brief, what is noble, he seems to be the true
self lover. Therefore, a man also can be called a self
lover in a praiseworthy sense. The virtuous man assigns
himself the noblest goods; he satisfies his soul's highest faculty--the intellect <u>(nous)</u>--and obeys it faith-
fully. But to love anything or anyone means to love the
best in him. Therefore, the man who loves and follows
his intellect is a true lover of self. This can be
proven by the following arguments.

    a. As in the state, the sovereign or the ruler is
        considered the state in the fullest sense, so
        in any other whole, the dominant part is
        considered the whole. The sovereign is man's
        intellect. Thus, a man who loves and obeys
        his intellect, loves and obeys himself as a
        man in the fullest degree.

    b. A person is called incontinent to the extent
        that his intellect is not in control of his
        emotions and actions. On the other hand, the
        continent man is the one whose intellect controls
        his emotions and actions. A self-controlled man
        is a true and full person because he follows
        his intellect's guidance. When we say that
        the continent man loves and follows his intel-
        lect, he truly loves himself.

    c. We regard a man as being an independent and voluntary agent when he deliberates and makes decisions according to his reason. Such a man guides himself. He is united to himself in the unity of purpose and action. He truly loves himself.

It is clear that the good man values his intellect most of all and lives according to its guidance. Thus, the good man will love himself in the fullest sense. He differs from an evil self-lover because he lives according to reason and the other according to passion, one pursuing what is good and noble, the other desiring what is merely expedient--in reality, what is harmful to him.

Those who strive to do good receive the approval and praise of all. And their example attracts others so that everyone achieves wellbeing and each member possesses the greatest of goods, that is virtue.

Two remarks are appropriate here resulting from the above discussion of two types of self-lovers.

It is best for a good man that he love himself, because by doing so, he will benefit both himself and others. And it is unfortunate that an evil man loves himself, since by following his base desires, he is liable to harm both himself and others by depriving himself of virtue and others of material goods.

As a result, the evil man does what he ought not to do; he acts against his intellect. But the intellect always chooses what is best for a man. On the other hand, the good man obeys, respects and loves his intellect.

Finally, the accusation that any self-lover does everything for his own interest should be exploded forever for this is not the case of the virtuous self-lover. He performs many actions in the best interest of his friends and his country. Moreover, he will sacrifice his own interests for the sake of his friends. Indeed, if necessary, he is ready to give his life for them. Let us be more specific.

a. As to giving his life for his friends, he would rather live nobly for a year than lead an indifferent existence for many years. Those who die for virtuous motives may live a brief life, but by sacrificing their lives for their friend's sake, they perform more nobly in one single act of the highest self-sacrifice than in many lesser good deeds. And so they lose their lives but gain moral nobility. Hence, they love themselves in the truest manner.

b. The good man is ready to lose money and external goods for his friend's sake. When he gives money to his friend, his friend gains wealth, but he himself gains moral excellence. Hence, he assigns himself the greater good, and, thus, he loves himself more.

c. The good man would sacrifice honors and even public office for his friend's benefit. This shows again that he readily gives away honor and position for the higher good which is the nobility of his soul. Hence, he is the true lover of himself.

d. Finally, the virtuous man may even prefer to let his friend perform noble actions instead of himself. In this case, it is the good man's merit to be the cause of his friend's good deeds. He is delighted to see his friend capture praise and nobility by doing virtuous deeds. Here again, our good man takes the better part for himself; he is the true lover of his self.

Briefly, true self-love toward true self is not selfishness or self-centered egoism. In fact, when the good man sacrifices his goods and his life for his friend, he may lose his fortune, health and even his life, but he is gaining moral nobility. That is the highest good he gains for himself as befits the true lover of his true self.

PART III

FRIENDSHIP AND HAPPINESS

Chapter 9

Does a Happy Man Need Friends?

The following discussion of the problem of whether or not a happy man (eudaimōn) needs friends, touches upon the concept of the happy man's self-sufficiency (autarkeia) and the role of friendship in his life.

Aristotle examines first the assumptions for and against the view that the happy man needs friends, and finds out that in all probability, he does. To prove that he does, he uses various characteristics of a happy man's personality in the first part of this chapter. In the second part of this section, Aristotle proves that the happy man by his nature needs friends.

I.   Opinions for and against the view that a happy man needs friends.

1. The opinion against it is proposed first. The supremely happy man (makarios)is supposed to be self-sufficient--hence, he does not need anything from others. To have a friend means to have another self that might complement what is missing in our own lives, but that we cannot provide ourselves.

2. The opinion for it is proposed next in several arguments.
a) It seems unacceptable to assign a happy man all the good things but deprive him of friendship which is one of man's greatest possessions.[23]

b) It is characteristic of a good man to do good, which includes giving rather than receiving benefits. But the happy man is good and excellent, and his outstanding characteristic is to do good. He, then, needs others whom he can benefit whether they are total strangers or friends. However, it is more noble that he does his friends good rather than strangers.

221

3. Finally, it seems strange that a supremely happy man should live his life in isolation. No man would choose to enjoy all his goods alone. Man is a social and political animal (zōon politikon) and his natural condition is to live in society, sharing his goods with others, loving and enjoying the company of other human beings, and, in turn, being loved by them. In other words, he does not need fellow citizens only for sharing in the community of various services; he needs real friends to live with him in the communion of their feelings and thoughts.

After presenting the two opinions about the happy man's need for friendship, Aristotle is ready to examine the grounds upon which the above assumptions are based. The purpose is to show that each of the two opinions has some grain of truth.

1. The opinion against

The proponents of the first opinion that the happy man needs no friends, in all probability have in mind useful and pleasant friends. Indeed, the supremely happy man has no need for useful friends because he is self-sufficient. He has no need--or very little--for the company of pleasant friends because he lives the most pleasant life and is truly self-content. But people think mistakenly that since a happy man does not need useful or pleasant friends, he needs no friends at all. He needs, as we shall see next, virtuous friends.

2. The opinion for

A happy man's need for virtuous friends may be proven by several dialectical arguments:

(1) Happiness is an operation (energeia). Energeia is that doing which is stretching from static or inoperative potency (dynamis) to static or perfect act (entelecheia). The happy man does not possess happiness as an act, a permanent or fixed state that, once possessed, would leave him happy without doing anything. On the contrary, the happy man actualizes his happiness bit by bit in acting toward and achieving gradually his self-fulfillment. This is a human condition. Only god is pure act, hence, always perfect: he suffers neither the state of imperfection, potency, nor the gradual process

222

toward his full actuality. On the contrary, humans are
bound by the law of development from less to more, and,
unfortunately, also from more to less. The happy man
cannot escape his human condition. But his activity--
the continuous quest for happiness--is pleasant and
satisfying in itself because it is good and noble. It
pleases him very much.

In spite of that, men are by nature better able to
observe others in action than themselves and make value
judgements of their action. While acting we are absorbed
in the process as agents and it is difficult for us to be
at the same time cool observers of it; we are even less
able to be the judges of our own best actions. However, we
may easily become observers of the actions of others,
especially of those who have high moral standards. The
supremely happy man may identify himself with them,
recognize himself in them, see them as an extension of
his self, of his sensations, of his thoughts and of his
virtuous actions. Hence, he needs virtuous friends in
order to strengthen, through their example, his quest
for happiness.

(2) The life of the happy man should be very pleasant.
Pleasure comes from activity. But it is hard for anyone,
and the happy man is no exception, to be continuously
active by himself alone. The activity of friends, especially of those who excel at virtue, is a joy for a good
man. It is a stimulus for his virtuous actions. He will
continue to go on living a good life, doing noble deeds
because he is spurred by his pleasure at the sight of
his friends' good actions.

(3) The society of good men united in good activity
helps the happy to practice better virtuous living as
Theognis[24] would say.

II. The above reasons for the happy man's need for
friends prove the point, but they do not express the real
cause for the happy man's need of friends. We have seen
so far that friends meet certain limitations of a happy
man: he is not the best judge of his actions' value;
he should be helped in his continuous quest for happiness
by his friends' example; and he practices virtue better
in the company of noble people rather than alone. Now,
in the second part of this chapter, Aristotle is going to
argue that the need for friends springs from the very
nature of the happy man.

The argument which follows is a strictly scientific one. It is based upon the properties of the subject in question. Physics (physikē) or natural science[25] is the science which treats of man. From the natural science point of view, man is a special kind of substance, a rational animal (zoon logikon). It will be shown that a virtuous friend is essentially desirable to a happy man because he is a rational animal, and as such, both he and the happy man exhibit certain characteristics.

The following psychological argument is presented step by step so that the middle term--rational animal-- may more clearly mediate in proving the happy man's need for friends.

1. Animals have a sense life, that is, they are the species of living body which has the capacity to sense. Man also has the ability to sense, but his distinctive characteristic is the ability to think.

2. Capacity is defined by its activity, the nature of which consists in the realization of the capacity. Life in man is defined by the capacities of sensation and thought. Therefore, a man's life is fully defined by what he actually senses and thinks. What men desire when they desire life--and all men desire life--is not simply to be able to sense and to think, but actually to sense and think.

3. The essential characteristics of life as Plato says, [26] are, measure, definiteness, determination, proportion. Life is something definite (hōrismenon); what we sense and think is something definite or deter- minate. Therefore, life is something intrisically good and pleasant. And what is good is certainly good and desirable to the happy man. In fact, his life is to him the most desirable and his existence most blessed. Ad- mittedly, we do not talk here about the vicious, corrupt and painful life because such life is not good or, in Platonic terms, such life is without measure and propor- tion.

4. Human life is sensation and thought. Both are accompanied by the consciousness that we are sensing and thinking. But to be conscious of our vital activities is to be conscious that we are living and existing.

5. Life is, as we said, intrinsically good and plea- sant. Our consciousness of life means that we have in us

something intrinsically good and pleasant. Therefore, the consciousness (aisthanesthai) of life, i.e., of sensation and thought, is itself something intrinsically good and pleasant.

6. It was shown[27] that the good man's friend is another self to him, and the good man feels toward his friend as he feels toward himself.

7. Hence, since it is desirable that a good man live a good life, so, or nearly so, he desires his friend's good life. We saw above that the consciousness of one's sensation and thought as intrinsically good makes human life desirable. Therefore, it is desirable for a good man to have a sympathetic consciousness (synaisthanesthai) of his friend's sensation and thought.

8. The sympathetic consciousness is obtainable and enriched in the best way by living with one's friends. The good man ought to share his friend's consciousness of the good life. This is done by living and conversing together, and sharing one's thoughts and feelings with one's friend's thoughts and feelings. This intellectual communion among friends is the real meaning of living together among good men. It is not enough to eat at the same table, as the cattle graze on the same field, to truly share in the life of each other on a human level.

In conclusion, the supremely happy man needs all that is desirable to him. But his life, i.e., his sensation and thought, are desirable to him in the first place. A friend's existence is equally desirable to him for his friend is his other self. If he has no friends, he is deficient in something that is intrinsically desirable. Hence, without friends, he cannot be a fully happy man.

In the first part of this chapter, Aristotle argued that a happy man needs friends because of the limitations of his nature. Our happiness is not pure act but the gradual actualization of our self-fulfillment. In the process of passing from potency to act we need the help of others. Man is a social and political animal, and political society offers him the possibility of satisfying his quest for happiness.

In the second part, Aristotle places the roots of the need for friends in the happy man's self-consciousness. Man is a rational animal. He needs friends who are an extension of his self-consciousness. He forges his friendship with them in a sympathetic consciousness of his friends' feelings and thoughts.

Chapter 10

Should the Number of Our Friends Be Limited?

Aristotle has analyzed in the preceding chapter the need for friends as it concerns the happy man. He considers now the need for friends in view of their number.

The following question is raised: how many friends should one have? Should he have as many friends as possible? The general answer must be found in the middle: a man should not live either without friends or with too many.

A more specific answer refers to various kinds of friendships. It is not possible to have many useful friends because one has to return their favors. Life is not long enough to let us repay the numerous gifts and services of many useful friends. Moreover, by returning favors to many, we are distracted in our own virtuous life. Therefore, we do not need many useful friends.

Similarly, a few friends of pleasure are enough. Humans need pleasant companionship but as in an adult diet only a small amount of sweets is recommended, so a few pleasant friends are sufficient for a man so that he may have joy in their company for a short time.

How many virtuous friends should we have? Is there a limit to the number of our virtuous friends as there is a limit to the number of citizens in the city-state? Ten adult male citizens do not make a city-state, but one hundred thousand adult male citizens are too many for a city-state. Thus, even if Aristotle does not fix the number of citizens sufficient for a city-state, it must be found somewhere between the too small number, ten citizens, and the too large number, one hundred thousand. Therefore, with respect to virtuous friendship, it is clear that we should not have many friends. Three reasons, taken from the three characteristics of friendship,[28] suffice to convince us that many virtuous friends are not desirable.

1. Friends are those who live together in peace and harmony. It is obvious that it is not possible to associate closely with many friendly people and share our thoughts and feelings with them. This is particularly true of virtuous friends who deserve our undivided attention.

2. Our friends should be friends among themselves to make our association with them possible. Otherwise, if they are not mutual friends but each lives outside the

circle of our friends, it becomes impossible for us
associate with so many people living apart and do it
the same time. But it is not often that our friends
happen to be mutual friends.

3. The true friend shares in his friends' joys
and sorrows. Yet, it is hard to rejoice with one
friend and mourn with another at the same time.

In conclusion we may say: friendship consists in
an excess of love which can be felt for only one or for
very few. One cannot intensely love many people and
cultivate truly intimate relations with them. The very
nature of the perfect friendship in which love is the
highest and the most intense, precludes the dividing
of that love among many. This is a human condition,
a limitation of human love, a reality that cannot be
ignored. After all, whatever the highest achievement
is, it must be rare. Therefore, an intimate virtuous
friendship is possible only with few people.

The preceding conclusion seems to be corroborated
by life experience. Not many people make up the friendship among hetairoi, a friendship that has been forged
from early childhood. Moreover, the friendships cele-
brated in poems and stories are those between two
people.[29]

What, then, may one say about those who boast a
host of friends, who say they are on familiar terms with
many? One may safely say that they are no one's
friends. They are called obsequious for the excess of
external pleasantness that they show. They are, however,
friends in a civil way as is usual among citizens.
One can be a 'friend' to many citizens even as a
virtuous person. However, this "political friendship"
is not deep enough to deserve the name of friendship.
The concord among citizens which is identified with
their friendship consists in their having one mind in
important civic affairs. The good man is ready to
follow the concord in important civic matters. But it
is impossible for a good man to have a truly meaningful
and intimate friendship with many virtuous men so that
he loves them for themselves. He should be happy to
have a few virtuous men as his friends.

Chapter 11

Do We Need Friends Both In Prosperity and Adversity?

The need for friends is approached here from a
specific angle: are they more necessary in times of
prosperity or in times of adversity or misfortune?
The general answer would be that in adversity one needs
friends to assist and to help him; in prosperity one
needs friends with whom he can share and whom he can
benefit.

Hence, friends are more necessary in adverse times.
In such a case the useful kind of friend is necessary.
It is, however, more noble to have friends in prosperity, when people look for good men in order to do them
good and to live in their company. Undoubtedly, the
very presence of friends is pleasant in both prosperity
and adversity. To prove this, Aristotle turns first to
adversity and then to prosperity.

A.   In adversity pain is lessened when friends
share in sorrow. The explanation of this fact varies.
One may think, first, that friends help us carry our
burden of sorrow, helping us feel it less. Another may
think that the very sympathetic presence of friends
brings joy to their afflicted friends. Whatever the
case may be, it is certain that a friend's presence
does lessen his friend's pain.

Further explanation of the presence of friends in
adversity is now in order.

The presence of a sympathetic friend can be
viewed from a double angle. The very presence of a
friend is a comfort to those in sorrow. Friends express
their sympathy by their countenance and their words,
for they know our character and what gives us grief or
joy. It is a pleasure to be able to have those who par-
take in our distress so close. On the other hand, it
is painful to see friends pained by our misfortunes
because everyone avoids causing pain to his friends.

For that reason, men of strong personality do not
let their friends share their grief unless their misfortune is extreme,[30] because they cannot bear the pain
which their pain causes their friends. They simply do
not want others to join in their sorrow because they do
not enjoy lamentations. On the contrary, women and men

228

of womanish character are pleased to have friends join
them in their mourning. But we should imitate, as in
other cases, as well as in this one, the man of more
noble character.

B. In prosperity, however,it is good to have
friends present both for pleasant and leisurely conversation and for knowing that they are pleased with our
good fortune.

Aristotle ends this chapter with some moral advise.

First, concerning a man in sorrow:

a. As much as we have recommended that a man should
call friends to share with him in his good fortune, for
the good man is expected to benefit others, so we must
say that a man should be reluctant to call on friends to
share in his misfortune.

b. However, he should ask his friends to visit him in
his sorrow only when this causes them little trouble and
is a great help to him.

Second, concerning the friends of the man both in
misfortune and in prosperity.

a. On the other hand, it is fitting that we console our
friend in his distress even if uninvited. For it is a
friend's duty to confer benefits especially upon those
who are in need. In this case, a friend's action is
more noble if he does it unasked, spontaneously, and his
friend in distress acts more virtuously, unwilling to
burden him with his trouble.

b. A man should readily join his friends in their
properity, for a prosperous man needs friends to enjoy
his good fortune.

c. However, we should not push ourselves to visit
a well-to-do friend. We should do it reluctantly and
modestly for it is not noble to be eager to receive benefits. Nevertheless, we should not get a reputation for
being unpleasant in rejecting our friend's benefits.
After all, the presence of friends is desirable in all
circumstances.

Chapter 12

Should Friends Live Together?

The last question of this book: should friends live together? has been answered positively[31]. Aristotle returns to the subject of intimacy between friends not to add anything but to end the study of friendship with friendship's most appealing characteristic.

One can compare friendship to sensual love in which the lovers desire to see each other as much as possible. Thus, they enjoy the sight of their friend because it is sight more than any other sense, by which they detect the beauty of their beloved and which makes them fall in love with each other and persist in mutual love.

Similarly friends enjoy seeing and living with (syzēn) each other. There are several reasons:

1. Friendship is an intimate association which requires a physical presence and an exchange of benefits between friends, but reaches deep into the mind and heart of friends. This is true, in particular, for a virtuous friendship which is a communion (koinōniā)[32] or an intimate sharing of thoughts and feelings with others. But people share themselves with one another by living together. Hence, living together seems to be most proper to friendship.

2. As a man is to himself so he is to his friend. His friend is his other self or an extension of his self. And just as the awareness of his existence is pleasant to a man, so the consciousness of the existence of his friend pleases him too. But this consciousness of one another's life grows precisely when friends converse and live together.

3. Every man wishes to share with his friend whatever makes his life worth living. Some drink together, some play together, and exercise together in various sports, hunt together and study philosophy together. Since they love these activities most of all, they are delighted to share them with their friends. It is, therefore, highly desirable to live with friends.

Some conclusions from the above premises on friendship may be profitably mentioned at the end of this chapter and this book.

1.   Concerning evil men one must say that their
friendship makes them wicked since they pursue evil
deeds together. But their character, and, consequently,
their friendship is unstable.

2.   Concerning good men, one must say that their
friendly living together increases their virtue,
as Theognis said, "you will learn noble deeds from noble
men."[33] The example of a friend's life is inspiring:
the company of the good man increases our eagerness to
live a virtuous life; the open relationship between good
men makes it possible for them to correct each other when
they see fault in each other's conduct.

BOOK IX

FOOTNOTES

1. <u>N.E.</u> VIII, vii - 1158b 27-28.

2. <u>N.E.</u> V, vi - 1132b 31-33.

3. <u>N.E.</u> VIII, iii - 1156b 9-12.

4. <u>N.E.</u> IX, i, 4 - 1164a 20.

5. Plato. <u>Protagoras</u> 328b-c.

6. <u>N.E.</u> VIII, xiii - 1162b 6 - 13.

7. <u>N.E.</u> I, iii - 1094b 11-27; <u>Ibid.</u> vii - 1098a 26-29; <u>II</u>, ii - 1103b 34 - 1104a 5.

8. <u>N.E.</u> VIII, xiii - 1162b 23-25.

9. <u>N.E.</u> VIII, i - 1155a 32-34; <u>Ibid.</u> iii - 1156b 19-24.

10. <u>N.E.</u> VIII, v - 1157b 22-24.

11. These three (five) basic sentiments of friendship are listed in two more places of this chapter, but in both cases, the third is dealt with first.

12. <u>N.E.</u> VIII, 2, 3-4 - 1155b 32-1156a 5.

13. <u>N.E.</u> IX, v, 3 - 1167a 5.

14. <u>N.E.</u> IX, vi, 1 - 1167a 25.

15. At the beginning of the sixth century B.C., Pittacos was elected the sole ruler of Mytilene unanimously so that he could introduce necessary political reforms into the constitution. After ten years of ruling Mytilene in such a worthy manner that he was numbered among the seven Greek wise men in antiquity, he resigned and entered private life, in spite of the citizens' request to continue in power.

Hence, as long as he ruled, there was an agreement regarding the government between him and his citizens. When he resigned, there was a disagreement between him and the citizens because of his decision to rule no longer.

16. Euripides. Phoenician Women, verses 588 ff.

17. Euripos, the narrow Strait separating Euboea from Boetia, at the town of Chalcis, was famous for its violent and frequent, seven times per day, ebbs and tides, and thus it became a symbol for changing things.

18. Epicharmus, a Greek comic poet, lived in Sicily in the first part of the fifth century B.C. Very few fragments of his poems are still extant. The quotation "looking at the seamy side" (frg. 146 Kaibel) means literally: looking at the piece of tapestry from the opposite, wrong side. Figuratively the sentence means: looking at life or human nature, in the context above, from the bad side.

19. N.E. IX, vii, 4 - 1168a 9.

20. N.E. VIII, viii, 3 - 1159a 27 - 1159b 1.

21. Cfr. N.E. IX, iv.

22. N.E. IX, viii, 2 - 1168b 5-10.

23. It is written in the text as follows: "The greatest of external goods" (N.E. IX, ix, 2 - 1169b 11). This is a utilitarian, though widespread, notion of friendship. Aristotle neither agrees nor disagrees in this place with such a view. He simply presents the opinion of others. Later on he will take an explicit stand that the happy man does not need useful friends. He needs virtuous friends only (Ibid. IX, ix, 4 - 1169b, 24).

24. Theognis, a poet of elegies, lived in the second half of the sixth century. The saying to which Aristotle points is: "you will learn noble things from noble people" (Theognis, line 35, Diehl 3).

25. More accurately speaking, the science of man is psychology. However, from Aristotle's viewpoint any philosophical treatment of the psyche (soul) is a branch of physics, for the soul is a form of natural bodies which are alive.

26. Philebus 64b - 65d - 66a-b. Socrates argues that beauty, truth and goodness are characterized by measure and proportion. The same characteristics are applicable to the whole of reality, hence, also to life.

27. N.E. IX, iv, 5 - 1166a 27-33.

28. N.E. VIII, v, 2-4 - 1175b 17-24; Ibid. IX, iv,
    1-2 - 1166a 1-10.

29. Such friendships were those, for example, of Achilles
    and Patroclus, Orestes and Pylades, Theseus and
    Pirithous.

30. "Unless their misfortune is extreme" (our underli-
    ning). The text for the word 'misfortune,' gives
    the Greek alypia. An obvious meaning of alypia is
    the absence of pain. But if there is no pain in us,
    there is no need for friends to console us. Some
    commentators give to the word alypia the meaning
    of insensitivity to pain. But if the grieved man
    is insensitive to pain, he would not need friends
    to comfort him. Apelt has substituted atychia for
    alypia. Atychia, not alypia means misfortune. And
    the meaning then is acceptable: unless his misfor-
    tune is extreme. In that case even the man of
    strong character needs friends. More about this
    text can be read in Gauthier-Jolif. L'Éthique à
    Nicomaque, Vol. II, Part II, 765-766.

31. N.E. VIII, v, 1-4 - 1157b 5-24.

32. Koinōnia is a community of interest in useful
    friendship, particularly among citizens who share
    the same services. Koinōnia is a community of
    virtue in virtuous friendship. But virtue is a
    result of an individual's choice and practice, and
    it cannot be communicated to others as are external
    goods and benefits. However, virtuous friends en-
    joy similarity in their virtuous characters. Their
    community is that of spirit, of feelings, of
    thoughts, of good deeds. Such community is deeper
    than that of interest or pleasure. It is the com-
    munity of the intimate sharing of one another's
    minds. It is a communion of two minds and two
    hearts.

33. N.E. IX, ix, 7 - 1170a 12. C fn Ft. 24.

BOOK X

PLEASURE, HAPPINESS, CONTEMPLATION; ETHICS AND POLITICS

There are three distinguishable parts in Book X of the <u>Nicomachean</u> <u>Ethics</u>. The first examines various opinions on pleasure and gives Aristotle's definitive view on the meaning of pleasure. The second examines the meaning of human happiness and finds it ultimately to consist in the contemplation of reality and the best of reality. The third shows the connection between ethics and politics and announces the program of political science.

For various reasons the subject of pleasure is connected with ethics.

    a.   Among all things pleasure seems to be related to humankind in a special way.

    b.   The young are educated on the basis of pleasure and pain.

    c.   It is extremely important for the formation of moral character to love that which ought to be loved and hate that which ought to be hated. But, by choosing what is pleasant and avoiding what is painful, people learn to love what should be loved and to hate what ought to be hated.

Therefore, there is no doubt that the subject of pleasure has a legitimate place in the study of morals.

PART I - PLEASURE

Chapter 1

Two Opinions on Pleasure

The controversy on the important subject of pleasure (hedonē) has grouped the participants into two camps:

1. Those who call all pleasure good and even the highest good. Such was the opinion of the mathematician, astronomer and philosopher, Eudoxus.

2. Those who call all pleasure evil. Among them some are certain of it. Such was the claim of Speusippus who succeeded Plato as the head of the Academy. Followers of Speusippus believe that it is in the interest of morality to treat pleasure as evil due to the fact that most men are so inclined to pleasures that they are enslaved by them.

Aristotle wants to show his disapproval of the idea of pleasure as evil even before he formally attacks it in Chapter 3. He tells us that evil pleasure goes against human nature. Humans naturally seek pleasure, but no one seeks evil by nature. The truth of the virtuous mean of feelings and actions should square with the facts of human nature. Human desire for pleasure is a natural fact and must as such be openly approached. Aristotelian ethics follows Aristotelian metaphysics, i.e., it is a realistic approach to the world of things. Ethics must realistically approach the world of human actions and feelings as they are. The test of truth in theory and practice is its correspondence to the facts.

> "...but it is by the practical
> experience of life and conduct that
> the truth is really tested, since it
> is there that the final decision lies.
> We must therefore examine the con-
> clusions we have advanced by bringing
> them to the test of facts of life. If
> they are in harmony with the facts, we
> may accept them: if found to disagree,
> we must deem them mere theories."[1]

236

Chapter 2

Opinion of Eudoxus: Pleasure is the Good

The arguments of Eudoxus for his opinion that
pleasure is <u>the</u> good are the following:[2]

1. All rational and irrational things desire pleasure.
    But what is desirable is good; therefore, pleasure
    must be good. In fact, pleasure is the most
    desirable thing for which all aim. But that which
    is the most desirable is the best. As a result,
    pleasure is the good or supreme good.

2. The same conclusion follows from a study of pain.
    Since pain is avoided by all things, its contrary,
    pleasure, must be the object of desire of all
    things.

3. The most attractive object of desire will be that
    which is chosen for its own sake and not for the
    sake of something else. Pleasure is such an object.

4. In addition, pleasure makes something which is
    already good even more desirable, even more of a
    good, but what is good can be increased only by
    another good thing. Therefore, pleasure is the good.

The fourth argument is not convincing to Aristotle.
Plato, he says, rightfully had used the last argument to
prove that pleasure is not the good.

1. The pleasant life is made better and more desirable
    by wisdom.

2. In addition, if pleasure were the essential good, it
    could not be made more desirable by the addition of
    any other good.

Putting aside the last argument, Aristotle believes that
Eudoxus' opinion is tenable. Speusippus' objection to
the first argument that the testimony of irrational
creatures is of no value, is rejected by Aristotle because both irrational and rational creatures seek
pleasure.

Aristotle also rejects Speusippus' counter-argu-
ment that the opposite of pleasure is not pain but a
neutral state as nonsense. The universally-sought for

object is necessarily good. Finally, Aristotle opposes
those who say that it does not follow that pleasure is
a good if pain is an evil. Aristotle believes that mankind pursues pleasure as good and avoids pain as evil
by universal consent. In Chapter 5 Aristotle will show
that pleasure is not the supreme good.

In conclusion, Eudoxus was more right than his
opponents, but he was wrong in not discriminating between the different kinds of pleasure and in saying
that pleasure is the supreme good.

Chapter 3

Speusippus: Pleasure is Evil

Speusippus thought that pleasure must be evil
because:

1. It is not a quality, therefore it is not a good.
    Aristotle answers that this argument proves too much.
    It would be equally valid against virtuous acts and
    even against happiness, neither of which are quali-
    ties: Virtuous acts and happiness are good
    activities.

2. It is not defined, not determined, it admits of
    degrees.

    a. If the argument means that there is a higher and
        lesser intensity in feeling pleasure by dif-
        ferent people, the same can be said of justice,
        temperance and other virtues: one is more or
        less just and temperate than others.

    b. If the argument points to the various forms of
        pleasure, it could be applied only to the mixed
        pleasures and not to the pure ones with no ad-
        mixture of pain. Mixed pleasures are analogous
        to health which admits of degrees in various
        individuals or the right but different propor-
        tion of elements in the human bodies of individuals.

3. It is not something final or perfect as the good is.
    Pleasure is some sort of motion, change or process.

This argument appears to be erroneous for the following
reasons:

    a. If pleasure were a movement it would have to be
        subject to speed and slowness. But, it is not
        possible to feel pleasure either quickly or
        slowly. Although a person may <u>become</u> pleased
        either quickly or slowly, one cannot <u>be</u> pleased
        at various speeds.

    b. It cannot be a process of generation, because
        generation and dissolution presuppose a common
        subject. In the first place, its subject is not
        the body as Speusippus thought, but the soul
        which is a simple entity.

c. Plato and his followers believe that pain is a
    lack of something (as hunger is a lack of food)
    and pleasure a replenishment. Evidently for
    them pleasure would be only in the body. But
    how can this explain pleasures of intellectual
    learning and memory, and even of sight, hearing,
    and smell where pain is not involved?

4. Platonists trying to support their teaching that
    pleasure is evil put a strong emphasis on disgrace-
    ful pleasures. Aristotle makes the proper distinc-
    tions as follows:

    a. It may be said that these pleasures are not
        really pleasant to a person of good disposition;
        they are pleasant to people of vicious dis-
        position.

    b. Although pleasures may be said to be desirable,
        they cannot be desirable when springing from the
        wrong sources. For example, wealth is desirable,
        but not when it has been acquired by treason.

    c. We may say that pleasures differ in kind.

        -- Some come from noble sources and some from base.
           For instance, it is not possible that the just
           man's pleasure be felt by the unjust and that
           the pleasure of a musician be felt by a non-
           musician.

        -- As opposed to the pleasure of flattery, the
           pleasure of friendship seems to make it plain
           that pleasure is not a single good, that there
           are different kinds of pleasure. The friend
           seeks our good; the flatterer seeks to please
           us. The friend is praised, the flatterer re-
           proached.

        -- Difference in pleasure is also seen in the choice
           of adult understanding over the pleasures of
           childhood. (Adults are expected to refuse to act
           disgracefully, although to do so may be pleasant
           and without painful consequences.) Furthermore,
           mature people choose things bringing no pleasure.
           Accompanying pleasure, if any, is considered only
           incidental and not sought after for itself. Such
           is our striving for knowledge and virtue.

In conclusion, we may say that Speusippus erred because he neglected to make several important distinctions. The following is a summary of a few important ones:[3]

a. Pleasure is not the supreme good.

b. Not all pleasures are desirable and good.

c. Not all pleasures are evil.

d. Moral and intellectual pleasures are desirable in themselves due to their specific quality or sources.

Chapter 4

The Concept, Conditions, and Role of Pleasure

Aristotle proceeds in the following two chapters
to present his own definitive view of the nature of
pleasure. The problem is where to put pleasure in the
hierarchy of human ends. Thus, Aristotle's first concern is to reject once again Speusippus' opinion that
pleasure is only motion towards an end. Like the act
of seeing, the pleasure we feel consciously seems complete and satisfactory at any moment of its duration.
If pleasure is felt at all, it is felt as a whole. We
experience it all at once. As a result, pleasure cannot be a motion, process, change, or transition from a
potential to an actual state aiming at completion when
the end of motion is reached. Every motion is characterized by specific parts, specific duration, differing
specific movements, and completion only when the end is
reached. But pleasure is not divisible and occurs in
any given moment as something whole and complete. "The
specific quality of pleasure on the contrary
is perfect at any moment. It is clear therefore that
pleasure is not the same as motion, and that it is a
whole and something perfect."[4]

Even though pleasure has been promoted to the
realm of ends, Aristotle still seems to leave it unde-
fined. What is that whole and complete feeling of
pleasure at any moment of its existence? From an earlier
study[5] we know that pleasure is perfect activity
(energeia); from the following, we will learn the more
refined concept that pleasure perfects activity. However, we are not told here what it is which perfects
activity in itself. Implicit in the study is the plain
answer that pleasure is a feeling of satisfaction
acquired through the activity of human faculties. Since
activity aims at some end or goal of human life,
pleasure is at its highest when resting satisfactorily
in the possession of the human highest goal--human well-
being.

The conditions of pleasure are those of activity
on every level. Every sense is active in relation to
its proper object; and the best sense activity is that
of the best-conditioned sense in relation to the finest
of its objects. Such activity is the most complete and
the most pleasant. Although there is always some
pleasure whenever senses and objects (colors, sounds,

flavors) are properly related, the greatest pleasure arises when both senses and objects are at their best. Similarly, when these proper conditions prevail for imagination and memory, and for intellect and reasoning power, we take the greatest pleasure in imagining and remembering, reasoning and contemplating. In conclusion, when directed to their finest objects, the unimpeded activity of the healthy senses, memory and imagination, reason and intellect constitute pleasant activity. Pleasure necessarily accompanies healthy activity.

The role of pleasure is to complete or perfect activity by stimulating, accompanying, intensifying and consummating it. Pleasure is not a part of activity: it is a perfection superimposed on it "like the bloom of health in the young and vigorous."[6]

The question arises: why are we not continuously pleased? Is it a question of growing weary? Since pleasure accompanies activity, and since no person can be continuously active, pleasure cannot be continuous. Pleasure subsides when activity subsides and ends when it ends: it cannot last forever because activity cannot last forever. Moreover, pleasure diminishes with repetition, for activity becomes relaxed.

One might think that people desire pleasure because they desire life: as an activity, life is necessarily related to pleasure. It can also be said that men pursue their favorite interests because they give them the most pleasure; for instance, a musician enjoys hearing tones and an intellectual delights in solving human problems. The question arises: shall we choose life for the sake of pleasure or pleasure for the sake of life? The two, pleasure and life, seem to be inseparable. "For there is no pleasure without activity, and also no perfect activity without its pleasure."[7]

Chapter 5

Kinds and Value of Pleasures

Pleasures, like activities, differ in kind. The
activities of thought differ in their objects from the
activities of senses as do the   pleasures which perfect them. Proper pleasure intensifies an activity.
Those who are fond of music make progress in their art
by enjoying it. Therefore, pleasure is proper to
activity and differs according to the activity. Difference in pleasures is even more apparent from the
fact that activities can be hindered by pleasures
arising from other sources. Such is the case of a musician engaged in a discussion of human problems, but if
he suddenly hears music he will no longer be
able to pay attention to the discussion. Also, if one
is simultaneously active at two things, the more pleasant activity drives out the other. "Hence, when we
enjoy something very much, we can hardly do anything
else; and when we find a thing only mildly agreeable,
we turn to some other occupation; for instance, people
who eat sweets at the theater do so especially when the
acting is bad."[8]

Since some activities are good, some bad, and some
indifferent, it follows that there are good pleasures:
these perfect the functions proper to man. Other pleasures are bad: these foster the activities improper to
man. There are, finally, indifferent or neutral
pleasures. Activities and pleasures are so linked and
interdependent that some people identify them. However,
although the two are not divided or separate they must
be carefully distinguished.

An important distinction regarding the order or
hierarchy of pleasures is now introduced. Pleasures of
mind are superior to pleasures of the senses. Among
the senses there is a certain order of higher and lower
pleasures. Since sight is superior to touch and
hearing, and smell to taste, the pleasures involved follow the same gradation. "Sight excels touch in purity,
and hearing and smell excel taste; and similarly the
pleasures of the intellect excel in purity the pleasures
of sensation, while the pleasures of either class differ
among themselves in purity."[9]

What is that criterion of "purity" that makes the
qualitative difference between higher and lower pleasures?

Purity is measured by the closeness to and the remoteness of pleasures from matter. The more one faculty has the capacity to apprehend form without matter, the more pure its activity, and consequently, its pleasure. Matter is the principle of limitation, imperfection and potentiality. Form is the principle of openness, perfection and actuality. The lower pleasures gravitate around material activities; the higher pleasures tend towards the fullness of form which is reached through immaterial activities.

Animals have proper pleasures in accordance with their proper activities. These are more or less the same for every species, but among animals, there may be a considerable variation. Horses, donkeys and dogs delight in different things. For instance, because of what he is a donkey would prefer hay to gold. A difference in pleasures is found particularly among men. What delights some people is a cause of pain to others. What is sweet to a healthy man may not be sweet to a sick man. We know that a definite standard determines which pleasures are good and noble, and which bad and base; we know it from the activities they perfect. However, despite the fact that the definition of good pleasure furnishes an objective criterion for judging pleasures, human weakness renders our application of it less than effective. Aristotle suggested that the wise man of good character be allowed to judge; for, as the bad man's activities are accompanied by bad pleasures, so the good man's activities are accompanied by good pleasures which are fitting models of ethical action. We look at the wise man to seek the true meaning of real pleasures. What the good man finds unpleasant may, of course, be pleasant to others, but only because they are in an unvirtuous condition. Disgraceful pleasures should not be called pleasures except, perhaps, insofar as they are related to a perverted sense of pleasure. Of those pleasures which are thought to be good, those which are proper to man will be the ones corresponding to man's proper activity or activities; that is, to the activities of the perfect and supremely happy man. Pleasures arising from secondary activities will be secondary. An intellectualist by education, Plato's disciple Aristotle gives primacy to man's proper pleasures i.e. those connected with intellectual activity.

PART II

HAPPINESS AND CONTEMPLATION

Chapter 6

Happiness is an Activity

After completing his study of the nature of pleasure Aristotle next examines the subject of human
happiness (eudaimonia). The reader is reminded of what
Aristotle previously said about human happiness. Happiness is not simply a habit (hexis) but an activity
(energeia) of the human faculties, an activity desirable
in and for itself, final, self-sufficient, and lasting.[10]
There are three kinds of activities considered desirable
for themselves: agreeable amusements, actions in conformity with virtue and contemplation.

The first item, amusements, cannot be the purpose
of human life. However, too many people find amusement
a substitute for happiness. But they are wrong. Excessive amusement may hurt our body and property. Those
who indulge the most in amusements are poor judges of
what human happiness should be. Tyrants spend their
leisure time in all sorts of amusements. Children are
another group of humans who need play and amusements for
their development. (We may add: modern-day playboys
live for the pursuit of pleasures and amusements). Virtue and reason, the two necessary ingredients of happiness,
are not found in the groups noted; and furthermore, amusements sought for their own sake are not valuable and pleasant to the good man. What the good man finds valuable
and pleasant is always in connection and in accordance
with virtue. Finally, amusement is a kind of rest and
relaxation from labors and a restoration of energy needed
to continue working. Thus, Aristotle had no doubt that
"to make amusement the object of our serious pursuits and
our work seems foolish and childish to excess." On the
contrary, "Anarchasis' motto, 'Play in order that you
may work,' is felt to be the right rule."[11] Since amusements cannot be desirable in and for themselves but instead to promote renewed activity, the latter is more
likely to be the source of happiness. Of course we mean
activity in conformity with virtue.

Which virtue? There are moral and intellectual
virtues. Moral virtues, ruled by practical wisdom

246

(<u>phronesis</u>) engender in man a disposition towards good emotions and actions. Moral virtues make man as man good. Moral life is the life of man as a composite being (body and soul), ruled by practical reason that controls his emotions and actions; it is the life in which all feelings and strivings are in conformity with moral virtue. A virtuous life involves serious purpose and steady effort; it is the life of a free man exercising choice and deliberation. Consequently, a free man who lives a virtuous life develops his higher faculties and controls his lower or irrational appetites, feelings, urges, instincts. Slaves, on the other hand, as human instruments of their owners, not being able to deliberate and to make choices for themselves, can lead a little if any virtuous life under the guidance of their masters.[12]

Intellectual virtues, on the other hand, ruled by theoretical wisdom (<u>sophia</u>), develop theoretical reason or intellect (<u>nous</u>) and make man god-like in intellectual activity and consequent happiness. The next chapter will further discuss intellectual excellence.

Chapter 7

Contemplative Life

"But if happiness consists in activity in accordance with virtue, it is reasonable that it should be
activity in accordance with the highest virtue; and this
will be the virtue of the best part of us."[13] Our
intellect (nous) is a faculty within us which Aristotle
calls divine or godlike. The intellect's activity is
contemplation (theoria), a direct intellectual grasp of
reality. This sublime contact with reality through
theoretical knowledge is a task of theoretical wisdom
or philosophy. True philosophers are wise and true
contemplatives.

Why is human happiness ultimately found in theoria?
Theoria is the highest human intellectual activity:
it is the activity of the highest human faculty (nous),
and it is also the activity of the nous concerning the
highest objects of reality as follows: being qua being
as grasped in metaphysics, being qua abstract quantity,
as studied in mathematics and being qua changeable but
not particular, as apprehended in the philosophy of
nature.

Theoria is furthermore:

-- the most continuous (lasting)of all our
   activities,

-- the most desirable and most pleasant of all
   human actions,

-- the most self-sufficient activity--a philosopher,
   strictly speaking, needs no friends or possessions to contemplate,

-- loved for its own sake, an end-in-itself, and
   not a means to some further results.

-- a kind of repose requiring leisure, "for we are
   busy in order that we may have leisure, and
   carry on war in order that we may have peace."[14]

On the other hand, the practical (moral, political) virtues as activated in political and military
pursuits are unleisurely, distracting and involving.
Statesmen are concerned with power, prestige and the

people's welfare. Politics is not the happiness of the
statesman or of the people. If properly used, it is the
means to happiness. Military man engages in wars when
necessary, but wars are dangerous not only to body but
also to soul. Military science and performance is only
a means to victory, and victory leads to the peace and
well-being of citizens. The contemplative life is far
above the stress and strain of both politics and military
pursuits. Only the life of intellect and its contemplation makes man completely happy.

The contemplative life is, it must be said, beyond
mere human nature. It depends on the divine in man. To
live according to divine intellect is to live a life that
is divine and far above mortality. As a result, we must
as much as possible make ourselves immortal, making every
effort to live according to the divine spark in us, the
intellect (nous).

> "if then the intellect is something divine in
> comparison with man, so is the life of intellect
> divine in comparison with human life. Nor ought
> we to obey those who enjoin that a man should
> have man's thoughts and a mortal the thoughts of
> mortality, but we ought so far as possible to
> achieve immortality, and do all that man may to
> live in accordance with the highest thing in him;
> for though this be small in bulk, in power and
> value it far surpasses all the rest."15

Aristotle breaks the confines of a closed universe and
invites us to open humanism: man is not the end-in-him-
self. Man is destined to become godlike. His nous is
his destiny. He cannot settle for less than the contemplative, godlike life.

At the summit of his thinking about human happiness,
Aristotle seems to return to Plato with whom he has often
disagreed. Aristotle tells us that the nous is man's
best and most proper faculty; therefore, the nous must
also be the most proper 'part' of human nature. Hence,
he rushes to conclude "...the intellect more than anything
else is man."16 Did Aristotle, for a moment set aside the
substantial body-soul unit and return to Plato's theory
that the soul is tied temporarily and accidentally to the
prison of the body? One thing is certain from the above
discussion. The life of the nous, contemplation, is the
happiest for man. Contemplation is the very essence or
form of human happiness. In the final analysis, Aristotle's
ethics and politics are intellectualist human endeavors.

249

Chapter 8

The Excellence of the Contemplative Life

Aristotle has compared the life of pleasure with the life of moral virtue.[17] In Chapter 8 he compared moral and intellectual goodness, the life of phronimos to that of sophos. The former is truly human; the latter is more divine than human. Still, Aristotle favors the latter as the most excellent and consequently the happiest human life.

He does not reject the moral life. He assigns to it, however, an ancillary role: the preparation of men for lives of contemplation. The moral life of man qua man which is ruled by phronesis and shaped by moral virtues of courage, temperance and justice, is inherently dependent upon many things. Moral virtues depend upon the human condition: they depend upon the bodily constitution and human character; they moderate human actions and emotions and respect human needs. Moral virtues dispose man to follow the guidance of phronesis but phronesis itself depends upon theoretical wisdom (sophia) for universal principles of human conduct which are not devised by practical wisdom (phronesis). Moreover, moral virtues depend upon externals. A statesman, exercising his political prudence, is concerned most of the time with the bodily and economic needs of his citizens. A generous man needs money to exercise his virtue. A courageous man needs bodily strength to attack his enemy. A just man needs others in society to do them justice. Therefore, since moral life depends upon so many things, it is far from being self-sufficient. Hence, it is manifest the excellence of intellectual goodness that does not need all those things or very little of them. But the wise man is a human being, living in a society, needing material goods, and thus, a wise man should live a morally good life. By doing so, he will be a truly happy human being even if only in a "secondary degree."

There is another reason why intellectual goodness excells over moral goodness. Gods are not morally good, and need not be because they live perfectly active and happy lives. What kind of activity is proper for Gods? To say that they are doing just actions by making contracts, returning deposits, settling their accounts in trials would be demeaning. It would also be demeaning to say that Gods are brave by enduring and attacking dangerous situations, engaging in liberal actions among themselves, or that they are temperate by subduing their bad passions. "If we go through the list we shall find that all forms of virtuous conduct seem trifling and unworthy of the gods."[18] Yet gods are very much alive and supremely happy. If we take away practical and productive activity from a rational being, the only one that remains is contemplative action (theoria). Therefore, the activity of gods must be contemplation. Contemplation of what? According to Aristotle, God is Pure Form and Pure Act, and this Pure Act is the contemplation of oneself. The contemplation of the Pure Form or supreme reality without any mixture of matter or potency is the thinking of the pure thought, of the Pure Form.

Aristotle characterized divine life in his Metaphysics by saying, "its thinking is a thinking of thinking" (in the original Greek text: noēsis noēseos noēsis)[19]. Similarly, a little further, Aristotle condenses his intellectualist concept of god by saying: god is "absolute self-thought throughout all eternity."[20] Significantly, he did not use in this case his term theoria for divine activity but that of Plato: noēsis. As a rule, Aristotle meets his teacher on the summits of his thought. Of course, even here the difference between him and his teacher exists: to Plato the queen Idea that permeates being, and particularly divine being is that of goodness, while Aristotle gives primacy to the truth of being, and to the truth of divine being in particular.

Similarly, the objects of intellectual human contemplation are those with no attached matter. These are intelligible forms that theoretical wisdom offers to the human mind: being qua being in metaphysics, being as abstract quantity in mathematics, and physical being detached from particular matter in physics. However, human and divine contemplation are only analogous: the difference is basic. In the divine contemplation there is a total identity and unity of subject intuiting (divine nous) and object intuited (god himself) while in human contemplation there is a similarity and union, not identity and unity of subject thinking and reality thought of. In spite of that difference, human contemplative activity is the closest to divine activity, and therefore, the happiest.

Regardless of the difficulties in achieving it, for Aristotle, the happiness of contemplation is envisioned in the context of this world. Aristotle is fully aware that since man is a composite being, his earthly happiness will involve a composite of mental, bodily and external goods used in conformity with moral virtue. But, as he often said, while this moral happiness is purely

251

human, contemplative happiness, on the other hand, resembles the divine. Intellect (nous) which grasps
reality immediately or intuitively, is set aside from
reason (dianoia) the discursive power of thinking as
well as from all other functions, faculties, and emotions
of the soul.

Human intellect is not only a separate faculty,
standing apart from all other faculties, but is also
separable from the body. Aristotle distinguishes the
active from the passive intellect and declares that the
active intellect is "separable [from the body], impassi-
ble [emotionless], and unmixed with matter since it is
essentially the activity."21 Active intellect will sur-
vive bodily death and may continue the life of contemplation even in the after-life. The difficulty surrounding the eternal life of contemplation is, however, serious.
Since nothing else will survive--neither reasoning, remembering, loving, nor the passive intellect whose function is to grasp ideas of reality given to it by the
active intellect through intelligible forms--how can the
active mind standing alone, indulge in contemplation?
In other words, in eternity neither the faculty intuiting
reality, passive intellect, nor the objects connatural to
human cognition, essences embodied in physical things,
will exist. How, then, will contemplation take place in
a separate active intellect?

Be that as it may in the after-life, Aristotle lists
more reasons for the excellence of the intellect over moral
goodness in this life. Animals, he says, being unable to
live a contemplative life, cannot be considered happy. He
admits that wise men or philosophers are humans and need
some external goods for their happy life. However, their
possessions are small and their dependence upon them,
smaller. Philosophers need to take care of their bodies
and their families, but moderately. The testimony of such
great thinkers as Solon and Anaxagoras confirms that man
can live a virtuous and happy life while having only
moderate means. However, regardless of what the famous
thinkers have said about the happy life with moderate
possessions, in moral matters, the facts of life are
standards for our value-judgments. The fact of life is
that wise men are the happiest among humans. Why?

The wise man exercises his intellect and keeps it in
the best state. He must, then, be the happiest of all humans. And, if there is such a thing as divine providence
--the divine care and guidance of human affairs--the first
on the list who are expected to be loved and cared for by
gods are wise men because they cultivate their intellect

and contemplate as gods do. They are dear to gods because they are godlike in their lives; they live right and noble lives. No wonder gods delight in guiding those humans who live as divine offspring.

Part III.   TRANSITION TO POLITICS

Chapter 9

How is Happiness to be Secured?

Now that the discussion on human lives dedicated
to moral virtues, to friendship, to pleasure, to contemplation has been completed, what is needed to secure
human happiness?   In practical matters the theory is not
enough.   Theory must be supported by practice.   Ethical
science influences only those who are educated from
childhood to build good moral characters.   The majority
of men follow their desires for pleasure and avoid
pleasures only for fear of punishment.

There are three sources to be taken into consideration when securing happiness.   These sources are human
nature or natural inclination to virtuous life; teaching
the theory of morals;   and habituation in living a
good, moral and intellectual life.

1.   As to human nature, none of the virtues are in-
     born or given by nature.   Blessed are those naturally
     inclined to a good life; however virtues are acquired
     by long and decisive practice.

2.   The teaching of morality is only beneficial to those
     who already possess a well-disposed moral char-
     acter.   As to the intellectual virtues, teaching is
     beneficial to those with the ability and willing-
     ness to learn.

3.   By the method of exclusion, then, the formation of
     good habits by the steady practice of virtuous acts
     is the only way to happiness, moral and intellectual.
     As a result, an important question is raised: how
     can man be helped to develop the good habit of doing
     what is right and noble?[22]

Good habits can be instilled only by following the
proper rules and regulations of the two human institu-
tions--the family, and the all-inclusive community of
civic life, the city state (polis).   According to
Aristotle, the family begins the process of education
while the state crowns the process.   Not only the young
in the family, but also adults in the state are guided
towards living good and happy lives.   In fact, the
family begins the process of education and the state

cements it through its laws. Laws guide men's lives, laws are educators of citizens, because they are expressions of the legislators' practical wisdom who create laws in accordance with the good human lives of their citizens. Legislation, as we know already[23] is higher than political science. The former deals with universal rules for good human conduct, the latter with the particulars of citizens' lives, and it is exercised in assemblies and juries. Legislation is an architectonic science, exceeding that of domestic rule in the family and practical daily politics. For the greeks, law-givers are not assemblymen, but either the founders of the state or special bodies of wise, aged, and ex-perienced men.

The rule of state law carries more authority and is less resented than paternal rule. Furthermore, the laws of the state may adequately compel and punish those refusing to obey them. The laws of state supply the citizens with necessary discipline. A well-disposed citizen of good moral character will obey the laws, and by doing so, acquire a set of good habits leading to the practice of a virtuous life.

Aristotle thinks that, unfortunately, laws enacted for helping citizens to lead good and happy lives are rare (Sparta, for example, made laws that aimed directly at the education of its citizens). Therefore, every man should learn to become a lawgiver--first in his family and then in his state. A father is better able to legislate for his family because a close tie of affection between him and his family exists. Further-more, it must be said that private education and indi-vidual guidance can be worked out with more detail and with more attention to each individual's private needs.

Nevertheless, only those knowing the general rules take the best care of particular cases. Medicine, for instance, is the science of healing everyone, not simply of healing Socrates or Callias. Science is based upon universals and the science of legislation is based upon universal insights into the rules of human conduct. Assuming that laws make us good, the study of legislation is necessary for everyone wanting to better not only him-self but also his friends and fellow men.

How can we become good legislators for our fellow men? We would naturally first turn to the experts--teachers. Since legislation is a branch of political science, one would think that politicians would teach us the science of legislation. But they do not. Politicians practice politics more through their native ability and experience than by knowing the theory of political life and legislation. On the other hand, Sophists boast that they may teach everything including legislation. But they reduce politics and legislation to a subspecies of rhetoric. Their method is purely eclectic in their approach to legislation. They tell us that all we must do is to collect the most respected laws and use them for current and future generations. But they do not try to understand the value of these laws or discern which are to be retained and which to be rejected or reformulated. Since the science of legislation is often neglected or improperly handled we must review the study of this most important branch of human knowledge. Since laws are the products of political life, our immediate task is to study political science through examination and analysis of the various kinds of constitutions devised by man for establishing political states. First, we will review the opinions of the previous thinkers on the best constitution, then we will review the collection of constitutions.[24] We will try to find out which constitutions preserve and which destroy states. Finally, we will study the best form of a constitution, the best laws and customs under it.[25]

From Book X as well as from Book I of the <u>Nicomachean Ethics</u> we must conclude that Aristotle did not separate ethics from politics.[26] Ethics, which is concerned with the morality and happiness of man <u>qua</u> man, introduces the study of the morality and happiness of man <u>qua</u> citizen. The two sciences deal with the same subject in different contexts: ethics in the context of human nature, human needs and moral character, politics in the context of the city-state. Both ethics and politics try to create in man a set of good habits in order to foster his practice of a good and happy life.

CONCLUSION

AN OVERALL-GLANCE AT THE NICOMACHEAN ETHICS

Looking back at Aristotelian ethical theory we may point out the following milestones. We started with the study of the good as an end and found that this purposiveness is embedded not only in the universe but in human conduct as well. The logical study of ends and means leads us, then, to the concept of the supreme good for man, his total well-being or eudaimonia.

Happiness (eudaimonia) consists in a life lived in conformity with virtue, whose nature Aristotle found to be the mean between excess and deficiency in feelings and actions. Since the very essence of moral virtue lies in the deliberation and choice of the virtuous mean, they, together with the impediments to and modifiers of the voluntary act, were closely examined.

After clarifying the issues of human ends, virtue and choice, Aristotle devoted a great deal of the Nicomachean Ethics to the study of individual moral and intellectual virtues. Ethics is the science of the good life; as a result, Aristotle discussed the variety of moral virtues exercised in daily life. The study of the principal virtues—temperance, courage, magnificence, magnanimity, justice—was necessary since these virtues control emotions and actions. The study of intellectual virtues was necessary in order to discover the rule or guiding principle by which the right mean is found in feelings and actions. The study of continence and incontinence was necessary to visualize fully the human condition, its weakness of the appetite in spite of the vision of right reason. The study of friendship was necessary to see mutual human love as a counterpart of and supplement to justice in social life. Aristotle should be credited for placing the study of friendship in the framework of ethics.

Finally, eudaimonia, the ultimate end of man's striving, was examined last. Aristotle first turned to the problem of pleasure which is too often identified with human happiness, in order to distinguish and clarify the relationship between the two. Although we have seen Aristotle's recognition of the great importance of moral happiness leading to the contemplative live, there is no doubt that he considered contemplation the essence of

human happiness. In the final analysis, Aristotle's
ethics is an intellectualist ethics, retaining its ultimate connection with the pure intellectualism of Plato's
ethics.

However, Plato in the <u>Republic</u> also sees in the
harmonious life of the three classes the great example
of harmony and happiness in the soul of individual
citizens. Aristotle ends his ethics by inviting us to
study the great art of legislation because the laws of
the polis are guides and educators of men in their
effort to secure their happiness. The study of constitutions (the way of life of different city-states will
be the subject of Aristotle's <u>Politics</u>).

BOOK X

FOOTNOTES

1
N.E. X, viii, 12 - 1179a 20.

2
A detailed comparison of the opinions and criticism on and of pleasure presented in Book VII, xi-xiv and here in Book X, i-v is expertly made by A. J. Festugière, Aristote. Le Plaisir. Paris: Librarie Philosophique J. Vrin; 1960. Introduction, pages vii-xx.

3
N.E. X, iii, 13 - 1174a 8-12.

4
N.E. X, iv, 4 - 1174a 5.

5
N.E. VII, xii, 3 - 1153a 15.

6
N.E. X, iv, 8 - 1174b 30.

7
N.E. X, iv, 11 - 1175a 20.

8
N.E. X, v, 4 - 1175b 10.

9
N.E. X, v, 7 - 1176a 1-5.

10
N.E. I, vii - 1097a 15-30; 1097b 1-30; 1098a 1-30; 1098b 1-10.

11
N.E. X, vi, 6 - 1176b 30.

12
    Politics, I, v, 3, 6, 9, 10, 11 - 1259b 20-30;
1260a 5-15, 32-42; 1260b 3-8.

    "for the slave has not got the deliberative part at
all."

    "And we laid down that the slave is serviceable
for the mere necessaries of life, so that clearly he
needs only a small amount of virtue, in fact just enough
to prevent him from failing in his tasks owing to intemperance and cowardice."

    "For the slave is a partner in his master's life..."

    "It is manifest therefore that the master ought to
be the cause to the slave of the virtue proper to a
slave..."

13
  N.E. X, vii - 1177a 12.

14
  N.E. X, vii, 6 - 1177b 5.

15
  N.E. X, vii, 8 - 1177b 30.

16
  N.E. X, vii, 9 - 1178a 8.

17
  N.E. X, vi.

18
  N.E. X, viii, 7 - 1178b 15.

19
  Metaphysics, XII, ix, 4 - 1074b 35.

20
  Ibid. XII, ix, 6 - 1075a 10.

21
  De anima, III, v - 430a 18.

22
    This same doctrine of the three possible sources
of moral virtue has been developed in N.E. II, i.

23
N.E. VI, viii, 2-3 - 1141b 25-30.

24
Aristotle alludes here to the 158 constitutions of the Greek city-states that he has undertaken to describe and to comment upon in his Lyceum, and which his students have completed under his supervision. Only one, The Constitution of Athens has reached us.

25
With the exception of Book I (the theory of the household), Aristotle has given us in the above list a brief sketch of the contents of his Politics: the opinions of his predecessors are presented in Book II, constructive and destructive constitutions are analyzed in Books III-VI, and the best form of government is shown in Books VII and VIII.

26
On the subject of the relationship of ethics to politics and vice versa, see Introduction pp.xvii - xxi, Book I, Chapter 2 "Ends and Means".

GLOSSARY OF KEY TERMS IN ARISTOTLE'S <u>NICOMACHEAN</u> <u>ETHICS</u>

This glossary contains the key terms and words most frequently used in Aristotle's <u>Nicomachean</u> <u>Ethics</u>. The terms are given in their Greek <u>form</u>, <u>first</u> <u>in</u> Latin transliteration, then, in parenthesis, in Greek letters. The terms are listed according to the English, not the Greek alphabet.

Since it is rather difficult to find a precise English equivalent for any Aristotelian term, several variants are given. Instead of trying to offer a 'modern' explanation of Aristotle's terms, we prefer to let him tell us what he meant by each term. This means that for each term in this glossary, we will quote appropriate passages from Aristotle's works.

Quotations from the <u>Nicomachean</u> <u>Ethics</u> (hereafter referred to as <u>N.E.</u>) are taken from the translation of that work by H. Rackham (Loeb Classical Library). Quotations from other Aristotle's works are taken from the Oxford translation of Aristotle's works.

GLOSSARY

Adikēma (ἀδίκημα): wrong act injuring others when done in full knowledge but without previous deliberation. It can be done in a burst of passion. Since there was no deliberation, hence no choice, the offender is not guilty.

"When an injury is done knowingly but not deliberately, it is an act of injustice or wrong; such, for instance, are injuries done through anger, or any other unavoidable or natural passion to which mean are liable; since in committing these injuries and errors a man acts unjustly, and his action is an act of injustice, but he is not ipso facto unjust or wicked, for the injury was not done out of wickedness." N.E. V, viii, - 1135b, 20-25.

Agathon (ἀγαθόν): good.

"The good is that at which all things aim." N.E. I, i, 1 - 1094a 3.
"The good of man is the active exercise of his soul's faculties in conformity with excellence or virtue, or if there are several human excellencies or virtues, in conformity with the best and most perfect among them /intellectual virtues/." N.E. I, vii, 15 - 1098a 17-18.

Agathon, good has three kinds: kalon (καλόν):
noble or virtuous or honorable, which is sought for its own sake; hedy (ἡδύ): pleasant which appeals to senses; sympheron(συμφέρον) or chrēsimon (χρήσιμον): useful, beneficial, expedient is that which is a means to something else.

"There are three things /goods/ that are the motives of choice and three /evils/ that are the motives of avoidance; namely, the noble, the expedient, and the pleasant and their opposites, the base /aischron - αἰσχρόν /, the harmful /blaberon - βλαβερόν /, and the painful /lyperon - λυπερόν/." N.E. II, iii, 7 - 1104b 30-34.
"It seems that not everything is loved, but only what is lovable, and that this is either what is good /in itself/, or pleasant, or useful." N.E., VIII, ii, 1 - 1155b 18-20.

Agnoia (ἄγνοια): ignorance. Lack of necessary knowledge that a person should have in order to be able to act morally. Otherwise, acts done through ignorance are not voluntary and the person is not responsible for them.

263

"An act done through ignorance is in every case not
voluntary, but it is involuntary only when it causes ↓
the agent pain and regret...." N.E. III, i, 15 - 1110b
17.

Aidōs (αἰδώς): modesty, sense of shame, shyness.

"There are also modes of observing a mean in the sphere
of and in relation to the emotions. For in these also
one man is spoken of as moderate and another as exces-
sive--for example the bashful man whose modesty takes
alarm at everything; while he that is deficient in shame,
or abashed at nothing whatsoever, is shameless, and the
man of middle character modest." N.E. II, vii, 14 -
1108a 30-35.

Aisthēsis (αἴσθησις): sense-perception, sensation.
Its object comes from without, its change of the sense
is qualitative.

"Sensation depends, as we have said, on a process of
movement or affection from without, for it is held to
be some sort of change of quality." De anima II, v -
416b 33-35.

Akōn (ἄκων): unwilling (for person).

Akousion (ἀκούσιον): involuntary (act). Involuntary
act is done against one's will.

"⟨The act⟩ is involuntary only when it causes the agent
pain and regret." N.E. III, 1, 13 - 1110b 18.

Akrasiā (ἀκρασία): moral weakness, incontinence, unrestraint. When right reason is not distorted in its
vision of moral values, but perverted passion pursues its
object persistently in spite of the reason's dictates,
we have the state of character which is called moral
weakness. How can one act badly while seeing clearly
that he is wrong? The sense knowledge clouds the knowledge of reason.

"For the knowledge which is present when failure of
self-restraint occurs is not what is held to be knowledge in the true sense, nor is it true knowledge

which is dragged about by passion, but knowledge derived from sense-perception." N.E. VII, iii, 14 - 1147b 16-18.

Akratēs (ἀκρατής): morally weak person. He knows the right and does the wrong under the influence of passion.

"But there is a person who abandons his choice against right principle, under the influence of passion, who is mastered by passion sufficiently for him not to act in accordance with right principle, but not so completely as to be of such a character as to believe that the reckless pursuit of pleasure is right. This is the unrestrained man..." N.E. VII, viii, 5 - 1151a 20-24.

Alētheia (ἀλ ήθεια): truthfulness, sincerity, straightforwardness in conduct and conversation.

"...The straightforward sort of man is sincere both in behavior and in speech, and admits the truth about his own qualifications without either exaggeration or under-statement." N.E. IV, vii, 4 - 1127a 24-27.

Akolasiā (ἀκολασία): self-indulgence, intemperance, licentiousness, profligacy.

"It is clear that excess in relation to pleasures is profligacy, and that it is blameworthy." N.E. III, xi, 5 - 1118b 6.

Akolastos (ἀκόλαστος): a self-indulgent person, not corrected, spoiled man, an incorrigible man.

"The profligate therefore desires all pleasures, or those that are most pleasant, and is led by his desire to pur-sue these in preference to everything else." N.E. III, xi, 6 - 1119a 1-3.

Anankē (ἀνάγκη): necessity is the fact or thing or principle that cannot be otherwise. Absolute necessity means that the subject (God, spirits of the stars) must exist and that principles are true forever. Necessity by hypothesis means necessity under certain given pre-conditions. If certain results are to be achieved, then certain preconditions must be present. Ex. If there exists vision or has to be then such organ struc-tured as eye must exist or will have to exist. Physics II, ix - 200a 15-18.

Andreiā (ἀνδρεία):   courage, bravery.

"Courage is the observance of the mean in relation to
things that inspire confidence /excess/ or fear
/defect/." N.E. III, vii, 13 - 1116a 10.

The supreme test of courage is, Aristotle believed,
death in battle for one's own country.

"What form of death then is a test of courage? Presumably that which is the noblest. Now the noblest
form of death is death in battle..." N.E. III, vi, 8 -
1115a 30.

Antipeponthos (ἀντιπεπονϑός): reciprocity. The law of
proportion regulates the exchange of goods and services
in society. Goods and services are being paid by
corresponding or proportionate values (mostly by money).

"But in the interchange of services Justice in the form
of reciprocity is the bond that maintains the association: reciprocity, that is, on the basis of proportion,
not the basis of equality." N.E. V, v, 6 - 1132b 32-34.

Apodeixis (ἀπόδειξις): demonstration, demonstrative
method. The scientific method in which one argues his
position based upon the true and primary principles,
i.e., premises and conclusions which are necessarily
connected.

"Reasoning is demonstration when it proceeds from premises which are true and primary or of such a kind that
we have derived our original knowledge of them through
premises which are primary and true." Topics I, i -
100a 27-30.

Aretē (ἀρετή): excellence, virtue, goodness of character which enables man to perform his particular function
well. Its genus is hexis, and its differentia specifica
is mesotēs to be chosen /proainēsis/ by logos, and its
exemplar is the conduct of the prudent man (phronimos).
(See all these entries in this glossary).

"Virtue then is a settled disposition /hexis/ of the
mind determining the choice/proairesis/ of actions and
emotions, consisting essentially in the observance of the
mean /mesotēs/ relative to us, this being determined by

principle /logos/, that is, as the prudent man /phroni-
mos/ would determine it." N.E. II, vi, 15 - 1107a 1-3.

Atychēma (ἀτύχημα): misfortune, misadventure, accident.

"When the injury happens contrary to reasonable expectation, it is a misadventure." N.E. V, viii, 7 - 1135b
17.

Boulēsis (βούλησις): wish, desire. It refers to an
end, not to a means. Is it of the good or the apparent
good? Wish by its nature aims at the good not at the
evil. Why then do so many people wish the apparent and
not the real good? Pleasurable good misleads peoples'
appetites.

"....that what is wished for in the true and unqualified
sense is the good, but that what appears good to each
person is wished for by him...It appears to be pleasure
that misleads the mass of mankind..." N.E. III, iv,
4-5 - 1113a 23- 35.

Bouleusis (βούλευσις): deliberation about how to act. It
is an act of discursive mind (l.logistikos). Deliberation
ponders over the means that are here and now most suitable in view of the goal to be reached. And we deliberate about the means which are in our control.

"The term 'object of deliberation' presumably must not
be taken to include things about which a fool or a madman might deliberate, but to mean what a sensible person
would deliberate about." N.E. III, iii, 2 - 1112a 20.

Dialektikē (διαλεκτική): the dialectic method. The
art of discussing and arguing one's position from evidence which is based upon the opinions of others who
are competent.

"Reasoning is dialectical which reasons from generally
accepted opinions." Topics I, i, - 100b 18.

Dianoia (διάνοια): reason, intelligence, mind. It means,
in a narrower sense, discursive thinking which proceeds
from the known to the unknown. See logos logistikos.

Dikaiosyne (δικαιοσύνη): justice, honesty, righteousness.

"Justice then in this sense /the general sense/ is perfect virtue, though with a qualification, namely, that
it is displayed toward others." N.E. V, i, 15 - 1129b
25-27.

"Justice /in a particular sense/ is the virtue through
which everybody enjoys his own possessions in accordance
with the law." Rhetoric I, ix - 1366b 8-10.

Dianemētikon dikaion (διανεμητικόν δίκαιον): distributive
justice operates between the state and its citizens.
Citizens receive proportionately equal rewards (honor,
money, protection) for the proportionate contributions
to the political community.

Distributive justice "is exercised in the distribution
of honor, wealth, and the other divisible assets of the
community, which may be allotted among its members in
equal and unequal shares" according to their merits for
the state. N.E. V, ii, 12 - 1130b 30-35.

Diorthōtikon dikaion (διορθωτικόν δίκαιον): corrective,
directive, commutative justice operates between citizens
in their private transactions which are either voluntary,
when both parties consent to them, or involuntary when
at least one party does not consent to them. The equal
of the corrective justice consists in restoring the
state of affairs that existed before the injury or da-
mage occurred.

"The other kind /of justice/ is that which supplies corrective principle in private transactions." N.E. V,
ii, 12 - 1130b 30.

Oikonomikon dikaion (οἰκονομικόν δίκαιον) domestic justice
regulates relationships between husband and wife, parents
and children, master and slave. Since wife, child and
slave are dependents in various degrees upon husband,
father, and master they cannot rule themselves but are
ruled by the man who is the head of the household.
Hence, no complete justice is there to be looked in
households but one that is analogous to political justice.

"Justice between master and slave and between father
and child is not the same as absolute as political justice, but only analogous to them." N.E. V, vi, 8 -

1134b 8 - 10.

In fact, since neither children nor slaves are equal to
their father and master nor free, the degree of the domestic justice is low in their case. The highest degree
of domestic justice is that between husband and wife.
Ibid. 8-9 - 1134b 10-18.

Politikon dikaion (πολιτικόν δίκαιον): political justice is being exercised in the midst of the political
society whose citizens are equal and free.

"Political justice means justice as between free and
(actually or proportionately) equal persons, living a
common life for the purpose of satisfying their needs."
N.E. V, vi, 4 - 1134a 26-28.

Actually in aristocracy only aristocrats are fully
equal and free, in oligarchies oligarchs, and in
democracies all citizens (not slaves).

Nomikon dikaion (νομικόν δίκαιον): conventional,
legal, customary justice. It includes rules and regulations which change from one to another country, from
one to another time.

"A rule ⌊of justice⌋ is conventional that in the first
instance may be settled in one way or the other indif-
ferently, though having once being settled it is not
indifferent..." N.E. V, vii, 1 - 1134b 20-22.

Physikon dikaion (φυσικόν δίκαιον): natural, universal
justice. It includes rules that are unchangeable and
valid in all places and at all times.

"A rule of justice is of two kinds, one natural, the
other conventional. A rule of justice is natural that
has the same validity everywhere, and does not depend
on our accepting it or not." N.E. V, vii, 1 - 1134b
18-20.

Doxa (δόξα): opinion. Uncertain state of mind about
the things that may be otherwise.

"...it follows that it is opinion that is concerned with
that which may be true or false, and can be otherwise:
opinion in fact is the grasp of a premise which is
immediate but not necessary." Posterior Analytics
I, 33 - 89a 3-5.

Dynamis (δύναμις): power, potency, ability, capacity to change, and to be changed.

"That which contains a source of motion or change.... which takes place in another thing, or in itself qua other." Metaphysics V , xii, 5 - 1019a 35.

Eleutheriotēs (ἐλευθεριότης): liberality, generosity, virtue of a free man who disposes liberally with material goods, particularly with money.

"This virtue/liberality/ seems to be the observance of the mean in relation to wealth.... wealth meaning all those things whose value is measured by money." N.E. IV, i, 1-5 - 1119b 23-26.

Eleutheros (ἐλεύθερος): liberal, generous man.

"And of all virtuous people the liberal are perhaps the most beloved, because they are beneficial to others; and they are so in that they give." N.E. IV, i, 11 - 1120a 22-24.

Energeia (ἐνέργεια): activity, active exercise, actualization, partial actuality or existence or completion during the process of change.

"Actuality (energeia) means the presence of the thing, not in the sense which we mean by 'potentially.'" Metaphysics IX, vi, 2 - 1048a 32.

Enkrateia (ἐγκράτεια): moral strength, continence, self-restraint.

Enkratēs (ἐγκρατής): a morally strong person, strong moral character. He tends to follow the dictates of his right reason in spite of the strong desire which draws him to the opposite side. He knows that certain desires are base and refuses to follow them. Instead, he abides by his right reason's guidance.

"Opposed to the unrestrained man is another, who stands firm by his choice, and does not abandon it under the mere impulse of passion. It is clear, then, from these considerations that Self-restraint is a good quality, and Unrestraint a bad one." N.E. VII, viii, 5 - 1151a 26-28.

Entelecheia (ἐντελέχεια): (en-telei-echein means to have an end in itself, to be out of becoming): full or complete act or complete reality of a thing after the process of change is completed, and the thing does not strive beyond itself any more.

"For the activity /ergon/ is the end, and the actuality /energeia/ is the activity /ergon/; hence the term 'actuality' /energeia/ is derived from activity /ergon/ and tends to have a meaning of 'complete reality' /entelecheia/." Metaphysics IX, viii, 11 - 1050a 20.

Epieikeia (ἐπιείκεια): equity, fairness, gentleness, clemency. Equity goes beyond the letter of law and solves the problems of justice and injustice by natural sense of fairness. No law can cover all present and less all future cases. Hence it must be rather general. Some cases are bound to be exceptions to the general rule.

"This is the essential nature of the equitable: it is a rectification of law where law is defective because of its generality." N.E. V, x, 6 - 1137b 8-10.

Epieikēs (ἐπιεικής): equitable, fair, humane, honest man.

"And from this it is clear what the equitable man is: he is one who by choice and habit does what is equitable, and who does not stand on his rights unduly, but is content to receive a smaller share although he has the law on his side." N.E. V, x, 8 - 1137b 34-35 - 1138a 1-3.

Epistēmē (ἐπιστήμη): science, scientific or demonstrative (syllogistic) knowledge.

"Scientific knowledge, therefore, is the quality whereby we demonstrate," i.e., give proof by deduction from first principles and arrive at certain conclusions. N.E. VI, iii, 4 - 1139b 31-33.

Ergon, erga, (ἔργον, ἔργα): work, product, result of any art or skill, function.

"All art /both craftmanship and fine art/ deals with bringing something into existence; and to pursue an

271

art means to study how to bring into existence a thing
which may either exist or not, and the efficient cause
of which lies in the maker and not in the thing made..."
N.E. VI, iv, 4 - 1140a 12-15.

Ethos (ἦθος): moral character, fixed pattern of
feeling and acting.

Men "acquire a particular quality /character/ by con-
stantly acting in a particular way." N.E. III, v, 10 -
1114a 7.

Eudaimonia (εὐδαιμονία): the good life; the well-being
in man which is the result of his well-doing (eupraxia);
the supreme good of man; happiness.

"...the good of man is the active exercise of his soul's
faculties in conformity with excellence or virtue, or if
there be several human excellencies or virtues, in conformity with the best and most perfect among them,/i.e.,
theoretical wisdom/." N.E. I, vii, 15 - 1098a 16-19.

Eudaimon (εὐδαίμων): happy, usually in the sense of a
happiness attained by man through his own efforts. See
Makarios.

Euergesia (εὐεργεσία): beneficence, unselfish service to
others, promotion by action of the good of another for
that other's sake which is a proof of real friendship.

"A friend is defined as one who wishes, and promotes by
action, the real or apparent good of another for that
other's sake." N.E. IX, iv, 1 - 1166a 2-4.

Eunoia (εὔνοια): goodwill which is the first ingredient of friendship. Goodwill implies that one wishes
good to another for that other's sake. If the goodwill
is not accompanied by good deeds in favor of another
person it constitutes the beginning of inoperative
friendship.

"Speaking generally, true goodwill is aroused by some
kind of excellence or moral goodness: it springs up
when one person thinks another beautiful or brave or the
like..." N.E. IX, v, 4 - 1167a 20.

Eutrapeliā (εὐτραπελfα):wittiness

"In respect of pleasantness in social amusement, the
middle character is witty and the middle disposition
Wittiness; the excess is Buffoonery and its possessor
a buffoon; the deficient man may be called boorish, and
his disposition Boorishness." N.E. II, vii, 13 - 1108a
23-27.

Gnōmē (γνώμη); judgment, good sense, insight; considerate, kindly judgment of others; sympathy, lenience,
consideration of equity toward others.

"The quality termed consideration, in virtue of which
men are said to be considerate, or to show consideration
for others, is the faculty of judging correctly what is
equitable." N.E. VI, xi, 1 - 1143a 19-21.

Hamartēma (ἀμάρτημα): mistake, error. A wrong (injustice) done against others by mistake, out of ignorance.
The result comes unexpected and there is no malicious
intent.

"An injury done in ignorance is an error, the person
affected or the act or the instrument or the result
being other than the agent supposed; for example, he did
not think to hit, or not with this missile, or not this
person, or not with this result, but it happened that
either the result was other than expected...or the person or the missile." N.E. V, viii, 6 - 1135b 12-16.

Hēdonē (ἡδονή): pleasure both bodily and mental. Instead of giving us a definition, Aristotle describes the
function of pleasure. Pleasure is intended to perfect
the activity of human powers.

"...it follows that the activity of any of the senses
/and more so of intellect/ is at its best when the sense-
organ being in the best condition is directed to the
best of its objects; and this activity will be the most
perfect and the pleasantest." N.E. X, iv, 5 - 1174a
15-20.

Hekōn (ἕκων): willing (person). One who consents
willingly and understandingly to perform the act he is
performing.

Hekousion (ἐκούσιον): voluntary (act).

"Voluntary act would seem to be an act of which the origin lies in the agent, who knows the particular circumstances in which he is acting." N.E. III, i, 20 - 1111a 22.

Hetaireiā (ἡταιρεία): 'fraternal' association of the people who have much in common: they are about the same age, similar upbringing, the same social standing, of the same tribe. Hetaireia grew up from the expanded family ties, it became a political organization in the fifth century B.C., and in Aristotle's times, hetaireiai were probably no more than social clubs.

Hetairos (ἡταῖρος): member of hetaireia, comrade, companion, fellow tribesman, kinsman, friend from childhood. The companions have in common, the close age, similar upbringing, same social standing, same tribe. They have common homes, meals, work and play.

"Again the proverb says 'Friends' goods are common property', and this is correct, since community is the essence of friendship. Brothers have all things in common, and so do members of a comradeship. Other friends have special possessions in common, more or fewer in different cases, in as much, as friend-ships vary in degree." N.E. VIII, ix, 2 - 1159b 30-35.

Hexis (ἕξις) pl. hexeis (ἕξεις): characteristic attitude; habit established by repeated and orderly action.

"The dispositions /hexeis/ are the formed states of character in virtue of which we are well or ill disposed in respect of the emotions /and actions/." N.E. II, v, 2 - 1105b 26-27.

Homonoia(ὁμόνοια): concord, harmony. Primarily political concept: concord among citizens of a state. Generally: indispensable element of friendship: the quality of being of one mind on the practical matters of life and action.

"Now concord in this sense exists between good men, since these are of one mind both with themselves and with one another, as they always stand more or less on the same ground..." <u>N.E.</u> IX, vi, 3 - 1167b 5-7.

<u>Isos</u> (ἴσος): equal, fair. The equal or fair (<u>to ison</u>) means taking one's right share of the good and bad things in the community, neither more nor less, but even and equal.

<u>Anisos</u> (ἄνισος): unequal, unfair. The unequal or un-fair (<u>to anison</u>) means taking more than one's share of the good and taking less than one's share of the bad in the community. <u>N.E.</u> V, i, 11 - 1129b 6-7.

<u>Kakia</u> (κακία): vice, wickedness, habit opposite of vir-tue both by excess and by deficiency. Good action springs from right reason and good desire. Bad or vicious action springs from the distorted reason and perverted desire. The ultimate end of the vicious per-son becomes that which the wrong desire aims at and not what right reason dictates. Wrong pleasures are at the root of the vicious life.

"But men are corrupted through pleasures and pains, that is, either by pursuing and avoiding the wrong pleasures and pains, or by pursuing and avoiding them at the wrong time, or in the wrong manner, or in one of the other wrong ways under which errors of conduct can be logically classified." <u>N.E.</u> II, iii, 5 - 1104b 21-24.

<u>Kalokagathiā</u> (καλοκαγαθία): nobility, goodness. The term is made of two words: <u>kalos</u> and <u>agathos</u>. This is the Greek ideal of the 'gentleman,' the man who possesses the whole of virtue, physical, moral and intel-lectual and high social status as well.

"A man is noble ⁄<u>kalos</u> and <u>agathos</u>⁄ because he possesses those good things that are fine for their own sake and because he is a doer of fine deeds even for their own sake; and the fine things are the virtues and the actions that arise from virtue." <u>Eudemian</u> <u>Ethics</u>, VIII, iii, 6 - 1248b 36-38.

"Nobility [<u>kalogagathia</u>] then is a perfect goodness." <u>Ibid</u>, 1249a 18.

<u>Koinonia</u> (κοινωνία): community, association, partnership, any kind of group whose members are equal in rights and

duties, held together by common interest, and have
common work to do in view of their common aim. Such
groups are those that meet human natural need for good
human life as the family, village, and city-state does;
and all kinds of associations that meet human wants,
political, educational, economic, recreational and
others.

Aristotle did not leave any systematic study on the
key word <u>koinonia</u> in his social and political philosophy.
We have to restore its meaning from <u>N.E.</u> VIII, 9-12 and
<u>Politics</u>, I and III.

<u>Leitourgia</u> (λειτοὐργια): a service performed for the
public by a private citizen who defrayed the costs.
Such <u>leitourgiai</u> included services such as equipping a
warship, a tragic or comic chorus for its musical compe-
tition at public festivals, and training in gymnasia the
competitors for the gymnastic contests, etc.

<u>Logos</u> (λὀγος): speech, statement. Rational principle.
Reason. Argument.

a) <u>Cognitive sense</u>: An act of planning, reasoning. We
first conceive the plan then we move to work on it.
The plan and purpose is even more found in the
works of nature than in those of art.

   "....the reason forms the starting point, alike in
   the works of art and in works of nature." <u>De parti-</u>
   <u>bus animalium</u> I, i - 639b 15-16.

b) <u>Normative sense</u>: practical, deliberative reason
which understands and formulates rational rules and
thus guides the life of the good and wise man.

   Of the two irrational parts of the soul--the vegetative and the appetitive--the vegetative does not
   obey <u>logos</u>, but the appetitive does heed, more or
   less, the guidance of <u>logos</u>.

   "...the vegetative ⁄part of the soul⁊ does not share
   in rational principle at all; the other, the seat of
   the appetites and of desire in general, does in a
   sense participate in principle ⁄logos⁊, as being
   amenable and obedient to it." <u>N.E.</u> I, xiii, 18 -
   1102b 30-34.

276

Orthos logos (ὀρθὸς λόγος): right reason, correct rule
or principle, logos in a normative sense as the guiding
principle of human conduct. Right reason is the rational
ability which, by the mediation of practical wisdom
chooses for every virtue the right mean in emotions and
actions in the right set of circumstances.

"Virtue....is a disposition determined by the right
principle; and the right principle is the principle determined by Prudence." N.E. VI, xiii, 4 - 1144b 22-24.

Logos epistēmonikos (λ.ἐπιστημονικός): scientific
reason. It contemplates invariable, necessary, and
eternal realities.

Logos logistikos (λ.λογιστικός): deliberative reason.
It reflects upon what is contingent and changeable.

"It has been said before that the soul has two parts,
one rational and the other irrational. Let us now similarly divide the rational part, and let it be assumed
that there are two rational faculties, one whereby we
contemplate those things whose first principles are
invariable, and one whereby we contemplate those things
which admit of variation..." N.E. VI, i, 5 - 1139a 5-8.

Makarios (μακάριος): blessed, supremely happy man who
has god-given happiness.

"It follows that the activity of God, which is trans-
cendent in blessedness, is the activity of contemplation;
and therefore among human activities that which is most
akin to divine activity of contemplation will be the
greatest source of happiness." N.E. X, viii, 7 - 1178b
26-28. See eudaimōn.

Megaloprepeia (μεγαλοπρέπεια): magnificence, splendid
spending of money on a large scale from the motive of
public spirit which was exhibited by the wealthy citizens in Athens when they took the charge and paid
expenses for public services called 'liturgies' (see the
entry).

"It ⌊magnificence⌋ does not however, like Liberality,
extend to all actions dealing with wealth, but only
refers to the spending of wealth; and in this sphere it

surpasses Liberality in point of magnitude, for, as its name itself implies, it consists in suitable expenditure on a great scale." N.E. IV, ii, 1 - 1122a 20-24.

Megalopsychiā (μεγαλοψυχία): greatness of soul magnanimity, lofty pride, self-esteem, high-mindedness. It is a virtue by which a great-souled man pursues honors on the grand scale. He claims and deserves high honor and pursues it rightly.

"...it is evident that honour is the object with which the great-souled are concerned, since it is honour above all else which great men claim and deserve." N.E. IV, iii, 11 - 1123b 22-23.

Mesotēs (μεσότης): or to meson (τὸ μέσον): mean of virtue in emotions and actions.

"By the mean of the thing I denote a point equally distant from either extreme, which is one and the same for everybody; by the mean relative to us, that amount which is neither too much nor too little, and this is not one and the same for everybody." N.E. II, vi, 5 - 1106a 30-33.

Metabolē (μεταβολή): change is the transition from potency as potency to act.

"The actualization of what exists potentially, in so far as it exists potentially." Physics III, i - 201a 10.

Change being the actualization of a potency it exists only while the potency is being actualized and it is not yet fully actualized; it is an actualization which at every moment of its existence is incomplete. Ex. the change goes on only and only while, say, a bridge is being built-up.

Nemesis (νέμεσις): righteous indignation at the undeserved good fortune of others. The two opposite extremes to this virtue are the following ones: Excess: envy or sorrow at the good fortune of others. Defect: malicious rejoicing at the ill-fortune of others. N.E. IV, vii, 15 - 1108b 1-6.

278

Noēsis (νόησις): intellect, intelligence, thought, comprehensive intuitive vision. Platonic term used by Aristotle in few instances. See theoria.

Nomos (νόμος): law, rule, convention, custom. Law is a dictate of reason, a guardian of virtue: not only of justice, but also of bravery, temperance and others. The law is a guarantor of the republic's common good and a promotor of citizen's social and political happiness. It is the embodiment of what is right and just.

"...law on the other hand is a rule, emanating from a certain wisdom and intelligence that has compulsory force." N.E. X, ix, 12 - 1180a 21-23.

"The law is ⌊a rule of life⌋ such that will make the citizens virtuous and just." Politics III, v, 11 - 1280b 10.

Nous (νοῦς): intellect, intelligence, intuitive rational power which grasps first principles of being.

"If then the qualities whereby we attain truth, and are never led into falsehood, whether about things invariable or things variable, are Scientific Knowledge, Prudence, Wisdom, and Intelligenge, and if the quality which enable us to apprehend first principles cannot be any one among three of these...it remains that first principles must be apprehended by intelligence." N.E. VI, vi, 2 - 1141a 3-8.

Orexis (ὄρεξις), pl. orexeis (ὀρέξεις): desire, tendency, inclination, appetite for pleasure.

"...desire is an appetition of what is pleasant." De anima II, 3 - 414b 5.

"Pursuit and avoidance in the sphere of Desire correspond to affirmation and denial in the sphere of the Intellect." N.E. VI, ii, 2 - 1139a 20.

Pathos (πάθος): feeling, emotion, passion, experience of pleasure and pain.

"By the emotions, I mean desire, anger, fear, confidence, envy, joy, friendship, hatred, longing, jealousy, pity; and generally those states of consciousness which are

accompanied by pleasure or pain." <u>N.E.</u> II, v , 2 -
1105a 21-24.

To <u>philauton</u> (τὸ φίλαυτον): self-love, <u>not</u> selfish or
<u>self-centered</u> love. Self-love is the basis and model of
love for others. All five characteristic feelings and
actions that a real friend nurtures and does for
others are found in the good man's love for himself.
Thus, he lives in harmony with himself; he wishes sin-
cerely his own good to himself and works for it; he
desires his own life and security, and especially that
of his rational part; he enjoys his own company; he is
deeply aware of his own joys and sorrows. The good man
feels all the above for his friend whom he looks as his another self, or the extension of his person. <u>N.E.</u> IX,
iv, 2-6 - 1166a 10-30. IBID. viii, 3ssq--1168b, 14ssq.

<u>Philēsis</u> (φίλησις): friendly affection, an essential
element of friendship.

"Again, loving ⟨philesis⟩ seems to be an active experience, and being loved a passive one; hence affection
and the various forms of friendly feelings are naturally
found in the more active party to the relationship."
<u>N.E.</u> IX, vii, 6 - 1168a 19-22.

(φιλία):
<u>Philiā</u> friendliness, affability, agreeableness, amia-
bility toward others. This virtue differs from friendship in that it does not involve emotion or affection
toward others. Friendly man is amiable to all. He is a
pleasant companion. He is agreeable to all because of
his natural disposition and good character.

"...a man of this character takes everything in the
right way not from personal liking or dislike, but from
natural amiability." <u>N.E.</u> IV, vi, 5 - 1126b 23-25.

<u>Philiā</u> (φιλία): friendship. Mutual human love. A
bond of associates in various communities, private and
public ones. A conscious, reciprocal goodwill which is
based upon the good qualities of friends.

"To be friends therefore, men must (1) feel goodwill
for each other, that is, wish each other's good, and
(2) be aware of each other's goodwill, and (3) the
cause of their goodwill must be one of the lovable qualities mentioned above." <u>N.E.</u> VIII, ii, 4 - 1156a 3-5.

Philiā (φιλία): friendly affection or love which is
intense, intimate, and accompanied by a deep desire for
the company of one's friend.

"Love means friendship in a superlative degree and that
must be with one person only..." N.E. IX, x, 5 - 1171a
12-13.

"...love indeed seems to be an excessive state of emotion, such as naturally felt towards one person only..."
N.E. VIII, vi, 2 - 1158a 12-13.

Philiā (φιλία): three kinds of friendship are: the
noble, the useful, and the pleasant. The noble or the
virtuous friendship is based on the moral and intellectual qualities possessed and shared by friends. The useful friendship is based on a mutual exchange of benefits.
The friendship of pleasure is based on agreeable
feelings that friends derive from each other's company.

"There are accordingly three kinds of friendships, corresponding in number to the three lovable qualities /the
three kinds of good: the noble, the useful, and the
agreeable]....Thus friends whose affection is based on
utility do not love each other in themselves, but in so
far as some benefit accrues to them from each other.
And similarly with those whose friendship is based on
pleasure: for instance, we enjoy the society of witty
people not because of what they are in themselves, but
because they are agreeable to us." N.E. VIII, iii, 1 -
1156a 11-14.

"The perfect form of friendship is that between the
good, and those who resemble each other in virtue. For
these friends wish each alike the other's good in respect
of their goodness, and they are good in themselves; but
it is those who wish the good of their friends for their
friends' sake who are friends in the fullest sense,
since they love each other for themselves and not accidentally /for some benefit or pleasure/." N.E. VIII,
iii, 6 - 1156b 7-12.

Phronēsis (φρόνησις): prudence, practical wisdom that
guides moral virtues.

"It therefore follows that Prudence is a truth-attaining
rational quality, concerned with action in relation to
the things that are good for human beings." N.E. VI, v,
6 - 1140b 20-22.

Phronēsis oikonomikē (φ. οἰκονομική):   domestic prudence extends to the affairs of the family.

Phronēsis nomothetikē (φ. νομοθετική):   legislative
prudence of a founder of a city-state or of special law-
givers. It is a supreme and directive prudence.

Phronēsis politikē (φ. πολιτική):   political prudence deals in particular with the matters of the public
well being of citizens.

Phronēsis bouleutikē (φ. βουλευτική):   deliberative
prudence which helps assemblymen in their decisions.

Phronēsis dikastikē (φ. δικαστική):   judicial prudence which helps jurymen to utter right sentences in
various court cases.

"Prudence ⟨of social type⟩...is distinguished as Domestic Economy, Legislature, and Political Science, the
latter being subdivided, into Deliberative Science and
Judicial Science." N.E. VI, viii, 3 - 1141b 30.

Phronimos (φρόνιμος): prudent man, the man of practical wisdom. Prudent man is the one who is able, here
and now, to make the right choice of moral means which
will lead to the moral end.

"Now it is held to be the mark of a prudent man to be
able to deliberate well about what is good and advantageous for himself, not in some one department, for
instance what is good for his health or strength, but
what is advantageous as a means to the good life in
general." N.E. VI, v, 1 - 1140a 25-28.

Physis (φύσις): nature; physei (φύσει):by nature,
naturally. Nature is understood to be the source of the
spontaneous self-growth and self-arrest.

"Each of them⟨ the things constituted by nature, as
opposed to those made by art⟩ has within itself a
principle of motion and stationariness..." Physics
II, i - 192b 14-16.

Poiēsis (ποίησις): production, making, doing as contrasted with praxis. See praxis. Production is the
making of things, useful or artistic, that is, either for
utility or for beauty sake.

Polis (πόλις): city-state, state. Self-sufficing
political, social, economic and educational unit. City-
state exists for the good life of its citizens.

"When several villages are united in a single, complete
community, large enough to be nearly or quite self-sufficing, the state comes into existence, originating in the
bare needs of life, and continuing in existence for
the sake of a good life." Politics I, 2 - 1252b 28-30.

Politeiā (πολιτεία): constitution of the city-state,
constitutional government. Constitution determines the
distribution of offices, designates the subject of the
supreme authority, and fixes the end to be pursued by
the citizens of the state. Thus, the constitution has
not only administrative but also normative role to
fulfill: it becomes the way of life which is typical
for each state.

"...for a constitution is the regulation of the offices
of the state in regard to the mode of their distribution and to the question what is the sovereign power in
the state and what is the object /telos/ of each
community..." Politics IV, i, 5 - 1289a 15-18.

Praotēs (πραότης): gentleness, moderation of anger.

"Gentleness is the observance of the mean in relation
to anger." N.E. IV, v,1-2 - 1125b 26.

Prāxis (πρᾶξις); pl. praxeis (πράξεις): action or
practice as contrasted from theoretical activity; human
conduct guided by reason, acting, doing; activity that
primarily develops and perfects human being who performs it as different from production of things or products outside their maker.

"The class of things that admit of variation includes
both things made and actions done. But making is different from doing...Hence the rational quality concerned
with doing is different from the rational quality concerned

283

with making." <u>N.E.</u> VI, iv, 2 - 1140a 1-5.

The rational quality (virtue) concerned with actions done is practical wisdom (<u>phronēsis</u>); and the rational quality concerned with making things is art (<u>technē</u>). See entries.

<u>Proairesis</u> (προαίρεσις): choice, the deliberate decision concerning moral conduct.

"And then the object of choice is something within our power which after deliberation we desire, Choice will be a deliberate desire of things in our power; for we first deliberate, then select, and finally fix our desire according to the result of our deliberation." <u>N.E.</u> III, iii, 19 - 1113a 10-15.

<u>Propeteia</u> (προπέτεια): impetuosity, a kind of incontinence.

<u>Propetēs</u> (προπετής): the impetuous is a man who does not deliberate and is driven by emotion.

<u>Astheneia</u> (ἀσθένεια): weakness of character.

<u>Asthenēs</u> (ἀσθενής): a man of weak moral character. The weak man deliberates but lacking moral strength and under the influence of passion does not abide by the results of his deliberation. If the impetuous man would deliberate by preparing himself and his reasoning power when the emotion emerging is felt and seen, he would not be easily driven by emotion. Usually the keen (<u>oxys</u>) and the excitable (<u>melancholikos</u>) are prone to impetuous kinds of incontinence. Neither the keen nor the excitable wait for reason to guide them: the former because of his quick thinking and lively imagination, the latter because of his warm and passionate temper.

"But there are two forms of Unrestraint, Impetuousness and Weakness. The weak deliberate, but then are prevented by passion from keeping to their resolution; the impetuous are led by passion because they do not stop to deliberate: since some people withstand the attacks of passion, whether pleasant or painful, by feeling or seeing them coming, and rousing themselves, that is, their reasoning faculty, in advance, just as one is proof against tickling if one has just been tickled already. It is the quick and the excitable who are most liable to the impetuous form of Unrestraint, because the former are too hasty and the latter too vehement to wait for reason, being prone to follow their imagination." <u>N.E.</u> VII, vii, 8 - 1150b 20-28.

Sophiā (σοφία): theoretical or philosophic wisdom is a union of intuitive and scientific knowledge.

"Hence wisdom must be a combination of Intelligence and Scientific Knowledge: it must be the consummated knowledge of the most exalted objects." <u>N.E.</u> VI, vii, 3 - 1141a 19-20.

Sophos (σοφός): the wise man is he who knows both first principles of reality and the conclusions that follow from those principles. He sees and understands things and events in the light of highest truths.

"The wise man therefore must not only know the conclusions that follow from his first principles, but also have a true conception of those principles themselves." <u>N.E.</u> VI, vii, 3 - 1141a 17-18.

Sōphrosynē (σωφροσύνη): reasonableness, self-restraint, self-mastery, moderation, temperance. This virtue has been limited by Aristotle to mean the control of bodily pleasures in eating, drinking and sex.

"Temperance is the observance of the mean in relation to pleasures..." <u>N.E.</u> III, x, 1 - 1117b 25.

"Temperance therefore has to do with the pleasures of the body. But not with all even of these..." <u>N.E.</u> III, x, 3 - 1118a 2-3.

"...it is actually enjoying the object that is pleasant, and this is done solely through the sense of touch, alike in eating and drinking and in what are called the pleasures of sex." <u>N.E.</u> VI, x, 9 - 1118a 31-32.

Sōphrōn (σώφρων): self-restrained, self-controlled temperate man.

"...the temperate man desires the right thing in the right way at the right time, which is what principle (<u>logos</u>) ordains." <u>N.E.</u> III, xii, 9 - 1119b 16-17.

Synesis (σύνεσις): an ability to make correct judgements about practical matters of human life. In particular: correct understanding what other persons say
about practical matters of human life. N.E. VI, x,
2-3 - 1143a 5-15.

Technē (τέχνη): art, skill, rational ability to do
things, craftsmanship of any kind; technē includes both
fine arts and crafts.

"Art, therefore, as has been said, is a rational quality, concerned with making, that reasons truly."
N.E. VI, iv, 6 - 1140a 21-22.

Telos (τέλος): aim, end, goal of activity. Perfect,
complete, final state of affairs.

"That for the sake of which a thing is done." Physics
II, iii - 194b 33.

Theōria (θεωρία): contemplation; comprehensive and
intuitive vision of intellect; a direct grasp of eternal
and unchangeable truths. Theoria is itself its own end,
the grasping of the truth for its own sake. Theoria
is the activity of the nous.

"....scientific knowing ⎣epistēmē⎦ and intuition ⎣nous⎦
are always true: further, no other kind of thought except intuition is more accurate than scientific
knowledge. Whereas primary premisses are more know-
able than demonstrations, and all scientific knowledge
is discursive...it will be intuition that apprehends the
primary premisses." Posterior Analytics II, 19 - 100b
7-12.

Tychē (τύχη): chance, an event which forms exception
to the habitual rule of natural happenings. Chance
event happens either incidentally (ex. an architect who
built the house happens to be a musician too) or in a
purpose-like manner i.e., it produces end-like results
which might be an end of the purposive action of human
agent (ex. a man collects the debt from his client whom
he meets by chance in a store). Both meanings are put
together in the following definition of chance:

"an incidental cause in the sphere of those actions
which involve purpose" i.e., of those actions that might
happen as a result of choice. Physics II, v - 197a 5-8.

SELECTED AND ANNOTATED BIBLIOGRAPHY OF AND ON ARISTOTLE'S
WORKS AND, IN PARTICULAR, THE NICOMACHEAN ETHICS.

While the following list includes only a few useful works
on Aristotle for the student, the bibliography on the
whole Aristotelian opus can be found in the following
sources:

During, I.

Aristoteles: Darstellung und Interpretatio seines Denkens.
Heidelberg, 1966. Extensive up-to-date bibliography.

Philippe, M.D.
Aristoteles. Bern: A. Francke Ag. Verlag, 1948.
Series: Bibliographische Einführungen in das Studium
der Philosophie.
Edited by I. M. Bochenski. Freiburg, Switzerland.
Bibliography on Aristotle's works up to 1948.

Repertoire bibliographique de Philosophie: Section:
Socrate, Platon, Aristote.

This is an independent quarterly supplement of the
journal entitled Revue Philosophique de Louvain.

This is the best place to find bibliographies on Aristotle
in the major world languages from 1950 to date.

Parks, George B. and Ruth Z. Temple, eds.
The Literatures of the World in English Translation: A
Bibliography.
Vol. I. The Greek and Latin Literatures.
New York: Friedriech Ungar Publishing Co., 1968.

Mansion, Augustin
"Travaux d'ensemble sur Aristote, son oeuvre et sa
philosophie".
Revue Philosophique de Louvain, vol, 57, 1959.
pp. 44-70.

Here Mansion wrote an extensive review of three following books on Aristotle:

D. J. Allan. The Philosophy of Aristotle. London 1952.

D. M. Philippe, O. P. L'Initiation a la Philosophie
d'Aristotle. Paris, 1956.

"Aristotele nella critica e negli studi contemporanei".
An article published in Rivista di Filosofia neo-
scolastica, Dec. 1956.

Important studies and bibliographies on Aristotle's
works can be found in:

Aristotelian Society. Proceedings, (Old Series 1-3
1888-1896); (New Series 1900-date).

A Synoptic Index to the Proceedings of the Aristotelian
Society, 1900-1949.
Oxford: Blackwell, 1954. pp. 127.

Critical Editions

Aristotelis opera. I. Bekker, ed.

Berlin: Royal Prussian Academy, 1831-1870, 4 vols. text
and vol. 5 Index.

The Greek text of vols. 1 and 2 in which Aristotle's
works are printed, was edited by I. Bekker. Vol. III.
Aristoteles Latinus. Vol. IV Scholia in Aristotelem.

This is the first modern critical edition of the text of
Aristotelian writings. Volumes I and II contain the text
of Aristotelian works. Volume III contains Latin translations and Volume IV Scholia. The fifth Volume contains
an excellent Index Aristotelicus preceded by Fragmenta
Aristotelica.

Aristoteles - opera omnia

Bibliotheca scriptorum graecorum and latinorum Teubner-
iana. Leipzig, Teubner, 1868-1961.

Translations

The Works of Aristotle Translated into English

W. D. Ross and J. A. Smith, eds. 12 vols. Oxford University Press, 1908-1952.

First and complete English translation of the works of
Aristotle. This is a monumental work for which all the
findings of the 19th century textual and philosophical
Aristotelian scholarship have been utilized.

This translation is completely reprinted in the series
Great Books of the Western World, Vols. 8 and 9 and, for
the most part, in the following work:

McKeon, Richard, ed. The Basic Works of Aristotle.
New York: Random House, 1941.

The Introduction to all Aristotle's works emphasizes
particularly the method of Aristotelian philosophy.

Critical Text and Translations

Aristotle. Complete Works. Vols. 23. Cambridge, Mass.,
The Loeb Classical Library, Harvard University Press,
1926-1966.

Text and translation with introductions, notes and
bibliographies. The Greek, as well as the Latin classical works published in this series, are as a rule, the
best such editions in the U.S.

Grammars and Dictionaries

Aristotle - Lexicons

Hermann Bonitz, ed. Index Aristotelicus. Originally
vol. V in the edition of Aristotle's works by the
Prussian Academy.

Reprinted from the 1870 edition in 1. vol. by Berlin:
de Gruyter, 1961. A standard work.

Kiernan, Thomas P. ed. Aristotle. Dictionary. New
York: Philosophical Library, 1962.

This work contains first a long introduction (7-162
pages) which presents the content of Aristotle's writings.
The Dictionary gives the description and definition of
Aristotelian terms quoting the place in his writings
from which the definition has been taken.

Organ, Troy. An Index to Aristotle in English Translation. Princeton University Press, 1949.

Aristotle-Grammar

Fobes, Francis H. Philosophical Greek. An Introduction.
Chicago: The University of Chicago Press, 1957.
Pages xii, 322, vocabularies, Index: English and
Greek. A sound introduction and guide to the grammar,
terminology and reading of philosophical Greek

with illustrative examples from Plato, Menander and
Aristotle. A special feature is the comparison with
cognate Latin words and modern derivatives from
Greek which is done neatly by the use of distinctive
types.

Aristotle: Histories of Philosophy

Brehier, Emile. The Hellenic Age. Chicago: The
University of Chicago Press, 1966.

Copleston, Frederick, S. J. A. History of Philosophy,
8 vols. New Revised Edition, Doubleday and
Company, Inc., Image Books, Garden City, New York,
1962.

Vol. I. Greece and Rome, Part II: Aristotle and
Post-Aristotelian Philosophy.

Fuller, B. A. G. History of Greek Philosophy. 3 vols.
New York, 1923-1931.

The third volume is dedicated to Aristotle. Easy and
enjoyable reading.

Gomperz, Theodore. The Greek Thinkers. A History of
Ancient Philosophy, 4 vols. London: John Murray,
1910-1912.

Vol. IV. Aristotle and His Successors. New York:
Humanities Press, 1964.

Thonnard, F. J. A Short History of Philosophy. Translated from the revised and corrected edition by
Edward D. Maziarz. Desclee and Company. New York,
1955, Printed in Belgium. Page 1074.

Ueberweg, Fr. Grundriss der Geschichte der Philosophie.
Vol. I. Die Philosophie des Altertums. Ed. 12.
Berlin: Mittler und Sohn, 1926.

This is, besides Zeller, another classical text for the
history of Greek philosophy.

Windelband, Wilhelm. A History of Philosophy, Two Vols.
Vol. I. Greek, Roman and Medieval. New York:
Harper Torchbooks, Harper and Row Publishers, 1958.

The classic work of 19th century German scholarship.
This work is still useful to the student, in spite of
the new advances of Aristotelian scholarship.

Zeller, Edward. <u>Aristotle</u> <u>and</u> <u>the</u> <u>Earlier</u> <u>Peripatetics</u>.
    Two vols., 1897. Reimpression made by New York:
    Russell and Russell Company, 1965.

The same work has been translated by B.F.C. Costello and
J. H. Muirhead, New York, 1962.

<u>Introductions</u> <u>to</u> <u>Aristotle's</u> Philosophy

Allan, D. J. <u>The</u> <u>Philosophy</u> <u>of</u> <u>Aristotle</u>. London:
    Oxford University Press, 1952. Second edition,
    1963.

A most illuminating discussion of the essentials of
Aristotle's thought. The best part is one commenting
on Ethics.

Bambrough, Renford J. <u>The</u> <u>Philosophy</u> <u>of</u> <u>Aristotle</u>.
Chicago: Mentor Co., 1963.

Contains translations of selected texts, and very useful
introductions to the main branches of Aristotle's philosophy.

Bambrough, Renford J. <u>New</u> <u>Essays</u> <u>on</u> <u>Plato</u> <u>and</u> <u>Aristotle</u>.
    New York: Humanities Press, 1967.

Aristotle, entry in <u>Encyclopedia</u> <u>Britannica</u>, 15th ed.
    Macropaedia - Knowledge in Depth. vol. I. Chicago:
    Helen Hemingway Benton, Publisher, 1974. pp 1162-
    1171.

Excellent survey of Aristotle's vast philosophical
teaching for the general reader.

Grene, Marjorie. <u>A</u> <u>Portrait</u> <u>of</u> <u>Aristotle</u>. The Univer-
    sity of Chicago Press, 1963, Phoenix Books, 1967.
    Page 273.

Includes an excellent discussion on the influence of
<u>biological</u> <u>interests</u> on Aristotle's thought, and Chapter
One contains an important critique of works on Aristotle's
development.

Grote, G. <u>Aristotle</u>, Third ed. London: John Murray,
    1883.

Hamelin, O. Le système d'Aristote. Paris: Alcan,
    second edition, 1931.

Jaeger, Werner. Aristotle. Fundamentals of the History
   of his Development. First published in Berlin
   1923, Second ed. Translated with the author's cor-
   rections and additions by Richard Robinson. London:
   Oxford University Press, 1948.

This is the pioneer work on the development of Aristotle's
thought. See the development of Aristotle's ethical ideas
in Chapters 4 and 9.

Janczar, Barbara. Review Notes and Study Guide to the
   Philosophy of Aristotle. New York: Monarch Press,
   1964.

Lloyd, G. E. R. Aristotle. The Growth and Structure of
   His Thought. Cambridge University Press, 1968. Ch.
   10. Ethics.

A survey of Aristotleian intellectual development and
philosophy. It strives to surpass Jaeger's conclusions.

Mansion, A. La génèse de l'oeuvre d'Aristote d'après
   les travaux récents. Revue Nouvelle de Philosophie,
   1927, 307-341; 1928, 442-466.

Morawcsick, J. M., ed. Aristotle: A Collection of
   Critical Essays. Garden City: Doubleday and
   Company, Inc., 1967.

Mure, G. R. G. Aristotle. London, 1932. Reprinted in
   London: Oxford University Press, 1964.

Includes a brief account of earlier Greek Philosophy and
is particularly helpful on Aristotle's metaphysics and
logic.

Randall, John Hermann, Jr. Aristotle. New York:
   Columbia University Press, 1960.

Stimulating but open to criticism; it makes Aristotle
seem more modern than he is.

Rolfes E. Die Philosophie des Aristoteles als Natur-
   erklärung und Weltanschauung. Leipzig: Miner,
   1923.

Roland-Gosselin, M.D., Aristotle. Paris: Flammarion,
   1928.

Ross, W. D. Aristotle, 5th edition. First published
   in 1923. London: Methuen and Co., Ltd., 1949.
   New York: Barnes and Noble, 1964,

This is the best short presentation of Aristotelian philosophy in English.

Taylor, A. E. *Aristotle*. London, Nelson, 1943. New
      York: Dover Publications, 1955.

This is a stimulating short account of Aristotle's doctrines. Taylor is an outstanding Platonic scholar.

Veatch, Henry. *Aristotle: A Contemporary Appreciation*.
      Bloomington, Ind. Indiana University Press, 1974.

Aristotelian logic is presented with superb clarity and ease.

Voegelin, Eric. *Order and History*. Baton Rouge:
      Louisiana State University, 1972.

Vol. I. Israel and Revelation; Vol. II. The World of
the Polis--a penetrating analysis of the ancient Greek
writers; Vol. III---a profound study of Plato and Aristotle. A particularly successful study of Plato;
Vol. IV. In Search for Order.

Vogel, C. J. de. *Greek Philosophy: A Collection of
      Texts*. With Notes and Explanations. Leiden: E.J.
      Brill, 1967.

Vol. I, Thales to Plato. 3rd ed. 1963, 334 pp.
Vol. II, Aristotle. The Early Peripatetic School and the
      Early Academy. 3rd ed., 340 pp.
Vol. III, The Hellenistic-Roman Period. 2nd. ed., 1964,
      xv, 674 pp.
Bibliography and Indexes in each volume.

Wallace, E. *Outlines of the Philosophy of Aristotle*.
      Cambridge, England: Cambridge University Press,
      1883.

ARISTOTLE'S NICOMACHEAN ETHICS: SELECTED BIBLIOGRAPHY

The following list includes selected, useful books in
the vast field of Aristotelian scholarship covering the
Nicomachean Ethics. For a complete bibliography on the
work, consult the following:

Before 1912: O. Apelt. Aristotelis Ethica Nicomachea,
     recognovit Fr. Susemihl, editio tertia curavit
     O. Apelt. Leipzig, 1912, pp. xiii-xxix.

For 1912-1958: Gauthier, René A. and Jean Yves Jolif.
     L'Ethique a Nicomaque. Vol. II, pp. 917-940.

For 1958-1968: Ibidem, vol. I, pp. 315-334.

For 1968-1978: Repertoire bibliographique de Philoso-
     phie: Socrate, Platon, Aristotle. This is an
     independent quarterly supplement of the journal
     entitled, Revue Philosophique de Louvain.

Editions of the Text

Aristotelis opera. Ed. by I. Bekker, Berlin: Royal
     Prussian Academy, 1831-1870, vol. 2.

Aristotelis Ethica Nicomachea. Recognovit Fr. Susemihl.
     Editio tertia curavit O. Apelt. Leipzig, 1912.

Aristotelis Ethica Nicomachea. Recognovit brevique
     adnotatione critica instruxit I. Bywater. Scrip-
     torum classicorum bibliotheca Oxoniensis. Oxford:
     Clarendon Press, 1890. Pages 264. Ample Index.

Translations

Ross, W. D. Aristotle. Ethica Nicomachea. London:
     Oxford University Press, 1915. Included in the
     series The Works of Aristotle. Oxford Translation
     of Aristotle, vol. IX, 1925.

A good index helps the student find the various passages
relating to the given problem. The translation is quite
faithful to the Greek text, consequently, it is somewhat
obscure and oftentimes difficult to understand.

294

Ostwald, Martin. <u>Aristotle. Nicomachean Ethics</u>. Trans-
lated with Introduction and Notes. New York: The
Library of Liberal Arts. Indianapolis: The Bobbs-
Merrill Company, Inc., 1962.

Introduction, notes, bibliography, glossary of technical
terms are all very useful to students.

Rachkam, H. <u>Aristotle. The Nicomachean Ethics</u>. Text
and Translation. Cambridge, Mass., Loeb Classical
Library, Harvard University Press, 1926.

The translator seeks to express the meaning instead of
the letter of the often condensed text of Aristotle.

Thompson, J. A. K. <u>Aristotle. The Nicomachean Ethics</u>.
London: Whitefriars Press, 1953. Pocket edition:
Baltimore, Maryland: Penguin Books, 1953.

Warrington, John. <u>Aristotle's Ethics</u>. Edited and
translated. London-New York: Everyman's Library,
1963.

Commentaries

Aquinas Thomas, St. <u>Commentary on the Nicomachean Ethics</u>.
2 vols. Trans. by C. I. Litzinger, O.P. Chicago:
Henry Regnery Company, 1964.

Aquinas comments on the <u>N.E.</u> following the literal Latin
translation of William of Moerbeke. This is the best
medieval commentary on Aristotle's <u>Nicomachean Ethics</u>
considering the state of Aristotelian scholarship in that
era. The alphabetical indexes of the subjects in Vol. I
and of names in vol. II are very useful.

Burnet, John. <u>The Ethics of Aristotle</u>. Edited with an
Introduction and Notes. London: Methuen and Co.,
1900. Reprinted by Arno Press, A New York Times
Comapny, 1973.

Very useful introduction and extensive notes.

Festugière, A. J. <u>Aristote. Le Plaisir</u> (Eth. Nic. VII,
11-14, X, 1-5). Introduction, Traduction et Notes.
Paris: Librairie Philosophique J. Vrin, 1960.
First Edition 1936, Pages Lxxvi, 48.

This is the definitive study of the two treatises on pleasure in Aristotle's N.E.

Gauthier, René Antoine and Jean Yves Jolif. L'Éthique à Nicomaque. Introduction, Traduction et Commentaire. Deuxième Edition avec une Introduction nouvelle.

Tome I. Partie Première. Introduction par R. A. Gauthier, Pages 358.
Tome I. Partie deuxième. Traduction.

Tome II. Commentaire. Première Partie. Livres I-V, p.p. 434.

Tome II. Commentaire. Deuxième Partie. Livres VI-X, p.p. 986.

Louvain: Publications Universitaires, 1970.

The above commentary on Aristotle's N. E. is probably the best today. It is also the most comprehensive.

Grant, Alexander (Sir). The Ethics of Aristotle. Illustrated with Essays and Notes. In two volumes, Fourth Edition, Revised. London: Longmans, Green, and Co., 1885.

Greenwood, L.H.G. Aristotle. Nicomachean Ethics. Book Six. With Essays, Notes and Translation. Cambridge: At the University Press, 1909, pages 214.

Useful Introduction, text and good translation, miscellaneous notes, Greek and English index.

Jackson, Henry. Peri dikaiosynes. The Fifth Book of the Nicomachean Ethics of Aristotle. Cambridge: At the University Press, 1879. Reprinted by Arno Press, A New York Times Company, New York, 1973, pages xxxii, 125.

Good introduction, text and translation and excellent notes.

Joachim, H. H. Aristotle. The Nicomachean Ethics. A Commentary. Ed. by D. A. Rees. Oxford: The Clarendon Press, 1951. Second Ed., 1955., Pages 304.

A solid and oftentimes brilliant commentary for students wishing to delve into the meaning of difficult passages in the Nicomachean Ethics. However, it must be noted

that Joachim is a logician and more inclined to Aristotle's
theoretical philosophy. This helps to explain his commentary of the passages he finds particularly interesting.

Rodier, G. Aristotle. L'Éthique à Nicomaque. Livre X.
    Texte et Commentaire. Paris, 1897.

Schuster, J.B. De iustitia. Aristotelis Ethicorum ad
    Nicomachum. Liber V. cum commentariis Silvestri
    Mauri, S. J. illustravit. Romae: Universitas
    Gregorian, 1938.

Stewart, J.A. Notes on the Nicomachean Ethics of
    Aristotle. 2 vols. Oxford: The Clarendon Press,
    1892.

Text and commentary. Very useful for understanding
difficult passages.

Sullivan, Roger J. Morality and the Good Life.
    Memphis, Tenn.: Memphis State University Press,
    1977.

BOOKS AND STUDIES ON

NICOMACHEAN ETHICS

Adler, Mortimer J. The Time of Our Lives: The Ethics of Common Sense. New York: Holt, Reinhart and Winston, 1970, pp. 361.

The author says about this book that it is a "re-writing of Aristotle's Ethics for the Twentieth century."

Albert, E.M., I.C. Denise and S.P. Peterfreund. Great Traditions in Ethics. New York: American Book Company, 1953.

Allan, D. J. "Aristotle's Account of the Origin of Moral Principles." Actes du XI Congrès international de Philosophie. Amsterdam: North - Holland Publishing Company, 1953. Papers XII, 120 - 127.

Allan, D. J. "The Practical Syllogism", pp. 325-340 in Autour d'Aristote Louvain: Publications universitaires de Louvain, 1955.

Ando, Takatura. Aristotle's Theory of Practical Cognition. First edition, 1958. Third revised edition: The Hague, Netherlands; Martinus Nijhoff, 1971, pp. 344.

Arnim, H. von. Die drei aristotelischen Ethiken. Vienna. Academy of Arts and Sciences, 1926.

Arnim, H. von. Nochmals die Aristotelischen Ethiken. Vienna, 1929.

Austin, J. L. "Agathon and Eudaimonia in the Ethics of Aristotle." J. M. E. Moravcsik, ed. Aristotle. A Collection of Critical Essays. pp. 261-296.

Colle, G. "Les quattre premiers livres de la Morale à Nicomaque." Annales de l'Institut Superieur de Philosophie de l'Université de Louvain. 4(1920), 179-218 .

Gauthier, David. Practical Reasoning: The Structure and Foundations of Prudential and Moral Arguments and Their Exemplification in Discourse. Oxford: Oxford University Press, 1963.

Gauthier, R. - A. La morale d'Aristote. Paris: Presses
    Universitaires de France, 1958. Second ed. 1963.

Gillet, M. "Le Tempérament moral d'après Aristote."
    Revue Néoscholastique, 16(1909) pp. 185-214.

Hamburger, M. E. Morals and Law. The Growth of Aris-
    totle's Legal Theory. New Haven, 1951. Second
    Edition, 1965.

Hamelin, O. "La morale d'Aristote". Revue de Méta-
    physique et de Morale 30(1923), pp. 497-507.

Hardie, W. F. R. Aristotle's Ethical Theory. Oxford:
    Clarendon Press, 1968.

Hardie, W. F. R. "The Final Good in Aristotle's Ethics."
    Philosophy, XL (1965), 277-295.

Hartman, N. Die Wertdimension der Nicomachischen Ethik.
    Berlin, 1944.

Mann, Jesse H. and Gerald F. Kreyche. Approaches to
    Morality. Readings in Ethics from Classical Philo-
    sophy to Existentialism.

Part I. "Classical and Medieval Intellectualist Thought:
    Plato, Aristotle, Aquinas, pp. 24-60. with the
    Glossary of technical terms by Francis H. Eterovich,
    O.P. New York: Harcourt, Brace and World, 1966.

Mansion, A. Autour des Éthiques attribuées à Aristote.
    Louvain, 1931. (Revue Néoscholastique) 33(1931),
    80-107; 216-236; 360-380.

Milo, Ronald Dmitri. Aristotle on Practical Knowledge
    and Weakness of Will. Hhe Hague: Mouton and Co.,
    1966. P. 113.

In this study the author presents a critical exposition
and examination of Aristotle's analysis of two very
important and related concepts: "practical knowledge"
and "moral weakness" or "weakness of will" (Akrasia).
In the discussion of the first concept, the author gives
special consideration to the relationship between practical knowledge and action, in particular, because his
primary interest lies in Aristotle's treatment of the
problem of moral weakness.

Monan, J. Donald. Moral Knowledge and Its Methodology
    in Aristotle. Oxford: At the Clarendon Press,
    1968. Pages xiii-163.

A study of phronēsis (practical wisdom) and practical
syllogism in Protrepticus, Nicomachean Ethics, Eudemian
Ethics. See especially Chapters 4 and 5.

Moravcsik, J.M.E., ed. Aristotle. A Collection of
    Critical Essays. Modern Studies in Philosophy.
    Part IV. Ethics, 241-333. Notre Dame, Indiana:
    University of Notre Dame Press, 1967, p. 341.

The four essays written by Prichard, Hardie, Urmson and
Austin are mentioned in this bibliography.

Nowak, James Anthony. A Critical Study of the Aristo-
    telian Concept of Choice. Chicago, 1963. 74 pages.
    Master's thesis. Department of Philosophy. DePaul Univ.

Oates, Whitney. J. Aristotle and the Problem of Value.
    Princeton, 1963.

Oesterle, John A. Ethics: The Introduction to Moral
    Science. Englewood, New Jersey: Prentice-Hall, Inc.

This is, to my knowledge, the only attempt made by a
contemporary Thomist to recast the whole ethics into the
Aristotelian mold. Review questions, discussions and
suggested readings at the end of every chapter are extremely helpful to the student for understanding the
key-issues discussed in individual chapters.

Schächer, E. J. Studien zu den Ethiken des Corpus Aris-
    totelicum. Paderborn, 1940.

Prichard, H. A. "The meaning of agathon in the Ethics of
    Aristotle." Philosophy 10(1935), pp. 27-39.

Tracy, Th. J. Physiological Theory and the Doctrine of
    the Mean in Plato and Aristotle. The Hague, Neth-
    erlands: Mouton and Company, 1969. P. 396.

Urmson, J. O. "Aristotle on Pleasure." In J.M.E. Mor-
    avcsik, ed. Aristotle: A Collection of Critical
    Essays, pp. 323-333.

Walsh, James J. Aristotle's Conception of Moral Weakness.
    New York: Columbia University Press, 1963.
    P. 199.

Walsh, James J. and Henry L. Shapiro, eds. <u>Aristotle's</u>
<u>Ethics: Issues and Interpretations</u>. Belmont,
California: Wadsworth Publishing Company, Inc.,
1967. P. 123.

The following persons have contributed to this volume:

R.A. Gauthier, "On the Nature of Aristotle's Ethics",
pp. 10-29.
Frederick Siegler, "Reason, Happiness and Goodness,"
pp. 30-46.
John Dewey, "The Nature of Aims," pp. 47-55.
G.E.M. Anscombe, "Thought and Action in Aristotle,"
pp. 56-69.
Gilbert Ryle, "On Forgetting the Difference Between
Right and Wrong," pp. 70-79.
Vinit Haksar, "Aristotle and the Punishment of Psycho-
paths," pp. 80-101.
Hans Kelsen, "Aristotle's Doctrine of Justice,"
pp. 102-119.

Veatch, Henry B. <u>Rational Man</u>. <u>A Modern Interpretation</u>
<u>of Aristotelian Ethics</u>. Bloomington, Indiana:
Indiana University Press, 1962.

An appeal, interestingly written, for the restoration of
<u>logos</u> in ethics. The author insists that the norms of
conduct are more important for ethics than the linguistic
analysis of its terms.